History's Greatest Hits

History's Greatest Hits

FAMOUS EVENTS WE SHOULD ALL KNOW MORE ABOUT

Joseph Cummins

To Mimi, who is quite historical

Contents

Introduction

IF EVENTS ARE FAMOUS, YOU MAY say to yourself, gazing at the subtitle of this book, why in the world should we know more about them? They're *famous*, after all. And famous means well known, renowned, eminent, illustrious, celebrated. But, really, how much do you know about Hannibal's crossing of the Alps with a herd of elephants? It's *famous*, of course. But did you know that almost all the elephants died? And that one reason why the location of Hannibal's high and treacherous path across the mountains remained hidden for so many centuries is that it became a fiercely protected smuggler's route?

In many ways, being famous obscures the actual event, in the same way that fame blinds us to the human reality of a movie star or other celebrity. So what I've tried to do here is bring what really happened to life and place it within a historical context, to help the reader understand its significance. The Crusades, for example, are the subject of uncountable romantic legends, poems, novels, and films, and as myth-ridden as any famous event in history; but since these holy wars of the eleventh to thirteenth centuries still have a bearing on the religious conflicts of today, it's important to know the reality behind them.

Not all of *History's Greatest Hits* have had a major impact on subsequent history, of course, and many are famous for other reasons. Some are simply notorious. The Charge of the Light Brigade didn't change history, but reading about the brigade's commanding officer, James Thomas Brudenell, the Seventh Earl of Cardigan — a man one historian has called "unusually stupid" — reminds one in a salutary way about the inadvisability of putting idiots in charge. George Armstrong Custer was not quite as big an idiot as Brudenell, but led his men to their Last Stand just as recklessly — and here, of course, part of why we remember the event is that not one soldier of Custer's command survived: we are haunted by the ghosts of his Seventh Cavalry, and the ghosts of what might have been.

Many of the events described in this book have had a major impact on our cultural history, and in some cases have become part of our language. We all have our "last stands," meet our own "Waterloos," and mutter "Et tu, Brutus" when betrayed by a friend (although Caesar didn't actually say that as the knives struck home). Understanding these events enriches our general knowledge and enhances our appreciation of this shared history.

Drawing on in-depth studies of the protagonists of these events by other historians, I have also tried to impart at least a little of what was going on in the minds of certain great leaders – from Queen Elizabeth I and Christopher Columbus to George Washington and Winston Churchill. This, in turn, helps make these famous events more comprehensible.

Finally, I hope I have been able to tell a good story or two here. For many people, the last time they will have read about the Battle of Agincourt or the Great Fire of London or the Wall Street Crash was in some dry and musty schoolbook, but these events and others recounted here are absolutely fascinating (if sometimes horrible) and we shouldn't be able to tear our mind's eye from them if they are retold effectively. History in ancient times was an oral tradition – stories told and reenacted in front of an appreciative audience – and *History's Greatest Hits* aims to impart some of that spoken feel and bring these episodes to life once more.

The Ancient World

250 BC–500 AD

Hannibal Crosses the Alps

How One of History's Most Determined Leaders
Drove an Entire Army — and a Herd of Elephants —
over Western Europe's Highest Mountains

IN THE THIRD CENTURY BC, the ancient North African kingdom of Carthage fought the up-and-coming power Rome for control of the Mediterranean basin. This lengthy and bloody conflict took three wars — known as the Punic Wars — and one hundred years to resolve. In the end, Rome was the victor, Carthage, famously, the loser, the once-grand old city burned literally to ashes, its people sold into slavery, its very earth sown with salt, so that nothing could ever grow there again. After this victory, Rome was well on its way to establishing its thousand-year empire, while Carthage became merely an echoing and distant memory. Except, that is, for one man: Hannibal Barca, whose extraordinary feat of crossing the Alps with a large army — and a herd of battle elephants — has captured human imaginations for 2,500 years.

It's doubtful whether we would know anything about Hannibal were it not for a dogged Greek-born historian named Polybius, who, writing fifty years after the event in his *History of the Roman Republic*, even tried to trace Hannibal's route and talk to descendants of those who had fought with the legendary Carthaginian. What a word picture Polybius paints. He reports that, as Hannibal stood in the foothills of the Alps, with mountains of indescribable height looming behind him — mountains no army had ever crossed — he addressed his nervous troops in this way: "What do you think the Alps are? They are nothing more than high mountains ... No height is insurmountable to men of determination."

Hannibal had come up with an extraordinary military and logistical plan: a way to attack Italy, not by sea, which the Romans with their powerful navy could readily guard against, but from the north, after traveling through mountains many thought impassable. But it was not just his logistical adeptness that motivated his army

A bust of Hannibal, now in the Museo Nazionale in Naples, Italy. Hannibal Barca was Rome's sworn and deadly enemy.

to travel one thousand miles through hostile territory, from Spain, across the Pyrenees and through southern France to Italy. It was also the fact that he was one of the most determined and inspiring leaders in history, driven by what may have been a passionate hatred of Rome, but was certainly a passionate need to win at any cost.

"I WILL USE FIRE AND STEEL"

The Punic Wars – the name comes from the Latin word *Punicus*, meaning "Phoenician," for Carthage began as a Phoenician colony in the seventh century BC – were about territory and wealth. In the third century BC, Carthage, located in modern-day Tunisia, controlled much of the islands of Corsica, Sardinia, and Sicily, southeastern Spain, and a good deal of the North African coast to present-day Israel. Rome, on the other hand, was just emerging as the conqueror of many of the city-states of the Italian Peninsula, and wanting to extend its dominion into the Mediterranean. The First Punic War began in 264 BC as a battle for control of Sicily and lasted twenty-three years. Carthage lost and was pushed out of Sicily and forced to pay a huge indemnity to the Romans. It turned its attention to building up an empire in Spain, but the Romans weren't about to let that happen either.

In 221 BC, Hannibal Barca, the twenty-five-year-old son of a legendary Carthaginian commander, took control of Carthaginian forces in Spain after his father was killed fighting the local tribes. He immediately began an aggressive campaign against some of the wild Celtiberian tribes to the north; when he besieged the city of Saguntum (now Sagunto in Spain), which the Romans thought was rightfully theirs, they demanded that he be brought to Italy in chains. But Hannibal scoffed at the emissaries who demanded that he give himself up and break off the siege, and in 218 BC the city fell to the Carthaginians in an orgy of slaughter. Diplomatic relations between Carthage and Rome were then broken off and the Second Punic War commenced.

It was said that when he was still a child Hannibal had sworn an oath that "as soon as age will permit ... I will use fire and steel to resolve the destiny of Rome." The Romans who met him reported back that he was indeed possessed of a fiery hatred of Rome. Whatever it took now, Hannibal was not about to allow Carthage to lose another war to Rome, for he knew that it would mean the utter destruction of his homeland. Soon, he began to put his plan for an overland attack on Italy into motion.

A POLYGLOT FORCE

Estimates vary regarding the size of Hannibal's army: ancient sources put it as high as one hundred thousand, but it was probably between forty and fifty thousand, including ten thousand cavalry. It was a polyglot force – Celtiberian tribesmen, Berbers and Numidian cavalry from North Africa, Gauls from southern France, Greek infantry. All were mercenaries, commanded by Carthaginian officers – yet Hannibal, through extraordinary charisma, as well as common sense when it came to dealing with soldiers, managed to keep them in line.

Famously, Hannibal also brought forty war elephants with him on his journey across the Alps. Elephants had been used in combat for thousands of years by the time Hannibal employed them and were a potent force, the tanks or armored cars of their time. They were especially useful against isolated communities that had never seen them before, as Hannibal must have suspected would be the case with the tribes he would run up against on his journey. Hannibal's elephants were African forest elephants. Now extinct, they were about half as high as the Asian

elephant, although they were relatively speedy and more maneuverable.

As he led his army out of New Carthage (the modern-day town of Cartagena) in the spring of 218 BC, heading up the east coast of the Iberian Peninsula to Gaul, Hannibal knew that he needed to make his journey in time to cross the Alps before winter set in, or he and his men would almost certainly perish there. After crossing into Gaul and fighting off a warlike tribe near the Rhône River, Hannibal's cavalry scouts had the misfortune to encounter troops under the Roman commander Publius Cornelius Scipio, who happened to put into the nearby port of Massilia (now Marseille) on his way to attack Spain. This chance meeting changed Hannibal's entire approach to crossing the Alps, for he could not now cross via

Which Way to Italy?

The question that has plagued scholars for generations is: which way did Hannibal go? Most historians have Hannibal following the Rhône north to where it joins with the eastward-flowing Isère River. This would have taken him to one of numerous transverse valleys which he might have followed generally south, deep into the mountains, where he could have crossed at a number of passes – Great St. Bernard, Little St. Bernard, Mont Cenis, or Clapier.

But more recently, historians (including John Prevas in his authoritative *Hannibal*

Crosses the Alps) have speculated that the Carthaginian turned right before he got to the Isère and followed the Drôme River eastward and then the smaller Durance River to the pass he eventually crossed: the high, desperate, and snow-covered Col de la Traversette. This route fits very nicely with ancient sources. But it has been little studied in the field, mainly because until recently the Col de la Traversette was a smuggler's route that was quite dangerous to traverse, and there will be no agreement until archaeological evidence is found.

Hannibal's elephants were battle-hardened war machines, but did not fare well in the subzero temperatures of the high Alps.

any of the more accessible passes in the Maritime Alps near the Mediterranean because he felt sure the Roman fleet was dogging him. So he made a detour north, up the Rhône River, and then turned right and headed down a river valley through moun-tains that rose about five thousand feet high. It was now nearly the end of August, and he had little time left to make it over the Alps before the winter set in at high altitudes.

At this point, the strategy must have begun to seem reckless, even to the leader himself. Yet one of the reasons why Hannibal is considered such a brilliant leader by historians is that he never once considered turning back, not even now when he knew the Romans were aware of his presence and he had lost the element of surprise.

INTO THE ALPS

After Hannibal made his stirring speech, his forty thousand or so men, along with elephants and horses and retainers, moved into the Alps. As the soldiers climbed, they wound their way through ever-narrower defiles and canyons. Above them on cliff ledges were wild tribesmen, the Allobroges, whose shadowy presence was frightening and who soon launched an ambush that caught the Carthaginians in a gorge, but which Hannibal was able to bloodily repel.

Surprisingly, and suspiciously in the eyes of the Carthaginians, these tribesmen sent a delegation to Hannibal, claiming that they were impressed by the way he had defeated the Allobroges and offering to lead him to an easy pass to Italy. Hannibal acquiesced to this, warily, even asking for hostages to guarantee the Carthaginians' safe passage. However, there is evidence he may have been lost, and felt that following these men was his only choice.

The tribesmen led the Carthaginians through the mountains for about two days, then steered them into an extremely narrow ravine with a high wall on one side and a

"What do you think the Alps are?" Hannibal said. "No height is insurmountable to men of determination."

After a week or so, Hannibal approached the tallest mountains in the French Alps, the last barrier between himself and the fertile valleys of Italy. These mountains were thirteen thousand feet tall, a truly awe-inspiring sight, some with snow on their peaks even in September. If the Allobroges had been bad, the tribesmen who inhabited this region were worse. In writing of Hannibal's journey, the Roman historian Livy called them "shaggy, unkempt men perched upon the crags above, more horrible to look at than words can tell." It seems, from the accounts of Livy and others, that this unnamed group was populous – and obviously not afraid to take on a large force of men in ambush.

fast-flowing stream on the other. As the Carthaginian column entered this ravine, the tribesmen moved to block the front and back entrances, while others crept up high on the cliffs. At a signal, they pushed piles of rocks and logs down upon the soldiers and shot arrows to stampede the animals.

It was a horrible slaughter, with men crushed by rocks, or caught between the hooves of elephants and horses. It is possible that the army might not have survived except for the forethought of Hannibal. To protect against just such an attack, he had placed his heavy infantry at the front and back of the column. These soldiers were able to repel the tribesmen attacking at those points and eventually help the middle of the column fight its way though the pass. They were aided in this by the elephants, which badly frightened the barbarians, sending them reeling out of the way when they charged. After a long day's struggle, the Carthaginians escaped.

A HIGH AND DESOLATE PASS

But the hardest part of the journey was yet to come. The Carthaginians now had to cross one of the highest passes in the Alps. In attempting this, men by the hundreds, weak and exhausted, began to slip and fall, and their cries echoed across the mountains, horrible music to the ears of those left climbing. According to at least one chronicler, a snowstorm now hit the column, causing more men to stumble over the precipices. The only thing each man could see through the blinding blizzard was the man directly in front of him.

Panic set in as even that small amount of visibility began to dim. The roars of the elephants that thudded down the sides of the great peaks to their deaths were especially terrifying. The falling elephants were joined by many of the pack animals, who broke through the first soft layer of snow with their hooves, became stuck in the ice beneath, and were finally pushed off the sides by soldiers impatient to get through. The soldiers themselves were burdened by supplies in heavy packs, and one tilt off balance could send them, too, hurtling into the dark ravines that surrounded them.

Hannibal, who usually traveled at the rear of the line, strode past his terrified soldiers, exhorting them to move, reminding them, even with the wind howling in their ears, that the beautiful valleys of Italy awaited them. "The mighty barriers we have scaled are the walls, not only of Italy, but of Rome itself," he told his troops. "It is only one battle when we get down on the plains, or at most two, and the great city will be ours."

After three days, they reached the top of the pass and could look down upon the Po Valley of Italy. But the descent – down slippery, rocky slopes, where the back of the column trod on icy slush churned up by the front – cost even more lives than the climb. Finally, however, the army reached the lower slopes of the mountains, and entered a temperate zone – which must have seemed like Eden to them. Trees and grass grew in abundance and there was fresh game and fruit. Filthy, emaciated, and traumatized, they must have looked worse than any of the "barbarian" peoples who had tried to impede their progress. But they had made it.

TAKING THE BATTLE TO ROME

The cost of the journey had been high indeed. Estimates vary, but it appears that in the Alps Hannibal lost perhaps twenty thousand men. Only three elephants – perhaps just one – survived. Despite this, Hannibal had achieved his objective and was now in a position to attack the Romans. After resting his remaining twenty-six

thousand troops for nearly two weeks, Hannibal brought them to their feet and marched them south through Italy.

Hannibal was to spend the next fourteen years campaigning there, where he won numerous victories. This included his bloody and historic success at Cannae in 216 BC, where his force massacred fifty thousand Roman soldiers in one day. But he was never able to get the city-states of the Italian Peninsula to side with him, and Rome, after an initial shock, was able to rally, finally defeating Hannibal in 202 BC at the battle of Zama, in North Africa.

Soon thereafter, the Carthaginian commander went into exile. Rather than be captured by the Romans, he committed suicide on an obscure island. Despite this, no one could say that Hannibal had ever really been defeated.

The Assassination of Julius Caesar

*The Conspirators Who Killed in the Name of Democracy,
and Ended up Destroying the Roman Republic*

AT DINNER, THE MAN SUDDENLY asked his companions what manner of death they might hope for, and answered his own question by saying he wanted a quick, unexpected end. After he went to bed, the windows and shutters of his house were blown open, as if by a fierce wind, except that the night was calm. In his sleep, the man dreamed he was flying above the clouds, skimming, lighter than air, and he awoke just as he was reaching out to touch the hand of Jupiter.

That morning was the Ides, or middle, of March. As Julius Caesar rubbed the sleep out of his eyes, his wife, Calpurnia, told him that she had dreamed of his lifeless body lying bloody in her lap. She begged him not to go to meet with the Roman Senate, as he had planned to do. Her exhortations gave Caesar pause; Calpurnia was not prone to hysteria. Moreover, he recalled a soothsayer, Spurinna, recently telling him that danger would befall him no later than the Ides of March.

When Caesar's close aide Mark Antony arrived at his house, Caesar instructed him to postpone the visit. But then another friend arrived and convinced Caesar it would not be seemly for the *Pater Patriae*, or "Father of the Fatherland,", to cancel a meeting with the Senate. The friend's name was Decimus Brutus, cousin of another Brutus who awaited Caesar on the Senate floor, and he had murder in his heart.

Caesar listened to this man and left his home for the last time.

A CAUTIONARY TALE?

It is no wonder that omens (real or imagined) surrounded the death of Gaius Julius Caesar. The most pivotal figure in the thousand-year history of Ancient Rome was born in 100 BC in the month of Quintilis, a month that was later named after him: July. (No one really knows, however, if he was born by Caesarean section.) Caesar was altogether extraordinary. He was a brilliant military leader — brave, imaginative, beloved of his men — who advanced the fortunes of Rome immeasurably by conquering Gaul. He was also a fine writer, whose tales of his conquests, while sometimes self-serving, are always gripping. And he was a superb administrator who, despite being a patrician himself, sought ways to spread the wealth of Rome around.

Of course, the man had his faults. The story of the assassination of Caesar can be seen as a cautionary lesson in what happens if you fail to heed warnings, if you take personal hubris to excess. Shakespeare understood that Julius Caesar is a perfect figure for drama. His play about the Roman leader, which is one of the greatest tragedies in literature, focuses on a question all human beings ask themselves: can we ever change our destiny?

The story of Caesar's assassination also continues to fascinate us because of its political ramifications and ethical implications. The achievements of Caesar, and his popularity at the time of his death, make his killing, on the face of it, puzzling. Yet the assassins claimed to be acting for the good of Rome and most historians have argued that this was the case (though some, more recently, have claimed the opposite). This in turn raises the broader question, still much debated and just as pertinent in our own time, of whether it is acceptable to murder an individual or individuals for the benefit of the majority — whether it is justifiable, in other words, to kill in the name of democracy.

CONQUEROR OF ADVERSITY

As his litter was borne along the bustling streets of Rome, a man raced up to Caesar holding a note and thrust it into his hands,

A bust of Julius Caesar. An outstanding general, politician, and writer, Caesar has fascinated generations of historians.

begging him to read it. Caesar took the note and pocketed it, waving the man off. He was possibly a servant in the house of one of Caesar's enemies, or a repentant conspirator – historical sources vary. In the note, the plot against Caesar was revealed, but Caesar seems to have dismissed the man as some favor-seeker and tucked the note away without reading it. Whether he felt any disquiet at this point, following the earlier warnings and dreams, we do not know. But we know that Caesar was a man who had faced adversity before, and had always triumphed. Perhaps it was this confidence that pushed him on, to his death.

beginning a distinguished military career that would catapult him to power.

Caesar spent two years campaigning in Asia Minor. When Sulla died in 78 BC, he returned to Italy and built up a reputation as a politician. In 63 BC, he went to Iberia (present-day Spain) as governor and was instrumental in putting down rebellions there. By 59 BC, he had returned to Rome and attained the prestigious position of co-consul with Marcus Bibulus. However, true power resided with what modern historians call the First Triumvirate, formed by Caesar and his allies Licinius Crassus and Gnaeus Pompeius Magnus (Pompey).

Whether Caesar was a dictator in the making or a genuine populist reformer is still a matter of controversy.

Caesar was a member of one of Rome's original aristocratic families, the Julii. The Julii were not of the ruling oligarchy, the *nobilitas*, but they were well connected – fortunately for Caesar. When he was only sixteen, he ran afoul of the tyrant Sulla during a civil war that pitted supporters of aristocratic rule against those who favored a more democratic approach – an early instance of Caesar's populist leanings. Sulla ordered Caesar's arrest, but Caesar escaped to the Sabine region of Central Italy. Caesar's relatives prevailed on Sulla to spare him, but Caesar sensed that it would be prudent if he spent some time away from Italy, and so he joined the army,

The members of the Senate and the most powerful aristocratic families were at this time broadly divided into two opposing camps: the *optimates* (literally, "the best men"), who distrusted the populace and wanted to hold power close to the ruling oligarchies; and the *populares*, the reformers, who sought (or pretended to seek) to improve the lot of the common people. Caesar was a *popularis*, and, as part of the First Triumverate, he tried to pass a law that redistributed land to the poor, thus endearing himself to the underprivileged of Rome, the *proletarii,* or plebs. Whether Caesar was trying to create a power base for himself as a future dictator, as his enemies (and many historians) claimed, or whether he was a genuine populist reformer, is still a matter of controversy.

Caesar may have had a popular following, but at this point he didn't have an army. However, his heroic campaigns in Gaul, from 58 to 50 BC, not only won him and Rome great riches, but also earned him the loyalty of his legions. This aroused the fear and envy of the Senate, where Pompey had recently joined the *optimates* faction. It demanded that Caesar return to Rome and disband his army. Instead, Caesar marched across the Rubicon River in northern Italy with his legion – a violation of Roman law – and began a civil war that resulted in the ouster and death of Pompey and many of his supporters.

By 46 BC, Caesar had returned to Rome in triumph, and in the next few years he was showered with honors by the Senate, including the title of Dictator for Life. There was some suggestion that these flowery honorifics were, in reality, sarcastic bestowals by a group of senators who, increasingly, resented Caesar's power and popularity, and what must have seemed to them an almost socialistic redistribution of wealth. For, during this time, Caesar gave allotments of land to thousands of his army veterans and also to eighty thousand of the plebs of Rome – and made a point of giving even more farmland to twenty thousand Roman families with three or more children (in fact, as the historian Plutarch said, he provided "almost the whole of [the province of] Campania" to the poor). He also set up public works projects, such as draining marshes and repairing towns and cities, as a way of providing work to the unemployed. On occasion, he even doled out cash to soldiers and citizens straight from the treasury.

In Whose Interest?

Traditionally, in popular literature as well as works of scholarly history, Caesar has been portrayed as a man with a weakness for adulation, who, one step away from becoming a dictator, was brought down by senators who feared for the integrity and survival of the Republic. In the last decade, however, some historians – prominent among them Michael Parenti, author of *The Assassination of Julius Caesar: A People's History of Ancient Rome* – have not only questioned the motives of the assassins but also convincingly claimed that Caesar was one of a long line of democratic reformers killed by Roman oligarchs to protect their interests. Another was the tribune Tiberius Gracchus, murdered in 133 BC by thugs hired by Roman aristocrats unhappy with Gracchus's land reforms. Yet another was Tiberius's brother, Gaius Gracchus, who followed in Tiberius's footsteps as a reformer and was killed in 121 BC, along with 250 supporters, by death squads hired by the oligarchy.

The Death of Caesar, by Vincenzo Camuccini (1773–1844). The assassination has provided a rich subject for painters through the ages.

For a long time, historians have seen the plot that arose against Caesar as an attempt by patriotic (even democratic) Romans to stop a despot, but there is now a very strong point of view that those who decided Caesar must be stopped were the opposite of democrats — were in fact rich nobility out to stop what they feared would be a wholesale power shift from the haves to the have-nots.

THE LIBERATORS

As Caesar traveled to the Senate on March 15, 44 BC, the note that might have saved him tucked deep in his robes, the men who would kill him awaited nervously. Most of what we know about the plot to kill Caesar as well as his actual death comes from

Caesar's biographer Suetonius and the Roman historian Plutarch. (Shakespeare's play, *Julius Caesar*, although obviously fictionalized, is a fairly faithful rendering of Plutarch's version of the story.) The plot had begun with Gaius Cassius Longinus, who harbored an enormous grudge against Caesar, whom he called a tyrant, but whom he may also have feared was going to weaken the powerful aristocracy, of which Cassius was a prominent member.

Cassius's most important ally was his brother-in-law, a young nobleman named Marcus Brutus, who happened to be the son of Caesar's longtime lover, Servilia, and who may have held grudges against Caesar that were other than political ones. The conspiracy then grew to include sixty mainly aristocratic Romans, not all of whose names have come down to us. One was Decimus Brutus, a distant cousin of Marcus, who was in fact a close friend of Caesar's; others included Tillius Cimber and Publius Casca. These men called themselves "the Liberators," and, over a period of months leading up to March of 44 BC, met secretly, a few at a time, in each other's houses. While they railed against Caesar's supposed tyranny, they, as members of the Roman Senate, had a great deal to lose by Caesar's land distributions and his reforms. They all had their sweetheart deals with contractors and public officials, for one thing. For another, they feared that the great, unwashed rabble now following Caesar so slavishly might ultimately gain power and turn on them.

Something, obviously, needed to be done. Knowing that Caesar was leaving the country with his army on March 18 to attempt to suppress rebellions in parts of Asia Minor, the conspirators decided to take drastic action on March 15 — the Ides of March — when Caesar would address the Senate.

"THE IDES OF MARCH HAVE COME"

Accompanied by Decimus Brutus, Caesar arrived in front of the Senate House mid-morning. Climbing the steps, he confronted Spurinna, the soothsayer, who had warned him of danger.

"The Ides of March have come," he told Spurinna jokingly.

"Yes, they are come but they are not yet passed," Spurinna is supposed to have replied.

Present-day Rome's Largo Argentina was the site of Caesar's assassination, though little trace remains of the Senate buildings.

If he pondered that answer, Caesar gave no sign of it. He went up the steps of the Senate and onto the floor — without bodyguards, as usual, since he considered having them as a sign of fear. The Senate stood in respect. Caesar sat down in his chair but was almost immediately surrounded by the conspirators, who began to ask him questions, to distract him. Tillius Cimber handed him a petition to read. As Caesar waved it away irritably, Cimber suddenly yanked Caesar's robe off his shoulders, a signal that the attack should begin (and a potent symbol, for his purple robe was the symbol of Caesar's dictatorship).

The first blow was struck from behind by Publius Casca, but his nervousness caused him only to graze Caesar's shoulder. Caesar retaliated by jabbing Casca's arm with the stylus he used for writing, crying out, "You villain, Casca! What are you up to?"

He then tried to burst through the circle of assassins surrounding him, but was stabbed in the face by Cassius. Then Decimus Brutus, who had lured him out that day, plunged a knife into his side. Whirling desperately, but trapped on all sides, Caesar fought as hard as he could, uttering guttural cries, striking out with his stylus. The assassins slashed and stabbed in a frenzy, so much so that they wounded several of their own members.

Marcus Brutus was one of the last to plunge his knife into Caesar. Shakespeare has the dying dictator cry, "Et tu, Brutus?" but this is an invention. Suetonius claims that Caesar's last words, directed at Brutus, were, in Greek: "And you too, my child!" Plutarch merely says that Caesar wrapped his toga around his head and died at the foot of a statue of Pompey, with twenty-three stab wounds in his body.

UNINTENDED CONSEQUENCES

When they were done, the conspirators turned to the rest of the Senate, displaying their bloody knives and claiming that they had slain a dictator as a legitimate act of tryannicide (tyrannicide being legal under Roman law). But the senators were terrified and fled the Senate House. Anger and fear then swept through the city, paralyzing Rome. By the next day, when Mark Antony gave his funeral oration for Caesar, the common people of the city had turned against the senators, even those who had not helped kill their idol.

With Mark Antony in control of the legions — and Caesar's anointed heir Octavian soon to be a formidable presence — Brutus and his coconspirators were forced to flee the country. Thirteen years of civil war followed. In the end, the Roman Republic was no more. Imperial Rome, with Octavian as emperor, had begun, and would last for five hundred years of absolute rule.

The assassins, whether they were acting out of self-interest, or in a true belief that Rome faced a tyrant, had ironically changed the course of Roman history and halted the Republic in its tracks. Had Caesar not been killed, who knows what would have happened? The most likely outcome is that Caesar would have become a sort of benevolent dictator, using the devoted masses as a power base to keep the aristocrats in line, but at the same time greatly improving the lot of the *proletarii*.

For six days after Caesar's violent death, a comet appeared in the skies above Rome. Some people believed it was Caesar's spirit, flying through the sky, as in his dream. And in coins minted after the assassination, the comet is always shown. That's a sign of the power of Caesar's name, then and thereafter, whether he was a tyrant or *popularis*, or a little of both.

The Fall of the Roman Empire

The Beginning of Europe's Long Descent into Darkness

HAD THERE BEEN NO ROME and Roman Empire there would be no us. Founded around 510 BC, the Roman Empire had by the third century AD extended across millions of square miles, to the Rhine and Danube rivers in the north, North Africa in the south, Spain in the west, and Constantinople and beyond in the east. Throughout this territory, the Romans paved roads (some still in use today) through trackless wilderness, constructed towns, and built aqueducts to water them. Roman government held sway and the Latin language grew in influence.

The city of Rome itself, with its public baths, sewer systems, glorious buildings, and flourishing arts and poetry, was not only the center of Western civilization, but in a sense helped create it. Our Western systems of law, our cultures, and our languages — it is estimated that fifty percent of the words in English, for example, are of Latin origin — derive from ancient Rome. Even our sense of empire. These days, it's considered a bad thing to have an empire, but Rome's thousand-year hold over the world probably did more good than harm.

Not surprisingly, the rulers of this magnificent empire attained godlike status. Some, such as Julius Caesar and Octavian, even claimed they *were* gods. Even the less effective, more disreputable emperors like Nero had an air of grandeur about them.

So, given all these great accomplishments, how did Rome end up in 476 AD being ruled by Romulus Augustus, a twelve-year-old boy? His first name, fatefully enough, was the name of the legendary founder of Rome, but people mocked him and called him *Momyllus*, which means "little disgrace" — that's when they weren't sarcastically calling him *Augustulus*, which means "little emperor."

BARBARIAN INVASIONS

The eighteenth-century historian Edward Gibbon wrote a famous masterwork, *The History of the Decline and Fall of the Roman Empire*. Gibbon attributed Rome's "fall" partly to the "barbarian" (from the Latin word for "bearded") tribes who had long

The Barbarians Before Rome, by Evariste-Vital Luminais (1822–96), depicts Germanic soldiers approaching the outskirts of the city.

been bubbling and boiling around the edges of the northern Roman Empire, but also to the Romans themselves, whom, he claimed, became lazy and self-satisfied, depending on hired mercenaries (in some cases the same barbarians who would turn on them) to do their fighting. Many contemporary scholars, however, have rejected Gibbon's arguments about barbarian hordes as overly simplistic and paternalistic. Was Gibbon not merely viewing the barbarians from a contemptuous Roman point of view? Barbarians were, after all, mainly Germanic tribes on an empire-building mission of their own. In the view of some of these modern essayists, the Roman Empire never "declined"; it was merely transformed, becoming an amalgam of Germanic and Roman influences.

This provides us with a kinder, gentler — not to mention more politically correct — end to the Romans. But it ignores the very real trauma felt by this thousand-year-old civilization at the time. It also overlooks the impact of the subsequent decline of Western (read: Roman) learning, when much classical knowledge — including records of what was happening in the fifth century as Rome neared its end — was not "transformed," but irrevocably destroyed. As a result, Europe entered what has come to be known as the Dark Ages.

NEPOS USURPED

Romulus Augustus reigned from October of 475 to September of 476. Not much is known about him, except that he was thought good-looking. He was a kid caught in a big trap, really, one from which he was going to be lucky to escape alive, given the chaotic conditions prevalent in Rome at the time. Romulus had been named emperor by his father, a general named Flavius Orestes, who was part German and part Roman and yet had been named Master of Soldiers — commander in chief of the Roman army — by the then-emperor, Julius Nepos.

This was a sign of the deep barbarian infiltration of Rome, and a mistake on Nepos's part. For Orestes subsequently led a combined group of barbarian auxiliary forces against the emperor, sending him into exile (there are some who say that Nepos was really the last Roman emperor) and putting his own son, Romulus, on the throne. He probably did this so that he could rule from behind the scenes. But if he was expecting a bright new era in Roman history (or even just greater spoils), he was to be sorely mistaken.

A SLOW DECLINE

Rome had, in fact, been sliding from power since the middle of the fourth century, when the Huns, a nomadic people from Central Asia, had appeared on the Eurasian steppes and pushed other tribes westward in front of them. One of these tribes was the Visigoths, who settled on the banks of the Danube in about 376 AD, living there on the sufferance of Emperor Valens, head of the Eastern Roman Empire (the Roman Empire had been divided into two halves, Eastern and Western, by the Emperor Diocletian, in 285 AD, to make it easier to govern).

Valens's corrupt officials treated the Visigoths in a high-handed way, as if they were inferiors, stealing money from them and not listening to their complaints. As a result, they revolted, and defeated and killed Valens in the historic battle of Adrianople in 378, then swept with a vengeance through the Eastern Empire. The next emperor, Theodosius I, finally made peace with the

Visigoths in 382, but only after ceding them the territory they had seized – Thrace (now northern Greece and the Balkans). Rome looked eastward nervously.

Less than twenty years later, a charismatic young general named Alaric arose from one of the royal families of the Visigoths. Alaric was trained by the Emperor Theodosius and served as one of his top commanders, but after Theodosius died he turned on the Romans. He first invaded Italy in 400, but was defeated by the Roman general Stilicho in the Piedmont region, possibly because the Romans had captured his wife and family and were holding them hostage.

suffering from a plague, began to die by the scores. According to some sources, cannibalism was practiced. Finally, someone – legend has it that it was a rich Roman noblewoman who could no longer stand the plight of her city – opened the Salaria Gate, and, for the first time in seven hundred years, Rome was in the hands of a foreign invader.

As far as sackings went, Alaric's was relatively mild. Many Roman citizens were enslaved, but because of this there was a glut of slaves on the market and they could be bought back from the barbarians very cheaply. What the Visigoths were mainly interested in was food, and after obtaining

> While they did not build cities, the Huns were, like the Romans, intent on assimilating conquered peoples.

Around 408, Alaric tried again, this time in the middle of a civil war – a propitious time for an invasion, as it turned out. Alaric even briefly aligned himself with forces under his old foe General Stilicho, but, after Stilicho was murdered by the Romans, Alaric turned with purposeful vengeance and marched on Rome.

In August 410, panic gripped the citizens of Rome as Alaric settled in for a siege. The Emperor Honorius fled to Ravenna just as Rome began to starve. Thousands of slaves left their masters and slipped out through the city's gates, seeking better employment with the Visigoths. Honorius refused to bargain with Alaric; meanwhile, the people of Rome,

what little they could from the starving Romans, they set off south to sack more fertile parts of the country. But Alaric died of an illness shortly thereafter, and the threat was temporarily dispelled.

THE EMPIRE DISINTEGRATES

The respite for Rome was relatively brief, however, for soon it had to deal with Attila and his Huns, who had moved out of Asia pillaging and conquering. While they did not build great cities like the Romans, the Huns

Overleaf: *The Colosseum and the Arch of Constantine*, by Giovanni Paolo Pannini (1691-1765), ponders the glory that was Rome.

A nineteenth-century Italian portrait of Attila the Hun, the "barbarian" leader who very nearly toppled the Roman Empire.

— particularly the charismatic Attila, who saw himself as a world leader — were intent on assimilating conquered peoples. After first invading the Balkans and Gaul (where they were defeated at the battle of Châlons), they headed for Italy. In 452, Attila cut a great swath of destruction through the northern part of the country before heading for Rome. It is said that Pope Leo I then met with Attila and persuaded him not to attack the city, although it is more likely that Attila turned back because famine and disease were by then tearing his army apart. In any event, the Imperial City was spared.

Attila died the next year, and the power of the Huns waned, but in 453 the Vandals dealt Rome a devastating blow. The Vandals were a tribe from eastern Germany whose very name is now synonymous with wanton destruction. After taking a roundabout route to Rome — through Spain, hopping across the Mediterranean, devastating North Africa, and then sailing to Italy — they spent two full weeks sacking Rome and did not refrain from murder and plunder, before returning to North Africa.

Over the next twenty years, the Imperial City and the Roman Empire disintegrated. With the Italian Peninsula devastated by barbarian onslaughts and civil war, the struggling Roman government was unable to levy enough taxes to keep a standing army in the field. Increasingly, it depended on barbarian mercenaries. The Roman government was weak and obviously up for grabs. It was at this point, 475 AD, that Flavius Orestes was appointed — ironically, to protect the Roman emperor. As soon as he could, he betrayed him.

ROMULUS IN EXILE

After Flavius Orestes appointed Romulus emperor, he, too, fell prey to the tumultuous politics of the time. He had double-crossed the barbarians who had fought for him, refusing to give them land to settle on, and they joined forces and rose against him, led by the Visigoth Odoacer (a name that has numerous spellings). Orestes was captured and quickly beheaded on August 28, 476.

Then Odoacer marched on Ravenna, where Romulus Augustus held court, and immediately deposed him, in the autumn of 476, as easily as a big kid pushes a little one out of a sandbox.

Odoacer then sent an arrogant note to Emperor Zeno of Constantinople – then head of the Eastern Empire – to the effect that there would be no need to appoint a new Western emperor: he, Odoacer, would now rule. It is a sign of how insignificant a threat Romulus was that Odoacer did not bother to have him killed – he simply pensioned him off to Campania in southern Italy.

The fall of the Roman Empire was so quiet, one commentator has written, as to be "noiseless." But this was because by the time Odoacer pushed Romulus out, the power of Rome was already gone forever, lost in war and strife. The Eastern Empire, protected by better luck, a great wall built around Constantinople, and water (the Bosphorus separates Constantinople from Europe, and the barbarians were notoriously poor seamen) survived until the Ottomans conquered it in the fifteenth century. But the Western Empire was gone. For a time, Roman bureaucracy kept the streets paved, the water flowing through the aqueducts, and the books safe in their grand libraries, but these things were not of value to the new owners of the empire, and gradually fell into disuse and disrepair.

Some aristocratic Roman families cooperated with the Germanic tribes and thrived, but many of the inhabitants of Rome and other major Italian cities were enslaved. Others were left alone to work for their new masters, but because the barbarians had redistributed the land among themselves, these former Roman citizens were left in a condition approaching serfdom.

Times changed. Coins were not minted. The famous Roman pottery, which had spread across the empire, stopped being made. Local economies declined severely, as did the population of Europe. The great civilization of classical antiquity now entered a steady decline. The Dark Ages, which would last until about 1000 AD, had begun.

What Happened to Romulus Augustus?

There is much speculation, but not a lot of real evidence, as to what happened to the young emperor after Odoacer deposed him. It is known that he went to live with relatives in Campania, in southern Italy, with a pension of six thousand gold *solidi* a year. He may have become a scholar or a monk – there is brief mention of a "lovely letter by the holy brother Romulus" in correspondence, dated 507, between a North African bishop and an Italian diplomat. And around the same time, a secretary to Theodoric the Great wrote a letter to a Romulus about certain issues to do with a pension. But after this, all is silence.

The Middle Ages and Renaissance

1000–1500

The Battle of Hastings

The Norman Triumph That
Changed the Face of Medieval England

IN THE EARLY LIGHT OF THE October morning, the Saxon shield wall on the crest of the hill must have seemed impenetrable to the Normans gazing up the slope. The English *thegns*, or landed aristocrats, loyal to their Anglo-Saxon king, Harold, were covered with chain mail, wore strong helmets, and carried swords and long, double-edged Danish axes. They had planted their heavy semicircular shields on the ground, interlocking them so that there was not an inch of space between them. Behind this barrier were the so-called levies, the English peasants who, under the feudal system, were obliged to fight for their king. And, at the center of the line, astride his horse and protected by his bodyguards, was King Harold Godwinson. It was his intention to hold firm and triumph, or die.

Arrayed against the Saxons, at the foot of the hill, were the forces of the invader, William the Bastard of Normandy, soon to be known by the far more flattering sobriquet of William the Conqueror. William's forces were equal in number to the Saxons, but far more mobile and professional, including as they did cavalry and archers, and experienced Italian mercenaries. There were arrayed in three divisions or "battles": Bretons on the left, Normans in the center, and French on the right. It was William's intention to shatter the English shield wall, kill Harold, and take his crown.

The battle began with a song. According to a legend, William's minstrel and knight, Ivo Taillefer, begged his king to allow him the honor of charging the English first. William granted his request and Taillefer sped his horse toward the Saxons, where he tauntingly tossed his sword in the air while singing what was probably an early version of the epic *The Song of Roland*. When an enraged Saxon soldier charged out to challenge him, Taillefer decapitated him and took his head as a trophy — and as proof that God was on his side.

This detail from the Bayeux Tapestry shows William the Conqueror exhorting his troops prior to the battle with the English.

The Saxons believed differently, of course. As the Normans rushed up the hill, they shouldered close behind their shield wall and cried, "Ut! Ut!" – meaning "Out! Out!"

THE MEN FROM THE NORTH

At this moment, around 9 a.m. on the morning of October 14, 1066, the future of England hung in the balance. The Anglo-Saxons had controlled the country since the fifth century, after migrating there from Scandinavia or Germany, but they were now faced with a mass invasion of their lands by the Normans from northern France – who intended to stay.

distance across the English Channel, had become a tempting target. All the more so because the Duke of Normandy, William the Bastard (so named because of his illegitimate status), saw himself as the country's rightful ruler.

A PROMISE AND AN OATH

Strong links between England and Normandy had developed following the coronation of King Harold's predecessor, King Edward the Confessor, in 1042. Prior to assuming the throne, Edward had spent twenty-five years in exile in Normandy, where his mother had taken him to escape a Danish invasion and

Chief of a warrior race, William proclaimed, "I was brought up in arms from childhood."

The Normans had recently emerged as a formidable regional power. They were descended from Vikings who had occupied the Seine River valley in the ninth century – their correct name, *Normanni*, means "the men from the north." In the tenth and early eleventh centuries, they had conquered much of northwestern France while developing a reputation as skilled and ferocious warriors, united by strong kinship ties. The feudal system, which obliged tenant farmers and knights to fight for the landholders, provided manpower and supplies for the Norman campaigns, but led to an unceasing quest for more land. By the mid-eleventh century, England, just a short

subsequent period of Danish control. On his return to England following the reinstatement of Anglo-Saxon rule, he had taken with him a group of Norman advisers. This upset the Anglo-Saxon aristocracy, who rallied round Godwin of Wessex, a powerful English lord. Aided by William, Edward expelled Godwin from the country in 1051. But after Godwin's death, his son, Harold Godwinson, managed to return to England. There he regained much of the power lost by his father, so much so that King Edward – not the most strong-willed of rulers – made him a chief adviser.

In 1064, Harold was shipwrecked off the French coast and captured by the Duke of Normandy. William claimed that Edward had promised England to him in 1051 in return for his aid in expelling Godwin, and he had long since set his eyes on its throne and rich lands. He forced Harold to swear an oath on a saint's relic to support his "claim" to the throne once Edward, childless and purportedly celibate, died.

On his return to England, however, Harold simply explained that the oath had been forced from him under duress, and Edward himself denied making any promises to William. So, following Edward's death on January 5, 1066, there being no other heir to the throne, and with the full support of the kingdom's most powerful nobles, Harold was crowned king at Westminster Abbey.

This infuriated William. And William was not a person to trifle with. Just a boy when he succeeded his father as Duke of the Normans — "I was brought up in arms from childhood," he told people — he had had to be courageous and wise beyond his years just to survive. Sincerely believing that God was on his side, he resolved to amass a great seaborne army, take England by force, and depose Harold.

HAROLD BESIEGED

William's invasion fleet was an incredible one for the time — six hundred ships, which were to hold seven thousand men in all, including knights, archers, and infantry. For months, the coast of Normandy rang with these shipbuilding efforts. Meanwhile, to help justify his attack, William sought the support of Pope Alexander II, drawing attention to the fact that the prelate who had crowned Harold, Archbishop Stigand of Canterbury, had not been formally recognized by the Pope. Alexander, who was keen to establish alliances with powerful figures outside the Holy Roman Empire, agreed, and he sent a papal banner in support. This, in turn, helped William rally troops from all over northern France and beyond. The fleet was finished in early September, and when favorable winds arose on the 27th, William and his men set sail for England.

King Harold already had his hands full, because he was fighting off not one invasion force, but two. For there was another claimant to the throne, King Harald III Sigurdsson of Norway, who was descended from King Canute, once the ruler of both Scandinavia and England. Joining forces with Harold's estranged brother, Tostig, Harald III invaded England in September, landing in the northeast and defeating the armies of two northern earls before making camp at Stamford Bridge, near York. Harold reacted swiftly, marched north with his army, and, on September 25, defeated and killed both Harald and Tostig at the battle of Stamford Bridge. This was a major victory for England, and also marked the last time a Scandinavian army would attempt to invade the country.

William landed on the southeast coast of England three days later. Needing as quick a victory as possible, since he was operating on foreign territory, far from his base of

supply, he and his forces began pillaging the land, hoping to draw Harold into battle. It worked: Harold raced down from York, stopped in London to gather more forces, and then headed with all speed to the little village of Hastings, in East Sussex. There he arrayed his forces across the Hastings–London road, on Senlac Hill, about eight miles north of the town, a site now known as Battle Hill.

Harold's force of about seven thousand men was set up across the crest of the hill, with its flanks anchored on either side by woods and the massive forest of Anderida at his back — on the face of it an impregnable position. But Harold's forces were not as strong as they seemed, as they had been weakened both by losses at the battle of Stamford Bridge and by the reluctance of local peasants to fight another pitched battle.

"I'M ALIVE!"

After Ivo Taillefer made his fabled charge (one account has him riding into the Saxon lines and killing another two Saxons before being killed himself), William gave a command and a shower of arrows fell upon the English. The Saxon soldiers ducked beneath their shields as the arrows fell, and were little harmed — the Normans were shooting uphill and the distance was hard to gauge. In any case, since Norman archery

A vivid illustration of the battle of Hastings from a fifteenth-century French manuscript, the *Chronicle of Normandy*.

tactics depended on shooting back arrows already fired by opponents, and since the Saxons were without archers, the Normans were soon forced to stop firing in order to conserve their ammunition.

William then had his infantry charge straight up the hill at the densely packed English army, but these foot soldiers were unable to break through the shield wall and fell back, with many dead and wounded. Their retreat almost became a rout. At one point, the English right wing began to pursue the Bretons falling back on the Norman left, and although their commanders checked this advance, it was noted with interest by the Normans.

A rumor then rippled through the panicky Norman ranks that William was dead and he was forced to doff his helmet and ride in front of his lines, yelling, "I'm alive! I'm alive!" But he was faced with a problem: time was on Harold's side, not his. The longer the battle took, the more likely it would be that reinforcements would come to Harold's aide. As the day wore on, repeated attacks on the shield wall produced nothing but dead Normans.

The Bretons had continued to observe that when their men retreated, the English right wing was likely to pursue, at least partway down the hill. So at William's behest, the Bretons staged a feigned retreat and when the Saxons pursued, the Norman cavalry charged and slaughtered them. This happened at least twice during the course of the long battle, seriously weakening the English line.

AN ARROW IN THE EYE?

By late afternoon, the battle had come down to a bitter, brutal clash of two armies. The shield wall had fallen back on itself and tightened up as losses increased. But still the English and King Harold held on, even though the gaps in their lines were now filled with peasant levies whose fighting value was questionable. For his part, William knew that if night fell and he had still not found a way through the shield wall, he would be forced to retreat from the battlefield, leaving his forces in a vulnerable position.

Before preparing for one last assault, he ordered his archers to shoot another volley, this one high over the Saxon lines, where it fell, wreaking havoc among the closely

The Bayeux Tapestry

A depiction of the events surrounding the Norman Conquest of England, the Bayeux Tapestry is one of the most extraordinary artifacts we have from this era. Preserved now in Bayeux, France, it is extremely long and narrow — 230 feet long by 20 inches wide. Despite its name, it is not actually a woven tapestry, but a piece of cloth embroidered with panels, each showing a particular event. It was probably commissioned in the 1170s by Bishop Odo, William the Conqueror's half-brother, as a way of commemorating William's victory — and as a handy piece of propaganda, since the Norman point of view is the only one shown. As a source of information on medieval society and soldiery at the time, it has been invaluable to modern scholars.

packed forces. As the Normans advanced, King Harold, who was rallying his troops, looked up into the sky and was pierced by an arrow that hit him directly in the eye. Some stories have it that he pulled it out and continued fighting, half-blind, blood spurting down his face, flanked by his bodyguards, until he was cut down by a Norman knight. But there are numerous versions of Harold's end, some of which have his body hacked to pieces. The Bayeux Tapestry shows a figure being struck through the eye with an arrow, but some historians think this is not Harold, or that the arrow was a later addition to the tapestry – in medieval times, a missile in the eye was considered a just punishment for traitors and liars.

However it happened, Harold died on the field, and the Saxons, having no king left to fight for, fled down the back of the hill and into the forest pursued by the Normans. William was triumphant: England was his. That night, William the Conquerer camped on the battlefield, at the spot where he later ordered the building of Battle Abbey, his thanks to God for his victory.

Courage is an essential attribute for a king and William certainly had that – three horses were killed under him that day. But so is luck. And William's luck may well have included an arrow that found its way to the eye of the king of England.

A FUSION OF CULTURES

Since there was no one left in England who was strong enough to oppose William, he had himself crowned king on Christmas Day, 1066, although he soon faced several rebellions and did not secure England until the 1170s. With the Norman Conquest complete, England changed forever. Land was given to the Norman lords who had participated in the conquest, a traumatic process for the Saxon owners. (There was so much squabbling among the Normans over who owned what that the Domesday Book was created to solve the disputes, in turn becoming an invaluable record of the period.) However, the Normans left intact the Anglo-Saxon legal system – sheriffs, courts, taxes, names of counties.

In the longer term, the Norman invasion changed the English language – infusing it with French and Latin – and ensured that Catholicism would be the state religion (until the sixteenth century). It also tied England more strongly to the European mainland.

The Saxons had trouble adapting to the rule of the man they considered a tyrant. But was William such a tyrant? Probably not. Although he met the fierce resistance of the north of England after Hastings with blood and fire, he also knew when to be merciful, and he understood how to administer and apply laws.

William the Conquerer died in 1087, still holding the lands he had conquered. No one really knows what would have happened had William failed to conquer England, but the melding together of these two strong peoples created one of the most extraordinary cultures in the Western world.

The Crusades

*The Centuries-long Battle for the Holy Land That Left
a Legacy of Suspicion and Misunderstanding*

ON A COLD NOVEMBER DAY in 1095, Pope Urban II gave a powerful speech in France that had a momentous impact on the subsequent history not only of Europe, but also of the Middle East. Facing a crowd of clergy and other important church officials at the Council of Clermont in Auvergne, Urban described what he saw as a disturbing development: the encroachment of Muslim Turks on Byzantium, the former Eastern Roman Empire, whose Emperor Alexius had sent the Pope an urgent plea for help. But it was not just, or even chiefly, the Muslim Turks threatening Asia Minor that concerned Urban, but the forces of Islam that held the holy city of Jerusalem and "the Holy Sepulchre of the Lord, possessed by unclean nations." The Pope went on:

> Your brethren who live in the east are in urgent need of your help, and you must hasten to give them the aid which has often been promised them … The Arabs have occupied more and more of the lands of those Christians … They have killed and captured many, and have destroyed the churches and devastated the

empire. If you permit them to continue thus for awhile with impunity, the faithful of God will be much more widely attacked by them. On this account I, or rather the Lord, beseech you as Christ's heralds to publish this everywhere and to persuade all people of whatever rank, foot-soldiers and knights, poor and rich, to carry aid promptly to those Christians and to destroy that vile race from the lands of our friends.

Urban whipped the crowd into a frenzy, promising them that "all who die by the way, whether by land or by sea, or in battle against the pagans, shall have immediate remission of sins." His listeners shouted over and over again, "Deus lo volt!" – "God wills it!" And so the Holy Wars began.

A MIXED LEGACY

The popular view of the Crusades in the West was shaped first by the romantic literature that sprang up while the Crusades were occurring, and later by Hollywood. Early on, Crusaders were portrayed as soldiers of God on a divine mission to reclaim the Holy Land. However, some

*The Looting of Jerusalem after the Capture
by the Christians in 1099,* an illuminated
manuscript illustration dating from 1440.

representations of the Crusaders in today's literature and in films present the European knights as bloodthirsty thugs out only for gold and land, God or Allah be damned. Despite these stereotypes, however, the extraordinary importance of the Crusades in history remains. Scholar Thomas F. Madden has written that "whether we admire the Crusaders or not, it is a fact that the world we know today would not exist without their efforts."

In the century before the Crusades, Christian Western Europe was recovering from the ravages of the Dark Ages and fighting off attacks from various invaders — Vikings from the north, Magyars from Central Asia, and various Muslim peoples from North Africa, some of whom were

This fifteenth-century illustration shows the soldiers of King Baldwin I, the first Christian King of Jerusalem, battling with the Turks.

fighting their way up the Iberian Peninsula. However, as the century came to a close, the fortunes of Western Europe changed. More efficient farming techniques, most notably the introduction of a more efficient plow, improved living conditions and in turn gave rise to rapid population growth. The consequent revitalization of the economy bolstered Europe's armed forces. At the same time, reformist popes were seeking a way to turn Europe's nobles away from the internecine warfare of feudalism — and confront Islam in the Holy Land.

AN ELECTRIFYING EFFECT

Pope Urban repeated his speech several times throughout 1095 and 1096, and sent forth his clergy to spread the word all over Europe: all who wanted to fight the Muslims and return Jerusalem to the True Cross were to swear a pilgrim's oath and make their way to Constantinople by August 15, 1096, on the Feast of the Assumption, and from there set out for the Holy Land. In return, they would be granted indulgences for the remission of their sins. It's not known what Urban expected when he made this plea — some historians think his main aim was to unite warring European nobles — but there is evidence that he thought a few thousand knights at most would answer the call.

Instead, over one hundred thousand people joined the initial wave of the First Crusade, known as the "Peasants' Crusade." Despite the Church's efforts to harness and control this gathering – Urban futilely decreed that no women, monks, or children should take part – huge numbers of peasants and land-poor knights streamed east toward Constantinople, electrified by a new piety, filled with millennial dreams, and seeing their pilgrim's oath as a sure road out of their impoverished lives. A charismatic and zealous monk known as Peter the Hermit was one of their leaders. Peter, preaching throughout northern France, told mass gatherings of peasants to meet in Cologne, Germany, in April, well ahead of Urban's proposed rendezvous. Leaving from there in two different groups, this ragtag Crusade headed for Byzantium.

RIVAL RELIGIONS

As it is today, Jerusalem was a city holy to both Christians and Muslims. The Christians revered it as the place where Jesus was crucified and the site of the Church of the Holy Sepulchre. For the Muslims, it was the city where the prophet Muhammad was taken on a mystical night journey before being raised up to Heaven to meet the prophets Abraham, Moses, and Jesus. The Muslims knew it as *al-Quds* ("the Holy Place"). When they captured it from the Byzantines in 638 AD, they built one of the world's most beautiful places of worship: the Dome of the Rock.

The idea that European Christians ("Franks," as the Muslims knew them) simply set out at the end of the eleventh century to retake Jerusalem for no reason other than fervent anti-Islamic sentiment doesn't portray the entire picture. For, at the time, Islam did pose a very real threat to Christianity.

The older of the two religions, Christianity had arisen in the first century AD and spread to all parts of the Roman Empire (which then included Jerusalem and Palestine, out of which the Romans had pushed the Jews). At this time in the history of the Catholic Church, the religion was spread peacefully, by missionary work. By the seventh century, when Islam began to flourish on the Arabian Peninsula, the religion of Jesus Christ was the predominant belief in Europe and the Mediterranean basin.

But not for long. Emerging in the early seventh century, Islam taught that while Christians and Jews might live peacefully and practice their religion under Islamic rule, Christian states must be replaced by Islamic ones. Muslim forces took over Palestine, Syria and Egypt, crossed to Spain, and defeated Christian forces on the Iberian Peninsula. By the mid-eighth century, they had launched raids into France.

Conflict between the two groups continued for the next two hundred years. The Arabs were conquered in the eleventh century by the Turks, but the Turks then converted to Islam and carried on the battle with the West. Byzantium – the surviving eastern half of the Roman Empire based in

Constantinople – was threatened when the Turks conquered Asia Minor. Looking across the Bosporus Strait in 1095, the Byzantine Emperor Alexius I Comnenus decided to make a plea to Western Europe for help in fighting the Turks. It was this plea that prompted Urban's speech.

DESTRUCTION OF THE PEASANT'S ARMY

The undisciplined army of pilgrims launched by Urban's plea made its way across the Rhineland in the spring of 1096. One group, whipped to a frenzy by an anti-Semite German count named Emicho, participated

arduous journey to the Holy Land. There, they allied themselves with the Fatimid rulers of Egypt (not the first time Christians and Muslims would make temporary marriages of convenience during the Crusades) to defeat a large Seljuk Turk force outside Antioch. Then they turned on their allies and wrested Jerusalem from the Fatimid Muslims in 1099. When the Crusaders entered the city, they massacred Muslims and Jews alike.

THE SECOND CRUSADE

The First Crusade had been successful beyond anyone's dreams, liberating the Holy Land in near record time, opening

When the Crusaders entered Jerusalem in 1099, they massacred Muslims and Jews alike.

in horrific slaughters of Jews – whom they considered to be enemies of Christ – in the German towns of Metz, Worms, and Mainz. Arriving near Constantinople in the summer of 1096, the tattered army of the Peasants' Crusade engaged a force of veteran Turks, and was quickly demolished.

However, this army of peasants was followed by a much more formidable group of soldiers led by great European nobles including Count Robert II of Flanders, Count Stephen of Blois, and Godfrey of Bouillon, the Duke of Lorraine. In large part motivated by piety, these men put aside their differences, raised a powerful cohort of knights and made the long, extremely

Jerusalem to Christian pilgrims, and founding a new Christian realm in Palestine. Divided into four states (the counties of Edessa and Tripoli, the Principality of Antioch, and the Kingdom of Jerusalem), it consisted of a narrow finger of land between the Mediterranean Sea and the Jordan River. It was a sliver of Christianity surrounded by enemies, notably the Seljuk Turks in Syria in the north and Fatimid Egypt in the south.

In the middle of the twelfth century, Arab leaders arose who sought to unify the Islamic world. One of them was Imad Ad-din Zangi, a Seljuk Turk who seized Edessa, the northernmost of the Crusader States, on

Christmas Day, 1144, and murdered all its European Christian inhabitants. This prompted the ill-fated Second Crusade, preached by the fiery monk Bernard of Clairvaux and led by French and German armies under King Louis VII and the Holy Roman Emperor Conrad III. This was nearly a complete disaster – one of the lowest points was a foolish attack on Damascus, a Muslim-controlled city that had up to that point been a supporter of Christian Jerusalem – and the Christian forces retreated in disarray.

Heartened by this victory, Islamic forces under such leaders as Nur al-Din, the son of Zangi, attacked Crusader outposts. Thus the pattern for years of warfare was set, with Crusader castles being besieged by "Saracens," as the Franks called the Muslims (a word deriving from a Greek term that means "easterners"), and other Crusaders riding to the rescue.

Slowly, the Saracens whittled away the Christian holdings in the Holy Land. In 1174, Nur al-Din died and was replaced by the legendary Salah al-Din Yusuf Ibn Ayyub, known to history as Saladin, the most ferocious Islamic leader of his age or of almost any other. Saladin had fought as one of Nur al-Din's lieutenants, although he had spent a good deal of time trying to wrest power from his leader and his family. On succeeding Nur al-Din, Saladin portrayed himself as the unifier of Muslims and set out to drive the Christians from the Holy Land.

In this he was almost entirely successful, defeating two armies sent from Jerusalem at the battle of Hattin, near the Sea of Galilee, and finally entering Jerusalem in triumph in 1187. After this, only a few Christian cities held out, notably the port city of Tyre. Saladin had, for the time being, stamped out the foreign presence in his land.

THE THIRD CRUSADE

The Third Crusade is probably the best known in the popular imagination of both West and East, pitting against each other as it did two famous warrior-kings, Saladin and King Richard I, the Lionheart, of England (although the two never met in personal combat, as medieval legend liked to have it). With the Crusader States in Palestine teetering on the edge of extinction, Richard joined forces with Emperor Frederick Barbarossa of Germany and King Philip II of France to raise a sizable army. Here, the stereotype of a hungry nobleman heading to the Holy Land to seize land and enrich himself can be put to rest, since much recent research of medieval records shows that crusading was an extraordinarily expensive business for any prince, and was mainly undertaken at this point in time out of piety and hope for remission of sins – a not inconsiderable reward.

From the beginning, though, the Third Crusade was marred by ill fortune. Frederick fell off his horse and drowned while crossing the Saleph River in Anatolia, in 1190. Richard and Philip, once the closest of friends, began arguing as they sailed to the Holy Land. Once there, they managed to retake the city of Acre from Saladin, but Philip, ill and unhappy, then left the Crusade.

It fell to Richard to advance the cause, and

A nineteenth-century portrait of King Richard I, also known as Richard the Lionheart, the most famous, if not the most successful, Crusader.

he proved himself the leader history and folklore has painted him: bold, intelligent, and extremely brave. He swept along the coast of Palestine, leading his men to victory after victory. But whenever he struck inland to attack Jerusalem, he was unable to secure his supply lines against his marauding enemy. Ultimately, he was forced to make a truce with Saladin, whereby the latter allowed unarmed Christian pilgrims free access to the Holy City, but only on condition that Richard and his forces left the Holy Land.

THE LATER CRUSADES

There were four more Crusades in the thirteenth century, but none was ultimately successful. By 1291, the date conventionally given as the end of the Crusades, Islamic forces had succeeded in ousting all Christian forces from the former Crusader States. The Middle East was now completely controlled by Islamic rulers and would remain that way until the nineteenth century. However, the battle between Christianity and Islam went on elsewhere for hundreds of years, resulting in the fall of Constantinople to the Turks in the fifteenth century and the near-fall of Vienna in 1529 to the armies of Suleiman the Magnificent.

Paradoxically, despite the almost total victory of Islam over the Christian armies in the Holy Land, it was Europe that benefited the most from the Crusades. Exposure to Islamic science, mathematics, art, and military science invigorated European culture. The increased traffic between Europe and the Holy Land stimulated trade, and Europe came to best the Islamic world economically. In contrast, a resentful Islamic world retreated into isolation, the once sophisticated courts of the Muslim realms becoming cultural and economic backwaters.

Today, eight hundred years after they officially ended, the Crusades are still a matter of speculation and controversy. Just after the terrorist attacks of September 11, 2001, when President George W. Bush referred in a speech to "this crusade, this war on terrorism," there were many in the Islamic world who felt this raised the specter of Christian knights invading Muslim lands in an attempt to destroy a religion and a way of life. And so perhaps the most lasting effect of the Crusades was to have sown the seeds of suspicion between Islam and Christianity.

The Children's Crusades

There were numerous "popular crusades" during the years of crusading, by which most historians mean crusades that arose spontaneously, not at the call of a pope, but simply as a fervent expression of faith. The most famous one is the so-called Children's Crusade of 1212, which was actually two separate Crusades. The first began in Germany when a youth named Nicholas proclaimed that an angel had appeared to him and told him to gather a force and take back the Holy Sepulchre from the Saracens. Soon, seven thousand youths followed him to Genoa. Once there, they expected the Mediterranean to part in front of them. When it did not, they returned home, disappointed.

The second was led by a shepherd boy named Stephen, who said he had a letter from Christ to the King of France. Stephen led thirty thousand people to Paris to meet with the king, but when the letter was found to be a fake, the crusade dispersed.

No Children's Crusade reached the Holy Land. Scholars have even questioned whether such crusades really involved only children, since the world *pueri*, used by chroniclers to describe these groups, may also have meant a lowborn person, no matter what his or her age.

Magna Carta

*A King Yields Powers in a Document That Becomes
the Foundation Stone of Modern Human Rights*

IN JANUARY OF 1215, A GROUP of noblemen, mainly barons from England's northern counties, gathered together for a secret meeting at Dunmow Castle in Essex, England, the home of Lord Robert Fitzwalter. As well as Fitzwalter, who had organized the meeting, those in attendance included several influential figures, such as Eustace de Vesci, Lord of Alnwick Castle, and Geoffrey de Mandeville, the Earl of Essex, and at least one important cleric, Giles, Bishop of Hereford. At that moment, England was extraordinarily tense, on the verge of the chaos that precedes a civil war. Armed bands of the barons' men roamed the byways, trying to keep order.

The barons were in a state of great anger about this lawlessness, and they laid the blame for the situation squarely at the door of the ruler of the realm, King John. At their meeting, they resolved that they must confront him and demand changes that would improve their lot and the lot of their subjects. In particular, they wanted an end to the heavy taxes John was placing on his people in order to pay for his failed war against France. Before the barons disbanded, they stood together solemnly and took an oath, that they "would stand fast together for the liberty of the church and the realm."

A few days later, the barons arrived at Windsor Castle, where knots of worried royal advisers were meeting hourly with the king. Reluctantly, John agreed to hear them out. It was not a happy meeting. To prove the seriousness of their intent, the barons had come armed, and their contempt for the king was palpable. Once in his presence, they set out their demands for reforms to the laws regarding the distribution of land to, and the taxes levied on, the nobility. If they did not receive these and other concessions, they warned the king, they would go to war against him.

These were no empty threats, and John knew it. Ultimately, they would constrain the king to concede – to a degree unprecedented in England or in any other Western realm of the Middle Ages – certain basic civil rights, not only to his barons, but to all of his subjects. And this concession would be enshrined in one of the most

In his play *The Life and Death of King John*, Shakespeare had John poisoned in a monastery. In reality, he died of dysentery.

extraordinary and important documents of all time: Magna Carta. In turn, Magna Carta (properly speaking, "the" is not attached to these two Latin words meaning "Great Charter") would become a symbol of civil rights and subsequently be the basis for common law in England and, later, for the U.S. Constitution and Bill of Rights.

A DISASTROUS RULE

Was there ever a king in English history so hated and scorned as King John? It's hard to think of one who really comes up (or down) to his standards of cowardice, betrayal, greed, and incompetence, so

Richard to rebel against his father in 1189; this armed revolt ended with Richard, the elder and more powerful brother, being named Henry's successor. When Henry died, Richard — soon to be known to history as Richard the Lionheart — became king. Knowing John to be untrustworthy, he confirmed him as Lord of Ireland and married him off to a rich woman, on the condition that he stay out of England while Richard was away on the Crusades. True to form, John agreed — and then immediately broke his promise.

Worse yet, when Richard was captured and imprisoned on his way home from the Third

John was bleeding the kingdom, and particularly his barons, dry. He was also losing the trust of his people.

much so that even in this age of revisionist history, John resists rehabilitation. It can be said, however, that John came by treachery naturally. He was, after all, a member of the Plantagenet noble family, rulers of England since 1133 and a notoriously treacherous bunch. His three older brothers had all rebelled against his father.

John was born on Christmas Eve, 1166, the youngest of eight children of Eleanor of Aquitaine and King Henry II of England. Despite the fact that John was Henry's favorite child, the king had kept no royal land to give his youngest son, who thus became known to many as John Lackland. Aggrieved, John joined with his brother

Crusade, John refused to help ransom him and, indeed, allied himself with Richard's enemy, King Philip II of France, to seize Richard's lands in Normandy. Richard made his way back in 1194, and forced John to relinquish these lands. But when Richard died in 1199, without a legitimate son, John had himself crowned King of England. He managed to gain King Philip's support for this by ceding him large tracts of French land in Normandy. However, he then upset Philip and all of the French aristocracy by annulling his existing marriage and wedding the barely pubescent Isabella of Angoulême — right under the nose of her fiancé, and one of Philip's vassals, Hugh IX of Lusignan. In response, Philip began a campaign to oust John from his remaining French possessions.

WEARING THE COST OF INEPTITUDE

Not only did John then fight an inept military campaign against Philip and steadily lose English holdings in France, but he also demanded financial support for his ill-advised ventures from his own nobles, in the form of "scutage" – a fee paid in lieu of military service. Despite the fact that this form of payment had either fallen into disuse or was used to levy only very mild fees, John had increased the rates of scutage eleven times during his fifteen years in office.

And this wasn't the only financial burden the barons had to carry as a result of John's fecklessness. Earlier, he had alienated Pope Innocent III by insisting on filling, and thereby profiting from, ecclesiastical offices. (Essentially, John would insist on a fee from any prelate who sought a higher office, usually in the form of Church lands or money raised from Church land.) In response, the Pope held not only John, but the entire country, excommunicate, meaning that no one could get married or buried or be baptized in a church. To have this ban lifted, John was forced to pay the pope the large sum of one thousand marks per year. Much of the money he recouped from his barons.

John was bleeding the kingdom, and particularly his barons, dry. He was also losing the trust of his people, who had seen him break his word over and over. Popular myths sprang up that spoke of people banding together against the king to achieve freedom – one was the legend of Robin Hood. So while it was the barons who led the revolt against John, largely for their own reasons, popular consensus supported them.

THE MARCH ON LONDON

When the barons met King John in January of 1215, they demanded reforms that had been enshrined in King Henry I's Coronation Charter (or Charter of Liberties) of 1100. In particular, they alluded to a promise made by Henry, to "all his barons and faithful men," to abolish "evil customs" that had oppressed them – in particular, abuses by the king when it came to the unequal handing out of royal land and extracting money from his barons through taxes. Henry had put these tenets into writing due to a possible threat to his throne, but had subsequently ignored them almost completely.

John paid little attention, either, and after the January meeting, both sides prepared for war, filling war chests with money and arming their followers. John gathered those barons still loyal to him and swore them to a new oath of fidelity, not just to their king but also "against the charter." He sent emissaries to Pope Innocent in Rome, seeking to sway the Catholic leader to his side. In early March, in a brilliant public relations stroke, he began wearing the white cross of the Crusader, and made all his men wear it, writing to the pope that his baronial enemies were "worse than Saracens" – the name used by Crusaders for Muslims.

Naturally, this did not please the barons. In May, led by Fitzwalter, they marched on London. Fitzwalter and Eustace de Vesci had very personal reasons for wanting to temper John's power. Fitzwalter claimed that the king had attempted to rape his daughter; de Vesci declared that John had seduced his wife. Whether this was true or not, no one knows. But such tales brought sympathy to the barons' cause. When they marched on London, the citizens opened the gates of the city. The barons occupied this seat of the Crown without a fight on May 17. Now there was no way John could avoid negotiating with the rebels. Moving beyond their initial demands, the barons drew up a series of articles, which they sent to the king. Emissaries went back and forth. By June, the barons had what they wanted: a document that would curb the king's power to do damage to their lives and estates.

THE CHARTER APPROVED

To make the document official, King John and his barons met "in the meadow which is called Runnymede between Windsor and Staines on the fifteenth day of June," – a field alongside the Thames River, about 30 miles southwest of London. John attached his seal to the so-called Articles of the Barons and ordered that the document be copied and distributed. In return, on June 19, the barons swore their fealty to John.

Magna Carta questioned the authority of a king to rule solely as he pleased – in 1215, an extraordinary question indeed. As a corollary to this, it also guaranteed the cornerstone of modern civil rights, the right of *habeas corpus* – meaning "you shall have the body" – which signified that the Crown could no longer keep a free man imprisoned forever without trial. Other articles dealt with maintaining the barons' property rights, limiting scutage, and restricting certain of the king's feudal privileges. But the articles became extraordinarily important for one simple change, made at the last minute. In stipulating to whom the provisions of the charter applied, the barons altered the term "any baron" to "any freeman." As a result of this seemingly minor change, the rights of *all* English people were, for the first time, written in law – and the foundation stone of modern ideas of freedom was laid.

THE AGREEMENT ANNULLED

Yet a great historical irony of Magna Carta is that, while it accomplished many things, it did not accomplish what it set out to do in the short term: avert a civil war in England. At the time, no one really believed that the agreement – dubbed the "Great Charter" to differentiate it from the Coronation Charter of 1100 – would hold. Part of the problem were articles 52 and 61, which indicated that if there were any disagreement about a plan made by the king, it "would be settled by the judgment" of a committee of twenty-five barons – all of whom were John's enemies, naturally. King John had signed Magna Carta because he had been forced to,

King John signing Magna Carta at Runnymede on June 15, 1215. Within months, John would seek to annul the charter.

but no king could be expected to have his power abrogated in such a way. This was the ostensible reason why John, almost as soon as he returned from Runnymede, rejected the charter and in September convinced Pope Innocent, whose temporal influence extended across much of Europe, to annul "the shameful and demeaning agreement forced upon the king by violence and fear."

The barons, naturally, were infuriated by this – once again, the treacherous King John had broken his side of a bargain. A bloody civil war then raged throughout England, with the rebels obtaining the support of the French against John (in return for promising Prince Louis, later King Louis VIII, the English throne). John campaigned destructively, torturing captured prisoners and extorting money from civilians to finance his army. At least two-thirds of the baronage of the country fought against him, including many men

A page of the Magna Carta. The charter's creators could not have foreseen the lasting impact it would have on constitutional law.

who had formerly been close to him. But then, in October of 1216, John died of dysentery, and the war came to an end. John's nine-year-old son became King Henry III, the rebels were restored to their lands, without paying a penalty for treason, and Prince Louis ultimately withdrew his claim to the throne.

AN ENDURING SYMBOL

Yet Magna Carta survived. To gain support among the nobility for the new monarch, Henry III's regents revised the document to exclude provisions calling for "rule by barons" and reissued it in 1217, and again in 1225. The 1225 version is the best known today. However, Magna Carta remained relatively inconsequential in English law until the seventeenth century, when Sir Edward Coke, who had been Queen Elizabeth I's attorney general, as well as a leader in Parliament in opposition to King Charles I, resurrected Magna Carta in order to show that even the Stuart kings must be held accountable under law.

The charter was then exported with British colonists to North America – and there, in the mid-eighteenth century, adapted by American radicals, who were enraged at the levying of taxes against them when they were not afforded a seat in the British parliament. The rebels held that Magna Carta forbade "taxation without representation." This was not literally true, but the Americans continued to believe regardless that Magna Carta protected their liberties – the seal adopted by the colony of Massachusetts on the eve of the Revolution showed a militiaman with a sword in one hand and Magna Carta in the other. From these ideals, in just over ten years, the U.S. Constitution would be born and, in turn, greatly influence other constitutions around the world.

Ringing Out across the Centuries

Numerous copies of Magna Carta were made to be read out in various parts of the kingdom. Of these, four survive – two at British cathedrals, two in the British Library. The sixty-three articles of the document are written in Latin, with gall-based ink, on a single sheet of parchment. Some of the articles are very specific to the moment (Number 58: "We will restore at once the son of Llewellyn and all the hostages from Wales"). Others ring out across the centuries. Like Article 38: "Hereforth no bailiff shall put anyone on trial by his own unsupported allegation, without bringing credible witnesses to the charge." Or Article 40: "To no one will we sell, to no one will we deny or delay right or justice."

The Black Death

The Devastating Plague That Still Shadows Us

ALL OVER EUROPE, DOCTORS refused to heal the sick, priests ran from the dying whose souls they were supposed to save, and parents fled their children. People ate, drank, and made love manically. In Italy, groups of desperate people lay with their faces over foul and bubbling sewers, hoping that the stench they inhaled would somehow ward off the dread disease. In England, people tore their clothes off and marched through the streets, whipping themselves with scourges, singing:

Come here for penance good and well,
Thus we escape from burning hell.
Lucifer's a wicked wight.
His prey he sets with pitch alight.

Everywhere, the dead were buried six deep – stacked, in the words of one Italian chronicler, "like lasagna." But soon such descriptions stopped and even writing stopped. Those who survived became simply too weary, too numb, too familiar with horrible death to comment further.

In five years, beginning in 1347, one-third of Europe – twenty-five million people – died of bubonic plague. Even this figure does not reflect the true horror of the situation,

for many villages and towns lost eighty percent of their populations. A world that had burst forth from the Dark Ages and was moving forward into a new era suddenly found itself pockmarked with deserted farms, abandoned villages, collapsed churches, and zombie-like survivors. Two centuries later, the name Black Death ("black" referring not to the color, but to something awful or evil) was coined for this pestilence; but, at the time, people in Europe called it *la moria grandissima*, or *la très grande mortalité*, or the *huge mortalyte*. Meaning "the Big Death."

A DEVILISH DISEASE

Bubonic plague changed the course of world history and haunts humankind to this day. All subsequent epidemics – smallpox, cholera, influenza, AIDS – are a reminder of the terror of the Black Death, the specter of a world strewn with dead bodies, defenseless against an invisible killer. Even today, when medical treatment is light years ahead of what was available in the fourteenth century,

Dante and Virgil and the Plague-stricken, from an early edition of the *Divine Comedy*. Plague cast a great shadow over the Middle Ages.

with every new epidemic – be it AIDS or bird flu – we subconsciously fear the return of the Big Death.

For those experiencing this extraordinary plague in the mid-fourteenth century, the effect was horrific. No wonder they flagellated themselves through the streets, praying to God or trying to appease the Devil. Though it wasn't known at the time, the devil in this case was a hardy rat flea known to scientists as *Xenopsylla cheopis*, a ravenous little creature that lived (sometimes by the hundreds) on black rats and other rodents. *X. cheopis* carried a virulent plague bacillus known as *Yersinia pestis*. When *X. cheopis* chomped down on human flesh (which it was increasingly likely to do when rats began to die off, either from the plague or from hunger), *Y. pestis* entered the human body and the effects were deadly.

The illness caused by *Y. pestis* took two forms. Bubonic plague was caused by direct contact with the fleas and resulted in egg-shaped lumps, or buboes, at the site of the flea bite, usually in the armpit or groin area, followed by black-purple bruising and a horribly foul stench arising from the victim. It had a mortality rate of sixty percent and killed within five to seven days. But the main form of the medieval plague seems to have been the pneumonic variety, which infects

the lungs and is then spread from person to person through the air, without the aid of *X. cheopis*. The Italian cleric Matteo Villani, writing in 1348, quite accurately depicted the course of pneumonic plague: "[The victims] began to spit blood and then they died – some immediately, some in two or three days … And it happened that whoever cared for the sick caught the disease from them or, infected by the corrupt air, became rapidly ill and died in the same way."

A CREEPING PESTILENCE

In the Dark Ages, Europe's climate had been markedly cold, but in about 1000 AD it warmed up. Combined with improvements in agricultural technology (a new type of plow, for one), this led to marked increases in food production. By the beginning of the

Finding a Scapegoat

Beginning mainly on the European mainland, in the spring of 1348, the plague occasioned what has been called "one of the most vicious outbreaks of anti-Semitic violence in European history." People, desperate for someone to blame, claimed that the traditional outcasts, the Jews, had been putting poison into water wells. (Interestingly enough, fewer Jews may indeed have died of the Black Death, probably because they were more insular, tending to shun outsiders, and because kosher practices led to better personal hygiene and cleaner food.)

The hysteria reached a frenzied height with pogroms against the roughly two and a half million Jews who then lived in Europe. Kangaroo courts and quasi-legal proceedings sprang up, either sentencing Jews to death (burning at the stake was a favorite method) or exiling them and seizing their wealth and property.

In certain German cities, such as Strasbourg, hundreds of Jews were burned to death after being stripped naked and having their clothes searched for hidden money – presaging a greater holocaust that was to come centuries later.

1300s, populations had grown rapidly and urban centers were thriving and densely inhabited. At the same time, advances in shipbuilding and navigation sent traders far across the known world. Soon after the start of the fourteenth century, Europe was hit by what has become known as the Little Ice Age. Devastating storms and frigid weather destroyed crops. About 1315, a famine struck Northern Europe, which significantly weakened the survivors' immune systems.

Meanwhile, deep in Asia, bubonic plague was beginning its march. China was then involved in a lengthy and bloody war against the Mongols, during which great swaths of the countryside were laid to waste. Rats, no longer able to feed themselves in the forests, headed for populated areas. As the creatures starved and died, *X. cheopis* sought new hosts. The humans they encountered, their immune systems weakened by starvation, other diseases and stress, were perfect targets. By the 1330s, the plague had laid China to waste. Records are nowhere near as complete as those left in Europe, but historians estimate that China lost 35 million people out of a total population of about 125 million. Some scholars go further and say that one out of every two people in China died.

Near the end of the 1330s, *X. cheopis* began to travel. It went with traders as they followed well-worn routes across the wide plains of Mongolia and Central Asia. By 1345, the plague had hit the lower Volga River and by 1346 the Caucasus and Crimea. By the spring of 1347, it had

traveled to the outskirts of the town of Caffa on the north shore of the Black Sea, a bustling trading center, leased by Genoese merchants from the local Mongols, where goods, people, and ideas from East and West met. When some Genoese traders ran afoul of the local Mongol ruler, he besieged them in their town, but soon *X. cheopis* hit his troops and began cutting down his soldiers by the thousands. So as to make his Genoese enemies share his pain, the Mongol leader ordered the stinking, plague-ridden bodies of his dead catapulted into Caffa, and the Christians inside began to die.

The decimated Mongol army finally gave up the siege and left. The panicked Genoese then tumbled out of the town — those who were still living — boarded ships and headed for Italy. They stopped at Constantinople and other ports, spreading the plague into each town, and then finally arrived in Italy in the autumn of 1347. It isn't quite certain how even a few seamen survived such a long trip, alive and surrounded by plague — possibly they had stronger genes than others — but as the ships from Caffa pulled into the port town of Messina, in Sicily, those onshore were horrified. Vague rumors had reached them of this horrible pestilence in the East, but now, here it was, right before their eyes. An Italian friar later wrote that the sailors in these dozen or so ships carried "such a disease in their bodies that if anyone so much as spoke with one of them he was infected … and could not avoid death."

DEADLY TENTACLES REACH OUT

On maps historians have created, the Big Death looks like a multitentacled monster holding the world in a dreadful embrace. One tentacle reached south and west from Constantinople to cause horrible suffering in Damascus, Jerusalem, and Cairo, while another groped northward from Messina, reaching central and northern Italy in early 1348. Not surprisingly, the plague tended to follow medieval trade routes.

The Italian writer Giovanni Boccaccio (1313–75) lived through the plague in the city of Florence. He brilliantly captured the experience in his famous *Decameron,* the story

Previous page: *Danse Macabre,* painted in Germany in the late fifteenth century by Bernt Notke (1440-1509).

and had abandoned his property and any stranger who went in made use of them as if he had owned them." Neither approach did much good, though: the Black Death killed three-quarters of the population of Florence.

DECIMATED POPULATIONS

From Italy, the tentacles split off: one going north into Germany, another west to France and Spain. From France, the pestilence leaped across to southern England, landing

England's population would not reach the level it was at before the plague until the mid-seventeenth century.

of ten well-born young people trapped by the pestilence in a villa. In the introduction to this work, Boccaccio describes the terror in the city, where people were afraid "to speak or go near the sick" or even to touch their clothing. People espoused different philosophies. Some lived moderately "forming small communities … shutting themselves up in their houses where there was no sickness … avoiding all excess, allowing no news or discussion of death." But some did exactly the opposite, thinking "the sure cure for plague was to drink and be merry." These men and women entered houses, according to Boccaccio, and held orgies there – an easy thing to do because "everyone felt doomed

there in the summer of 1348. It probably entered the country through the port of Bristol, which lost half its population, and then spread outward, flourishing in the foul conditions of most medieval towns of the era, where sanitation was highly primitive. The disease arrived in London in November. Those who became infected lived scarcely two or three days, and soon London had lost one-third to one-half of its population. While the plague was a democratic killer – three Archbishops of Canterbury died, one after another – generally the poor died faster than the rich. This was no doubt because immune systems were compromised by poor nutrition; chroniclers at the time noticed this, as well: "The one who was poorly nourished with unsubstantial food fell victim to the merest breath of the disease."

Even harder hit were the villages of rural England, where a community of, say, two hundred people might be wiped out. The lifeblood of this society — its farms, livestock, and rural workers — was destroyed. Records describe one sad and horrible symbol of this: a mad peasant who, for years after the plague hit the county of Durham, in northern England, wandered the roads, calling out for his wife and children, who had died.

Historians estimate that the population of England and Wales in the early fourteenth century, before the plague struck, was six million people. It's possible that the plague killed fifty percent of this population; numbers did not rise to the same level again until the mid-seventeenth century.

A WORLD TRANSFORMED

The plague quieted down over the winter of 1348, giving false hope that it had passed, but sprang up again in 1349, burning through England to Scotland, leaping to touch eastern Ireland, then crossing the North Sea to Scandinavia, before devastating Moscow in 1352 and heading farther south. Finally, it died out (for the time being) near Kiev — exhausting itself on the endless and relatively empty Russian steppes.

The world was devastated, but the plague had brought a strange blessing. Europe had been overpopulated as the 1300s began, with people beginning to fight over

resources. Now, there was a ghastly amount of room. The few remaining farm workers were much in demand and could therefore insist on better wages and conditions. As a result, the standard of living of ordinary country dwellers improved.

The Big Death instilled in people paradoxical desires. One was to live life to the fullest — men and women began to marry and start families earlier. It also created an obsession with death and dying. One reflection of this was the new popularity of morality plays. For performances of one, *The Dance of Death*, people would gather, often in a graveyard or church, and take macabre pleasure in a spectacle that included a dancing skeleton choosing audience members and leading them to a grave. This would be followed by a sermon, the gist of which was usually close to the following inscription from a tomb of the period: "Dust you are, unto dust you return, rotten corpse, morsel, and meal to worms."

The plague was to return again in 1362 and in numerous smaller yet still devastating reoccurrences for centuries thereafter, right up until the 1600s. Another wave of plague swept through Asia late in the nineteenth century, and it was then that the role of *Y. pestis* and *X. cheopis* was discovered. Although this last plague pandemic was contained, *X. cheopis* still exists in wild rodents, and hundreds of plague cases are reported each year. These can be treated with antibiotics, and further global outbreaks have been kept at bay, but the dread fear of the Big Death still remains.

The Battle of Agincourt

*The Victory Against the Odds That Made
Henry V a Symbol of English Military Might*

*We few, we happy few, we band of brothers;
For he to-day that sheds his blood with me
Shall be my brother; be he ne'er so vile,
This day shall gentle his condition:
And gentlemen in England now a-bed
Shall think themselves accursed they were not here …*

William Shakespeare, *Henry V*

KING HENRY V'S UNEXPECTED, underdog victory at the battle of Agincourt made him a hero to the English people — and to anyone who has read William Shakespeare's play *Henry V* and thrilled to his "band of brothers" speech. While his triumph did not win England the Hundred Years' War, it saved his kingship, and furthermore became the battle by which England symbolically defined itself for the next five hundred years. This in turn helped English leaders inspire their people in times of crisis ranging from the Spanish Armada invasion of 1588 to the Battle of Britain in 1940.

Of course, the speech is pure fiction and the real-life Henry V was neither the raucous "Prince Hal" nor the good King Harry of Shakespeare's portrayal. He was instead a fairly brutal bloke who fought his way onto a throne he might otherwise have been excluded from, and thereafter invaded a country he had no right to invade. In other words, Henry was not unlike most other rulers of his time. On the muddy field at Agincourt on October 25, 1415, however, Henry V was extremely brave and extremely lucky — not a bad combination.

LANDING AT HARFLEUR

One morning in August 1415, in the French port of Harfleur in the English Channel, French soldiers manning the town garrison turned their eyes seaward and suddenly saw, to their astonishment, a vast fleet of ships approaching. Quickly noting that the fleet was flying the English red cross of St. George, the French defenders sounded alarm bells, which in turn echoed out over the choppy waters of the Channel to the invading force.

Leading the three hundred English ships was the twenty-eight-year-old King Henry V, who had come to reclaim land he thought belonged to the English throne. His struggle was the continuation of what would become known as the Hundred Years' War, a series of conflicts between England and France that continued for 116 years. It had begun in 1337, when the English King Edward III grew tired of French attacks on English territory on the French mainland. One way to stop this, he figured, was to give himself the title of King of France, on the somewhat far-fetched grounds that he was the only surviving male heir of his maternal grandfather, the deceased French King Philip IV. This would legitimize a war against France. Naturally, this was something that the *real* king of France, King Philip VI – Philip IV's nephew – was not happy about.

The conflict waged back and forth for seventy-five years or so, but by the time of Henry V's reign the French were in a weakened state – and Henry had decided to take advantage of this. His twelve thousand troops and huge siege engines took the port of Harfleur in five weeks, but at great cost. The French garrison put up a

A portrait of King Henry V of England. Henry's tonsure and pious pose belie a brutal and determined character.

strong defense, but finally capitulated, after which Henry expelled all the French inhabitants, planning on filling the town with English immigrants and turning it into an English port of entry in France.

During the siege, however, dysentery had ravaged Henry and his men, costing the lives of perhaps two thousand soldiers. Henry had been planning a major campaign in France after taking Harfleur, but now, with his army weakened, he decided to make his way north to winter at the English-held port of Calais. Leaving a small force behind to fortify Harfleur, he set off with nine hundred men-at-arms – mounted

not anoint him heir to the throne – not because of hard partying, but because they had serious political differences – there was no pious reconciliation. Instead, Henry forced his way into his father's bedchambers, followed by armed men, and, using threats, induced Henry IV to make him his heir. And so it was that in 1413, after his father's death, Henry V became King of England.

THE WAITING GAME

The French forces, perhaps twenty-five thousand strong, were led by the Constable of France, Charles d'Albret. D'Albret was no military genius, but he was smart enough to

Shakespeare's portrayal ensured that Henry V would become a legendary figure in English history.

knights – and five thousand archers, shadowed by a French army that was at least four times larger.

This situation might have fazed a less determined king, but not Henry V, who had clawed his way to the English throne. Shakespeare's description of him as a madcap partier who made a pious recon-ciliation with his father, King Henry IV – the prodigal son, returning – has only a kernel of truth. Henry, born probably in 1387, had become a hardened warrior by the age of sixteen, when he commanded his father's forces at the battle of Shrewsbury. He may have led a somewhat raucous life, but when the ageing and ill Henry IV would

understand that time was on his side. He didn't want to risk incurring a loss similar to the one suffered at the battle of Crécy, in 1346, another vital engagement of the Hundred Years' War, where Edward III's knights and archers had beaten off repeated French frontal attacks. So he rode hard on the English, keeping them away from favorable river crossings, harassing their flanks, and making sure their sickly and starving troops did not receive supplies.

Henry doggedly marched his men on toward Calais, finally crossing the Somme at a ford near St.-Quentin, but found his way blocked by the French near the village of Agincourt. It was now October 24 and the

French and English were, at last, facing each other. Henry had, however, maneuvered his army so that he had one crucial advantage: his men were at the head of a long, narrow strip of land flanked on either side by thick woods. He might have been outnumbered, but he was not going to be outflanked.

FOR ENGLAND AND ST. GEORGE

The night before the battle, it rained, hard. The French, certain of the annihilation of their foe — for how could twenty-five thousand not crush six thousand — drank and partied and shouted taunts, with French knights throwing dice for the opportunity to be the first to kill or capture the English king.

On the English side, Henry ordered strict quiet. He also commanded his troops to make their confessions to the priests traveling with the army, take a last communion, and prepare themselves for their possible deaths. Whether a pose or genuine, Henry presented himself as a religious man. He wore his hair in the short, pious style of monks, anointed himself with religious oils, spent hours in prayer, and had taken as his role model St. George, the warrior-saint. In fact, the English troops all wore the red cross of St. George, which had been used as a symbol of English patriotism at least since the First Crusade in 1099 — indeed, its use here helped establish it as the potent icon of English nationalism it remains today.

Did Henry make a "band of brothers" speech that night, as the rain poured down and the gibes of the French echoed around the English camp? Almost certainly not. But as light dawned the next day, he did something even more significant. He put on a royal coat over his armor that bore not only the three leopards that were another symbol of England but also the three gold fleur-de-lys of France, as well. This act of almost unimaginable arrogance in the face of an overwhelming foe, on enemy ground, inspired the English troops greatly. As did something a medieval soldier would take note of: as Henry rode out in front of his line of troops that morning, he wore no spurs, a sure sign that when the battle was joined he intended to fight on foot.

HENRY'S LETHAL WEAPON

In fact, all of Henry's men would fight on foot that day. At the center of his line were his dismounted men-at-arms, who wore full armor and carried swords, as one might expect, but whose main weapons were axes and maces, which were needed to batter through an opponent's armor. On either side of the men-at-arms was Henry's most lethal weapon: his five thousand archers.

These were English longbowmen, the finest archers in the world. They were well paid, professional, and highly skilled, and the French feared them greatly. The longbowmen could shoot their deadly broadhead arrows as far as 350 yards. At 55 yards, they could drive an arrow through any armor. They had decimated the French on any number of occasions and

This fifteenth-century depiciton of the battle of Agincourt shows captured French knights being led away by an English soldier.

they knew that they could expect no mercy from their enemy, who had hung three hundred English longbowmen after a French victory earlier in the Hundred Years' War.

To protect against their being ridden down by French knights, Henry had ordered the longbowmen to fashion wooden stakes, which would be placed in the ground in front of their ranks – a stroke of innovation that would help win the battle for him.

STARTING WITH A STANDOFF

Facing Henry's army were three lines of French knights, dismounted men-at-arms in the front, then cavalry, then Genoese crossbowmen. After some fruitless negotiations — Henry refused to make a deal or concede defeat — the two forces stared at each other across the narrow, ploughed field for hours, a typical medieval standoff. Finally, around noon, Henry realized that he had to make a move. Pointing his men onward, he led them at a slow march toward the French forces.

When Henry's army arrived within three hundred yards of the enemy, the English archers drove their stakes into the ground and let loose a volley. Thousands of arrows clouded the sky at once, arching up and up, then falling straight downward, planting themselves in the backs of horses, glancing off French armor with a clang, or, where a knight was unlucky enough to look up at the wrong moment, striking through a visor slit.

Enraged, the French cavalry charged along the flanks, determined to destroy the English archers. But the ploughed ground of the field, perhaps 750 yards wide, was soft and wet from the rain, bogging down the horses and causing some to slip and fall. Also, the woods on either side kept the horsemen hemmed in, unable to flank the English lines. As the French neared the enemy lines, the English longbowmen unleashed a deadly volley of arrows that cut through the cavalrymen's armor. Then the survivors were brought to a sudden halt by the wooden stakes. The longbowmen rushed out to surround them and, using sidearms such as long knives, axes, and heavy, long-handled mallets, literally hammered the French into the ground.

Now the main French force engaged the English line of men-at-arms, and a ferocious battle ensued. Medieval close combat relied on brute strength: the aim was to knock your opponent down and beat him to death with mallets or battle axes, or find an opening in his armor, through joints in the plate or the visor, and stab him until he stopped moving. At Agincourt, on the plowed fields slippery with mud and blood, some knights fell beneath piles of other knights and suffocated. The Duke of York, the most prominent Englishman to die that day, lost his life this way.

HENRY MAKES HIS MARK

At this point, the real Henry V began to resemble the legendary Henry of Shakespeare, for his gallant presence was felt everywhere on the field. The English soldiers saw him race to and from crisis points on the battlefield. Most of the time, he was accompanied by his bodyguards, but no bodyguard kept Henry from direct action. At one point, he raced to the aid of his brother Humphrey, the Duke of Gloucester, standing over the man's wounded body and, joined by his royal party, fighting off the Count d'Alençon and as many as eighteen French knights who had sworn an oath to kill him. A French knight charged in, eager to claim the English king as his prize, and a blow from the man's battle-ax knocked part of Henry's crown from his head and dented his helmet (today, you can see it on display at Westminster Abbey). But Henry and the English stood fast.

Gradually, the French retreated and Henry and his surviving force were left on the bloody field, surrounded by piles of dead and groaning men. Henry ordered his soldiers to begin taking the fifteen hundred or so French prisoners to the rear, but then heard the news that a French raiding force was behind his lines and sacking his unprotected baggage train. Fearful that the remaining French — who were formed into a battle line that alone outnumbered the English forces — would now assault him from the front, Henry made a brutal decision: he ordered the French prisoners slaughtered. No English man-at-war would perform this deed, as it was against the rules of chivalry (it may also have angered them because dead knights would bring no ransoms). So two hundred longbowmen went at the prisoners with knives and mallets. When news of this reached the French, they retreated, leaving the way open to Calais. The battle was now over.

A POTENT MYTH

Agincourt was a stunning English victory, as well as a terrible French defeat – the French casualties encompassed half of the nation's fighting nobility, including three dukes, ninety counts, and about fifteen hundred knights. The English lost perhaps four hundred men.

Directly after the battle, Henry marched to the English port at Calais, but, with his sick and tired army, was in no position to follow up on his victory and march on Paris. But two years later, in 1417, Henry invaded France again and won a series of victories against a French foe weakened by internal dissension. Thereafter, he was able, with the Treaty of Troyes in 1420, to have himself recognized heir to the throne of France and regent – the king, Charles VI, having ceded his rule as a result of his debilitating mental illness. To cement the deal, Henry married the king's daughter, Catherine of Valois, on June 2, 1420. But just as he was about to achieve his goal of becoming dual king of both countries, he died of dysentery, aged thirty-four, seven weeks before Charles's own death, in 1422.

Henry V then passed into history, his story being repeated in various medieval chronicles. When it reached William Shakespeare, he seized upon it to provide his seminal portrayal of the warrior king who overcame the odds to become a symbol of England's fighting spirit. Even if Shakespeare's depiction departs from reality, it is easy to see why Agincourt, and King Henry V, represent victory and brotherhood right down to the present day.

V for Victory?

There has long been a legend that the "V for Victory" two-finger salute, so famously employed by Winston Churchill during World War II, began at Agincourt. Supposedly, the French had threatened to cut off the fore and index fingers of any longbowmen they caught, so that they could never fire a bow again. Tauntingly, the English held up their intact fingers to show the French they could still shoot. It's a nice story, but almost certainly not true. Capturing English longbowmen and cutting off their fingers (and presumably letting them live to experience their discomfort) was simply not a rational strategy, since common archers would garner little or no ransom. Far better and easier to kill them, which is what the French usually did.

The Execution of Joan of Arc

How an Illiterate Country Girl Led Her Country to Victory,
and Became a National, Religious, and Feminist Icon

PUSHING AND SHOVING TO obtain the best vantage points, ten thousand spectators gathered in the main square of Rouen, in northwestern France, on the morning of May 30, 1431. For weeks, they had watched the trial of the Maid, as she was known, and heard ever more outlandish stories of her past. At the center of the square were four large platforms. On one sat the Maid's judges, on another her guards, on the third the Maid herself alongside her preacher, and on the last a wooden stake, which was planted in a mounded plaster base to raise it high, so that it was visible to everyone in the crowd.

Before the Maid was brought to the stake, ceremonies were performed. There were sermons, speeches, and prayers. It all took so long that some of the eighty English soldiers guarding the Maid began to taunt her and the cleric who was praying with her: "What, priest, will you make us dine here?" Finally, however, the Maid was chained to the post, with her arms high above her, and the crowd gasped as the wood was set ablaze.

THE VARIOUS LEGACIES OF JOAN

Saint, heretic, schizophrenic, feminist icon, illiterate shepherd girl, savior of France — you can take your pick when it comes to Joan of Arc. She has been the subject of countless studies, the protagonist of novels, plays, and operas, the basis of medical and psychological speculation, and the object of ongoing religious veneration. The Catholic Church canonized the Maid, as she was known, in 1920, and held her up as an icon of both womanly purity and strength. She has long been venerated by liberals and socialists in France for her humble origins and empathy for the poor, but also by conservative patriots as an example of early French nationalism. As a further example of the contradictory ways in which Joan has been used as a symbol, during World War II both the Vichy Regime (which cooperated with the Nazis) and the French Resistance used her image as an icon.

Joan of Arc at the Coronation of Charles VII
(1854), by Jean-Auguste-Dominique Ingres,
melds the warriorlike and saintly sides of Joan.

And all this for an illiterate country girl who was perhaps nineteen when she died. Yet the kernel of who Joan of Arc really was will always elude us — just as it did her inquisitors — since her shape shifts as ours does.

CAPTURE OF THE "SORCERER"

When Joan of Arc fell into the hands of the English occupiers of the French city of Rouen in 1430, it was as if she had been taken by the devil, for these men meant to do her a great deal of harm. "Fell into the hands" makes it sound like Joan's capture was merely a fortune of war, and it was not. In fact, having been captured fighting a valiant rearguard action against Burgundian French forces (who sympathized with the English) at Compiègne, she was sold to the English by her French captors for a goodly sum.

The English wanted to put to death this "sorcerer," as they called her, for she had been a great hindrance to their efforts to conquer France — in particular, she had been instrumental in making sure the French dauphin, or heir to the throne, Charles VII, became king of the country, rather than Henry VI, the young son of Henry V. But the English did not want to execute the Maid themselves, lest the French people who sympathized with Joan disapprove. Therefore, they brought together a panel of judges, chief among them Pierre Cauchon, Bishop of Beauvais, and had them try her on religious grounds, for heresy. After all, here was a woman who said God spoke to her on a daily basis.

VOICES IN BELLS

Joan of Arc (Jeanne d'Arc) was born, probably in January of 1412, to Jacques d'Arc and Isabelle Romée, at Domrémy, on the Meuse River. The family owned a small amount of land and Joan, along with a sister and brother, grew up helping to farm and to tend flocks, although Joan proved to be hopeless when it came to chores. This was partly because of her piety, which made itself evident when she was very young. Whenever a bell sounded for mass, she would drop whatever she was doing and head for the village church.

By the time Joan was thirteen or so, however, these innocent village bells signified something else: when the child heard them, she also heard voices from God. The voices (later accompanied by physical manifestations) were mainly those of three saints: St. Michael, St. Catherine and St. Margaret. Eventually, these voices informed her that she needed to save France — a country that, at the time, was quite in need of a miracle or two.

Joan of Arc grew up during the endgame of the Hundred Years' War, a perilous time to be living in France. England had just won a major victory at Agincourt, controlled the cities of Paris and Reims, and, as Joan was hearing voices from God, was besieging Orléans, the last loyal French city north of the Loire. English raids into the countryside — known as *chevauchées* — devastated the lives of poor farmers. To make matters worse, the French King,

Charles VI, was quite insane — Joan may have heard voices, but Charles VI thought he was made of glass — and a vicious internal struggle for power was taking place, with one faction, the Burgundians, siding with the English against the real heir to the French throne, the Dauphin Charles.

Into this desperate and chaotic situation stepped Joan, at the age of perhaps sixteen. Her saints had told her to drive the English out of France and bring the dauphin to Reims (the traditional site for French coronations) to be crowned. It is perhaps a sign of how desperate the French were that the dauphin actually met with Joan when she secretly left her home village and asked to see him at the French court at Chinon. Or it was a sign of how impressive Joan was, for this young woman, who by now was dressing in men's clothes (including armor, shield, and sword) in order to fit in with the rest of the army, was supreme in her confidence that the English siege of Orléans could be raised with her help.

Indeed, Joan not only lifted the siege at Orléans (despite being wounded by a crossbow bolt in the neck), but also helped capture several other towns in the English occupied zone, and finally escorted the dauphin to be crowned King Charles VII at Reims. She even led a failed attack against Paris (where she was wounded once again) before being captured. Joan's actions during this period had frustrated the English, who had been on the verge of success in France, but were now forced on the defensive — and by a woman, no less.

How did this peasant girl acquire enough military leadership and tactical acumen to win victories and bedevil the English? The short answer is, no one knows. Traditional historians, perhaps less inclined to give a woman credit for military skill, assumed she was merely a banner-waver during these campaigns — close in on the action, to be sure, but not a planner. But more recently, some historians have concluded that she may in fact have been a skilled strategist,

The Sound of Whose Voice?

Was Joan of Arc crazy? Some modern psychiatrists have diagnosed her with schizophrenia — certainly her voices and hallucinations fit into this pattern, and schizophrenia often begins in adolescence. But many historians have doubts about this, since Joan was actually able to function at a very high level, commanding men in battle and brilliantly parrying her questioners at her trial, something a schizophrenic would have difficulty doing.

Some experts have claimed that Joan's hallucinations may have resulted from organic causes — from mold spores, say, or a type of tuberculosis — but these explanations are not terribly convincing. We may just have to take Joan's word for it: that her voices were from God.

This fifteenth-century tapestry from Orléans shows Joan arriving at Chinon for her audience with the dauphin on March 6, 1429.

not merely an icon. Quite possibly, she simply displayed enough leadership qualities that the troops were willing to follow her and do her bidding.

IMPRISONMENT AND TRIAL

At Joan's trial, which began on January 13, 1431, this extraordinary military career was put on display by examiners, who were prosecuting her as much for the fact that she wore men's armor and clothing, wielded a sword in combat, sat perfectly atop a horse in a man's war-saddle, and led men into combat, as for any perceived religious apostasy. When the examiners asked her if she had ever been in a place where English

were killed (a coy way of getting her to admit killing an Englishman), she replied bluntly: "In God's name, yes! How gently you talk! Why don't they leave France and go back to their own country?"

During the trial, Joan was kept in a large tower of Rouen Castle, called the Tour du Trésor, later named the Tour de la Pucelle (the Tower of the Maid) after her. She had made several escape attempts before she arrived in Rouen, and so inside her tower room she was placed in leg irons that were chained to a huge piece of wood. An iron cage was also made for her, in the shape of her body, but whether it was used is uncertain. She was guarded twenty-four hours a day by a squad of English soldiers.

The trial itself consisted of repeated interrogations, many taking place in the royal chapel of the castle. Aside from Cauchon and the other judges, there were numerous assessors (learned men charged with giving an opinion of the accused, although they had no say as to her verdict) and other onlookers.

From the beginning, the judges were confronted with Joan's stubborn

about that and rather than tell you all I know I would prefer you cut off my head!" The judges continually set traps for her, at one point asking her if the voices told her to wear male clothing: "All that I have done is by the commandment of the Lord,", she replied. "And if He had commanded me to take another dress, I should have taken it."

And when she was asked if she believed that she was in a state of grace — essentially a trick question, for no true believer would really claim to know to whom God had given salvation — Joan gave an answer worthy of Solomon: "If I am not, may God put me in it; and if I am, may God keep me in it."

> The judges were confronted with Joan's stubborn individuality — her single most extraordinary trait.

individuality, her single most extraordinary trait, evident in a situation in which she was under extreme pressure. When asked to swear an oath to tell the truth, she replied: "I do not know what you will ask me about. Perhaps you will ask me things which I shall not tell you." (She finally agreed to take a very limited oath.)

After questioning her on her childhood and military matters, the examiners returned over and over again to the subject of Joan's voices. She could not (or would not) quite say what the saints she claimed to have seen looked like (although she described Michael as being quite handsome), and became irritated when pushed on the subject: "I have told you all I know

RECANTATION AND EXECUTION

Joan was proving no pushover; so much so that the embarrassed Bishop Cauchon decided to stop holding semipublic sessions of the trial. Still, the strain on Joan was enormous. Not yet twenty, without legal defenders or representation of any kind, she had only herself and her voices to rely on. And, while the voices came to her in prison — indeed, during the trial itself — she sometimes said that they were inaudible or confusing.

Battered on all sides, faced with a horrible death by burning, she agreed to publicly renounce her voices and make penance for the error of her ways. She did so on May 24, in the town's cemetery, with an executioner's wagon nearby, ready to take her to be burned if she faltered. She was then sentenced to life imprisonment. She made her recantation wearing women's clothing, possibly to show that she was cooperating with the authorities.

However, Joan could not keep this charade up. By the following Sunday, once again wearing men's clothing, which she apparently still had in her possession, she announced that she was hearing her voices again. There is some historical evidence that Joan was sexually assaulted in prison after her recantation, while wearing women's clothes. This is not conclusive, but if it is correct, it might explain why Joan put on men's clothing again; it is also possible that it was the trauma of the assault that resulted in the return of her hallucinations.

Whatever the case, on May 29, the court sentenced her to be burned at the stake, the next day. Despite the fact that Joan must have seen this coming, she was distraught on the morning of her death. "Am I to be treated so horribly and cruelly that my body, which has never been corrupted, must today be consumed and reduced to ash. Ah! Ah! I would seven times rather be beheaded than to be thus burned," she cried out, and could not be comforted.

Just before 9 a.m. on May 30, Joan was placed in a cart and brought to the market-place, surrounded by English guards. She was now, at this final moment, dressed in women's clothes – wearing a black shift with a black kerchief over her head, and she

Isidore Patrois' painting *Joan of Arc Being Led to the Stake* (1867) is today displayed in the Musée des Beaux Arts in Rouen, France.

wept profusely. After a priest gave a sermon, a miter was forced on her head and she was proclaimed a heretic and an idolater.

Now the religious men present, including Bishop Cauchon, left her to the secular authorities, although one priest accompanied her to the scaffold. As Joan was chained to the stake, it appeared that

she had begun hearing her voices again; those nearby heard her call out to St. Michael. She also exclaimed "Rouen, Rouen, shall I die here?" as if she could not believe her fate. She begged for a cross and one was shown to her.

Then the fire was lit. The huge noisy crowd fell into perfect silence as the Maid's shrieks and pleas rose up to the heavens. As the flames enveloped her, she began to cry out for holy water. Her suffering lasted a long time – the executioner later explained that the stake was placed so high up he could not reach the young woman to mercifully strangle her, as was customary in such cases. He was so moved by her plight that he wept. Yet by order of the authorities, he was ordered to rake the fire back after Joan died, so that the crowd could truly see that she was dead.

Then she was burned to ashes, and the ashes thrown into the Seine. All except her heart, which – according to a legend that sprang up – could not be burned at all.

The Spanish Inquisition

How a Desire for Political Unity
Spread Religious Persecution in Europe

O N FEBRUARY 6, 1481, SEVEN people were marched out from the Cathedral of Seville, led by chanting, black-robed Dominican friars. The seven were dressed in yellow robes, held votive candles – and wore nooses around their necks. And, as they were marched toward an open field outside the city, they were followed by a howling mob.

These seven people (six men and one woman) were *conversos*, Jews who had been converted to Christianity. They were being rounded up because they had, or were suspected of having, "relapsed," or secretly begun to practice their Jewish faith again. The *conversos* were the prime target of the Spanish sovereigns, King Ferdinand and Queen Isabella, who wanted nothing more for their country than that all worship the same God. Out of this desire was born the Spanish Inquisition, which was to have an infamous effect, not just on the *conversos*, but on Spain and the Catholic Church, as well.

The Spanish Inquisition (from the Latin word *inquisitio*, meaning "examination") lasted officially for almost four hundred years (it was not abolished until 1834), but was most active from 1480 to 1530. Not only did it result in the persecution and death of thousands of Jews, but it also led to the exile of almost half the Jewish population of Spain. Recent historians have posited that the role of the Catholic Church was a less active one than previously believed and have placed a good deal of the responsibility on Ferdinand and Isabella, and it is certainly true that the pope who first authorized the Inquisition was aghast at the horrors he had helped set in motion. But the official Church did little to stop the persecution and the fact remains that the prime instruments of the Inquisition – the face it showed to the public through its inquisitors and through those who publicly harangued the people about to be executed – were Catholic clergy.

"THEY AMOUNT TO THE SAME"

Ferdinand and Isabella of Spain were the most glamorous monarchs of their time, and the most focused. The theme of their entire reign can be summed up in one phrase:

unity for Spain. They married in 1469, royal cousins from the powerful provinces of Castile and Aragon, and following their coronation in 1475, oversaw the epic last stage of the eight-hundred-year-long *Reconquista* – the ouster of the Moors from Spain, which was completed with the conquest of Granada in 1492.

Tanto monta, monta tanto, Isabel como Fernando was their motto: "They amount to the same, Isabella and Ferdinand." And being devoutly religious Catholic monarchs, Isabella and Ferdinand both wanted all of Spain to worship Christ. In earlier times in the history of the Iberian Peninsula, three religions – Judaism, Islam, and Christianity

An auto-da-fé procession taking place in Spain in the late 1400s, as depicted in a nineteenth-century engraving.

– had lived together in a peace which, if by no means perfect, had been a workable one. But increasingly, in the late fourteenth century, Jews had been subjected to vicious pogroms in which thousands were massacred. Surviving Jews found themselves ghettoized and in many instances forced to wear red badges denoting their religion.

While many Jews fled the country, many more converted to Christianity. Known as *conversos* or "New Christians," they became a burgeoning new class in

Spanish society, often holding high positions not just in government, but in the Church itself. However, the anti-Semites in Spain, particularly among the clergy, never accepted or trusted the *conversos*. One such man, Friar Alonso de Hojeda, prior of the Dominicans in Seville, had the ear of Queen Isabella and, in 1475, came to her with an alarming report.

Hojeda said that he had evidence that, in the province of Seville, more and more *conversos* were reverting to their original faith. Some had had their children circumcised, others secretly celebrated the Jewish Sabbath, still others sat *shivah* for their dead and practiced kosher customs.

Was any of this true? Quite possibly, given that a large group of *conversos* had converted merely as a practical matter, to save their families from exile or worse. But much of it was no doubt paranoia, fueled by anti-Semitism or even a greedy desire for Jewish property. In the next few years,

however, reports from Dominicans in other provinces came into the royal court, giving detailed examples of the perfidy of these "crypto-Jews" and urging Isabella and Ferdinand to take strong action.

The monarchs were sufficiently concerned that they visited some of the provinces in question to see and hear for themselves. Isabella (whose chief confessor, Friar Hernando de Talavera, was himself a *converso*) was not at first convinced, but Ferdinand was, and ultimately brought Isabella into the fold. The two monarchs turned to Pope Sixtus IV, who, on November 1, 1478, issued a papal bull authorizing an inquisition. Not the first inquisition, of course – there had been others in history, going back to the twelfth century, when the Albigensian heresy was rooted out in France – but the one that was to become the most famous. It would take two years to get underway, but when it did, its purgative flames blazed high.

Stoking the Fires

Why did the Inquisition choose burning as a form of execution? According to canon law, the Church could not shed blood, so it therefore had to find another way to execute its heretics. For similar reasons, the Mongols used to put persons of royal blood in sacks and beat them to death, but the Church chose burning instead.

After the victims were tied to the wooden or stone posts, ropes were kept ready to

garrote them if they should recant at the last moment. After a series of incidents in which the prisoners refused to do so and continued to castigate the authorities and proclaim their innocence, all burning victims were gagged. It was considered an honor to be chosen to place the wood around the feet of a heretic. The fire was kept going, all night if necessary, until the heretic was nothing but ashes.

THE PUBLIC BURNING

The place that the *conversos* were being marched toward on February 6, 1481 was merely an open field, which the Inquisitors referred to as "the stage." But it very quickly became known as the Quemadero, or burning place. In the middle of the field were wooden stakes (later, these would be changed to stone ones so that they did not have to be continually replaced). The swelling crowd had come to watch these *conversos* burn.

Before that happened, there was to be some preaching. And the preacher was none other than Friar Alonso de Hojeda. Hojeda's sermon to the seven condemned *conversos* at Seville was a grandiloquent one, filled with exhortations to those who were true in their faiths to seek out idolaters and persecute them. The good friar quoted from the apocryphal preachings of St. Peter, which painted a picture of heretics "hanging by their tongues ... and under them a fire flaming and tormenting." When Hojeda was finished, a civil authority read out the details of each charge — one of the prisoners had eaten unleavened bread and kosher meat, another had attended a secret Jewish service, and so on.

Hojeda and his fellow Dominicans next offered the *conversos* kneeling before them a chance to repent their sins. This would not save their lives, but it would allow them the grace of being strangled before the fire reached them. Very soon, these first seven victims of the Inquisition at Seville repented and received this small mercy.

Satisfied, the Dominicans ordered that the *conversos* be chained to the wooden stakes. Loyal Catholics then eagerly stepped forward to pile wood high around the victims — the Dominicans had promised that performing this service would lead to indulgences for the remission of sins. Then, masked executioners whose normal task was to dispatch criminals came forward, and with quick efficiency garroted each prisoner with a length of leather rope. Finally, the flames were lit and the public burnings began.

THE GRAND INQUISITOR

A week later, Seville's second auto-da-fé began, but Friar Alonso de Hojeda was not present. On the day after his passionate sermon, he had become ill with what turned out to be bubonic plague, and he died before the next auto-da-fé could take place. Those who were inclined a certain way saw this as the hand of God upon him, but he was soon forgotten. For another Inquisitor was to gain prominence in Spain who would become the driving force behind the Spanish Inquisition. He was the Dominican Tomás de Torquemada.

Born in 1420, Torquemada was the nephew of an influential cardinal and theologian. He was a strange-looking man: tall, thick-browed, with a squashed and flattened nose, he resembled the sparring partner of some pugilist — not a star boxer himself, but a man who possessed dogged qualities of perseverance.

Since 1452 the prior of the monastery in Santa Cruz in Segovia, Torquemada was a confessor of both Isabella and Ferdinand, who admired him for his holiness. He never wore shoes, slept on bare wooden cots, wore hairshirts, and refused to touch meat. His modesty caused him to turn down an archbishopric offered him. But when the job of Grand Inquisitor was offered to him in 1483, he did not turn it down. This is interesting in light of the fact that most historians believe that Torquemada's maternal grandmother was a *converso*.

Torquemada has come down in history as a bloodthirsty fanatic, but this is an

genuinely horrified by the "severe tortures" being meted out to get the suspected heretics to confess. In a papal brief issued just before Torquemada was appointed in October of 1483, Sixtus explicitly rebuked not only the Inquisitors, but also Ferdinand and Isabella, who were, in practice, in charge of the whole affair. And, in a bull issued in April of that year, the pope went further, demanding that justice be given to *conversos* like any other suspected criminals – for instance, the right of counsel, the right to confront those who had accused them and the right of appeal. But this bull was for all intents and purposes ignored after Sixtus died in 1484.

Pope Sixtus IV, who had authorized the Inquisition, was horrified by the severe tortures being meted out.

inaccurate portrayal. Instead, he was the Adolf Eichmann – the Nazi functionary who oiled the bureaucratic wheels behind the Final Solution – of the Inquisition: the organizer, the man who set up procedures, the bureaucrat who made sure the paperwork was in order before the heretics were strapped to the rack. Under Torquemada, the Inquisition spread across Spain, from one Holy Office in Seville to nearly two dozen around the country.

SO MANY TO BE JUDGED

The first year of the Inquisition, after February 1481, was so harsh that even Pope Sixtus IV became alarmed. The Pope was

This is because his successor, Innocent VIII, was susceptible to pressure from Spanish diplomats, who put forward the case that the Inquisition was a matter for Spanish authorities to handle alone.

Ferdinand had informed Torquemada early in 1483 that he and Isabella now wished to expel all Jews (*conversos* or not) from the Kingdom of Spain, and so Torquemada had been preparing for this massive task. At the end of 1484, he gathered all his appointed Inquisitors about him in Seville and issued a set of instructions on the procedures that needed to be followed during the arrest, interrogation, and imprisonment or execution of heretics. Once again eerily foreshadowing the "banality of evil" of the ordinary means by which the Nazis went about their Holocaust, these instructions were all about efficiency and rapid processing. Everything went far more easily and cost less if the suspected heretic confessed quickly (expenses – paid for by Isabella and Ferdinand – were a big concern as the Inquisition wore on), so steeper penalties were put in place if he or she did not recant within thirty days. No one was allowed to confront their accuser. If the Inquisitors – a panel of Dominican clergy, usually – found that the *conversos* had made only a "partial" confession, torture could be used. The Inquisitors even developed their own chilling terminology: those who agreed to adhere to the One True Faith after torture or imprisonment were said to have "reconciled," while those who died in the flames were said to have been "relaxed."

Three tortures in particular were favored. In one, the accused was strapped upside-down on a ladder with a cloth over his or her face; then water was forced down the prisoner's throat until he or she passed out. In another, the prisoner had a rope tied to the wrists and weights attached to the feet, then was pulled up before being dropped suddenly. Last but not least was the rack, on which the prisoner's wrists and ankles were stretched and twisted.

Torquemada's instructions also set out procedures for the requisition of the property of the accused, which went either to finance the Inquisition, or directly to the

A nineteenth-century portrait of Tomás de Torquemada. A born administrator, Torquemada kept the Inquisition functioning efficiently.

crown, which received a third of all confiscated goods and properties, and usually granted some portion of that to wealthy nobles. This has led one historian to call the Inquisition "a vast land grab from wealthy and prominent landholders."

THE BLACK LEGEND

The Spanish Inquisition did not officially end until the last Holy Office disappeared in 1834. Torquemada died in 1498, after helping institute what would become Ferdinand and Isabella's Alhambra Decree of March 1492, which ordered the

expulsion of all Jews and Muslims from Spain within three months. Weakened by years of relentless Inquisition, perhaps forty thousand, or half the Jewish population of Spain, emigrated to Portugal, North Africa, or the Ottoman Empire, particularly Constantinople or Greece. In these places, they continued to speak a Judaeo-Spanish language and practice ancient customs which are continued by Sephardic communities in these areas to this day. Others chose to be baptized during this

Francisco Goya's *Inquisition Scene* (c. 1816) captures the macabre and at times absurd nature of the religious persecutions.

Catholic scholars have mounted a revisionist campaign that claims that the Inquisition was not nearly as bad as many people believe, was in fact a "black legend" invented by Protestant writers after the Reformation. These revisionists point out that not as many people died as was once claimed, that torture was relatively infrequent, and that Ferdinand and Isabella, not the Church, bear the chief responsibility. There is some truth to these claims, in the same way that there is truth to the claims that Torquemada was the manager of the Inquisition rather than a torturer. But the Catholic Church's (at the very least) tacit acceptance of Ferdinand and Isabella's persecution and ousting of the Jews fostered what historian Joseph Perez has called "the development of the insidious prejudice of blood purity," a prejudice that subsequently spread outward from Spain.

Whether or not the influence of the Church was less than people initially believed, the Inquisition increased the tensions between the Church and the Jewish religion, tensions that were further exacerbated by Pope Pius XII's failure to help Jews during the Holocaust. The Spanish Inquisition remains a dark stain, not just on the glittering reputations of Isabella and Ferdinand, but also on what had shown itself to be a cruel and intolerant church.

three-month period, in order to keep their homes and possessions, and in turn became fresh targets for the Inquisition.

In all, between 1480 and 1530, perhaps two thousand heretics, mainly *conversos*, were relaxed at autos-da-fé. In recent years, many

Columbus Arrives in the Americas

The Search for a Maritime Trading Route Joins Two Worlds

[We] set sail on Friday, August 3, half an hour before sunrise, steering for the Canary Islands of your highnesses, thence to proceed until I arrive in the Indies and fulfill the embassy of your highnesses to the Princes there … My plans involve such close attention to navigation and hard work that, considering all, I shall have to forget about sleep.

THIS PASSAGE IN CHRISTOPHER Columbus's journal is obviously written for the ears of his mentors, King Ferdinand and Queen Isabella of Spain, containing as it does a level of sycophancy that might impress a modern junior executive. Still, it rings with history. Columbus was setting off on a voyage that was the most important ever undertaken. Never before or since in the history of the world has such a vast discovery of unknown territory been made. Those on the continent of Europe whose eyes had been turned inward, or to the East, suddenly found a fertile new ground for nation-building. Within a few short years, Spain, France, England, Portugal, and the Netherlands were involved in a fierce race to grab as much land in the Americas as possible, and the balance of power was permanently altered in Europe.

For those who lived in the Americas, however, Columbus's landing would have to be called a singular disaster. Decimated as much by European disease as European steel (many native cultures were killed by smallpox before any of their individual members even saw a European), their way of life would be completely destroyed.

FINDING A WAY EAST

It wasn't as if the two worlds had never touched before, of course. The Chinese of ancient times may have traveled to Central America. The Vikings had crossed the Atlantic (at the time generally referred to as the "Ocean Sea") numerous times, sailing to Labrador and Newfoundland, and possibly points farther south, in the years between 1000 and 1300 AD. But, with the exception of one, short-lived settlement in Newfoundland, these journeys were trips to pick up timber or

No verified likenesses of Columbus exist, so even Sebastiano del Piombo's now-famous portrait was probably based on guesswork.

find good fishing, and contact with this unknown world was not exploited.

Columbus's infinitely more sophisticated voyage came about because of a desire by European countries, in particular Portugal and Spain, to find a sea route to Asia – in particular to the "Indies," as India and China were known. Pioneering a route from Europe to the lucrative trade goods of the East that avoided the long and perilous overland journey through Central Asia could bring fabulous wealth. Fabled mariners, the Portuguese had led attempts to reach the Indies by heading east via Africa and the Cape of Good Hope. But with most people of learning having accepted that the world was round, attention began to focus on the idea of reaching the East by sailing west. Attempts had been made as early as the late thirteenth century – but the mariners never returned. It was a voyage, everyone agreed, that was fraught with extreme peril.

ROYAL APPROVAL

About forty years old at the time of his legendary voyage, Columbus was born in Genoa, Italy, a city with a long-established seafaring and mercantile tradition. He probably went to sea by the age of ten and in later years plied the Mediterranean for various Italian city-states before going to work for the Portuguese and their king,

In this artist's impression, a priest blesses Columbus and his fleet as they depart from Palos, Spain, on August 3, 1492.

John II. Columbus proposed to King John that he should sail across the Western Sea to the Indies, but John rejected the proposal, being certain that the way to the East lay east via Africa. So Columbus took his idea to Ferdinand and Isabella, heads of a newly unified Spain following the expulsion of the Moors, and they agreed to back him.

Columbus was an odd figure, a mixture of arrogant loner and supplicant, an idealist convinced of his ideas, and an opportunist out to become "Admiral of the Ocean Sea," as he asked his sponsors to name him. Yet he was an undeniably brave and brilliant seaman. He knew from his extensive seafaring experience that two different wind systems operated in the Atlantic, forming a circulation. The northeast trade winds (*las brisas*) would push him across the ocean from the latitude of the Canary Islands, and the southwesterly trades, which blew farther north, would push him in the opposite direction. The question was, would they be strong enough to get him back home?

SECRETLY MAKING HEADWAY

Setting sail on August 3 from Palos in Spain, Columbus had with him three ships: the *Niña*, the *Pinta*, and the *Santa María*; his crew consisted of ninety men. The ships were caravels, two- or three-masted sailing vessels, although the *Santa María* may have been a *não*, a larger and heavier vessel, since, although it was Columbus's flagship, it always lagged behind the other two. At the beginning of the ocean crossing, heading west from the Canary Islands, Columbus recorded nothing but good sailing weather — strong westerly winds, blue skies, flying fish leaping through the air. "The savor of the mornings was a great delight," wrote Bartolomé de las Casas, Columbus's biographer, who abstracted the explorer's journal (the original no longer exists).

Columbus's crews were provisioned for a year, but he expected the voyage to take only a few weeks, since the geographies he had consulted had said that the Ocean Sea between Europe and the Indies must be very narrow at the twenty-eighth latitude, which was the latitude Columbus was following from the Canary Islands. In the first ten days of his voyage, the trade winds sped him along for 1160 nautical miles (a nautical mile is 1.5 regular miles). On his best day he made 174 nautical miles (261 miles).

This speed was a mixed blessing, however, for Columbus expected the outlying islands of the Indies to appear any day, and they did not. Concerned that his crew might begin to become fearful, he lied to them about the distance they had covered each day, always telling them they had traveled a lesser distance.

BEWILDERED AND BECALMED

In the third week of September, Columbus's ships encountered an alarming phenomenon: the Sargasso Sea. Looking like a great meadow of yellow and green grass, the Sargasso is made up of sargassum, a thick

weed. It is harmless to ships, but since no European had ever sailed through it before, the men did not know that. They were also much disturbed because they thought such weeds must presage land, yet there was no land to be seen.

Around this same time, the trade winds seemed to falter, and the ships were forced to sail much more slowly, tacking to find a breeze. They traveled only about 250 miles in five days, and the sea was so smooth the men were able to shout between vessels to each other, and dive off to go swimming. On September 25, a lookout on the *Pinta* shouted "Tierra! Tierra!" and everyone believed they saw a high mountain in the distance. Columbus even sank to his knees to thank God. But it turned out to be a mirage.

DESPAIR - THEN JOY

While Columbus recorded in his journal that "the sea was like a river" and the air "sweet and soft," the men were growing suspicious. To these sailors, Columbus was a foreigner, a Genoese, and not a very likeable one at that. As the ships moved farther and farther into the unknown, with no sight of land, they began to grumble openly. He tried to placate them (even as he continued to lie about the distances they were covering), but by October 10 (when the ships were about two hundred miles from the present-day Bahamas) had agreed that he would turn back within a few days if land were not spotted. He wrote in his journal:

"Here the men could no longer stand it; they complained of the long voyage."

Because of his desperation to find land, he ordered that the ships sail at night, a dangerous prospect in unknown waters if land is thought to be near. All hands therefore kept a sharp lookout. Around 10 p.m. on October 11, Columbus thought he saw a light flickering in the distance, but wasn't sure. (No one has ever decided what this light could have been, since Columbus was still too far from shore to have seen a fire.) But around 2 a.m. on October 12, Rodrigo de Triana, lookout on the *Pinta*, saw a white-sand cliff or beach gleaming in the distance and cried out "Tierra! Tierra!"

This time it was no false alarm. Columbus soon pulled alongside in the slower *Santa María* and marked the distance to this welcome apparition as about six miles. The ships tacked back and forth, waiting for dawn.

The voyage from the Canary Islands had taken five weeks. Steering through uncharted waters, using celestial navigation, and dead reckoning, Columbus had managed to find the optimal course to the Americas – a course that Spanish ships would follow for centuries to come.

A MOMENTOUS MEETING

Columbus had brought his men to an outlying island of the Bahamas, probably Watlings Island, though this is still debated. The island, which Columbus was to name San Salvador, was a low, curving landmass about thirteen miles long by six miles wide, protected by a coral reef. Once daylight arrived, Columbus and his men sailed their ships to an opening in the reef and entered a shallow bay. Floating in azure waters, off a beach of glistening sand, they suddenly saw a group of naked people run down to the shore and stare in astonishment at the Spanish ships.

Where Did Columbus Land?

Many historians believe that Watlings Island in the Bahamas fits the description of San Salvador, the island where Columbus first touched land in America. It is the right size, occupies the right geographical position, and has an inland lake, which was described by Columbus. But many other historians, including a team of experts hired by the National Geographic Society to make a five-year study, favor tiny Samana Cay, which

has some of the same features as Watlings, and may also have lain more directly in Columbus's path. Still other historians feel that Samana is too small and too arid to have ever supported a settlement like the one Columbus described (though recent archaeological findings seem to indicate at least some habitation of Samana at the time of the voyage). The debate will continue, but for now Watlings appears to get the nod.

Columbus, on the *Santa María*, ordered a longboat dropped to the sea, and he and a group of armed men rowed to shore. The captains of the other ships followed suit. Columbus carried the royal banner, while others in the party carried flags bearing green crosses and the letters F and Y (the initials of the Spanish king and queen). Once on shore, they fell on their knees and praised God for their salvation.

Ignoring the naked people approaching, Columbus took possession of the island in the name of Spain. Then he turned his attention to the islanders, who turned out to be friendly and gentle, and were probably reminded Columbus of the Gouache Indians of the Canarys — an ominous reference, for the Gouache were being hunted to extermination by the Spaniards.

Columbus passed out beads and "red caps" to these people, and accepted parrots, balls of cotton thread, and javelins in return. The Indians appeared to be poor, but one thing caught Columbus's interest: many of them had gold hanging from holes pierced in their ears or noses. Asking about this using signs, he thought they told him that the gold came from an island to the south, where there was a great king. So, after spending three days on San Salvador, Columbus

The template was set: enslaved Indians accompanying Europeans on a single-minded hunt for gold.

Taino or Arawak Indians. Although the Indians had never seen men like these or ships of such size, they showed no fear. According to Columbus, some of these people thought the Spanish were gods and threw themselves on the ground with their arms outstretched. Columbus spent a great deal of time describing them in his journal (much more so than the island itself, which probably disappointed him — it was not as lush as he had thought the Indies would be). The Taino wore their hair in bangs over their eyebrows and long down their backs, painted their bodies and their faces white, black or red, and had skin coloring that was neither black nor white. They

decided to leave and seek this island. He took seven Indian men with him as guides, giving them no choice in the matter. Thus the template was set for the conquest of the Americas: enslaved Indians accompanying Europeans on a single-minded hunt for gold.

SHORT-LIVED GLORY, LASTING FAME

Columbus continued exploring the islands for three months, hoping to find gold and the fabled land of the Indies or of Cipangu (Japan), which he also thought might be in these latitudes. At first it was a fruitless search. One of his captains, Martín Pinzón aboard the *Pinta*, abandoned Columbus and went off to search for gold on his own.

This reconstruction from the Naval Museum in Madrid shows Columbus and his entourage arriving on an island in the West Indies, and being greeted with gifts by the local Indians.

The *Santa María* ran aground on Hispaniola (now in Haiti and the Dominican Republic) and had to be abandoned. But Columbus was able to find gold on that island and even left a small European settlement behind. In January of 1493, he sailed north, found the southwesterly trade winds, and headed back to Spain, rejoined by Pinzón in the *Pinta*, who had also found gold.

When he arrived back in Spain, Columbus was given honors beyond his wildest imaginings. He was awarded the rank of "Admiral of the Ocean Sea" and made viceroy and governor of all the lands he had discovered. He was to make three more voyages to the Caribbean, though he never gave up insisting the Americas were the Indies, despite growing evidence to the contrary. Unable to renounce an idea that was obviously wrong, and angered by the

Spanish government's refusal to give him ten percent of all gold found in the New World as he had requested, Columbus died embittered and estranged at the age of fifty-five, in 1506. Meanwhile, and especially after Hernán Cortes landed in Mexico in 1519, Spain reaped the benefits of Columbus's momentous discovery. Wealth poured into its treasury, enriching and empowering the nation far beyond its previous status, just as it was about to take its position as a pre-eminent power in Europe.

Columbus had not found the Indies, nor had he really found a "new" world. Instead, as the historian John H. Parry has put it, he "established contact between two worlds, both already old." But from that moment of contact, the modern world – one of extraordinary interchanges between far-flung cultures, both for good and ill – has sprung.

The Early Modern Era

1500–1900

The Defeat of the Spanish Armada

The Sea Battle That Saved England, Began Its Long Rise to Maritime Supremacy, and Rewrote the Rules of Naval Combat

THE WEATHER HAD BEEN unseasonably cold all that spring and summer of 1588, with heavy storms and rain squalls rolling across England and turning the Channel into a cauldron of choppy waves and gale-force storms. The morning of July 29 dawned to unpromising gray skies. Mists hugged the ocean surface and fast-moving showers raced across the waves. Still, the watchers stationed at Lizard Point in Cornwall, at the southwestern tip of England, squinted dutifully off into the distance.

Later that morning, one of the guards, peering through his telescope, spotted the dark shapes of dozens of ships far out over the water. This was what they had been waiting for. Within minutes, torches were touched to piles of resin-soaked brush that stood at the ready. First one beacon burst into flame, then another and another, until a glowing necklace of fire lit up the southern English coastline, all the way from Cornwall to Plymouth, in whose harbor lay the English fleet. The fires were an alarm call, warning of the approach of the Spanish

Armada, the great invasion fleet that had been expected for some time and which, the English knew, posed the most serious threat their nation had faced for centuries.

For their part, the Spanish in *la felicísima armada* – "the fortunate fleet" – could see the glow of the fires and guess what they portended. The Spanish high command sent out an English-speaking captain in a small tender, who returned that night with four terrified English fishermen in tow. They revealed that the English fleet led by the Lord Admiral, Charles Howard, Second Baron Howard of Effingham, and his famous second-in-command, Sir Francis Drake, was coming to make a fight of it.

The ensuing naval battle would become a part of English folklore – it has long been recounted how Drake calmly continued his game of bowls after hearing the news of the Armada's approach, and how the whole of England reacted to the dark news with pluck and courage. But the battle also had a very real effect on subsequent events. Although more Spanish ships were eventually lost to gales and storms than to English cannon fire, England's victory began its rise to the status of a first-class naval power; it also marked a major shift in naval strategy, away from close-in fighting to the use of accurate, long-range cannon fire.

DEEP DIVISIONS

Long-standing differences and a succession of disputes led to this extraordinary battle between England and Spain. In a sense, the countries and their differences were embodied by their two rulers – Elizabeth I of England and King Philip II of Spain.

Elizabeth, daughter of King Henry VIII, was a Protestant, while Philip was a staunch Catholic who had once had close ties to England. He had been married to Mary Tudor, Elizabeth's Catholic predecessor, and had even intervened with Mary to save Elizabeth's life after a Protestant plot to put her on the throne instead of Mary was uncovered.

But after Mary's death in 1558 and Elizabeth's accession to the throne, the two monarchs and their countries had become enemies. This was partly the result of religious differences and partly because England had begun to flex its muscles, particularly at sea, which put it at odds with Spain, then the most powerful seagoing nation in Europe. English seafarers like Sir Francis Drake attacked Spanish shipping, seemingly with impunity; Elizabeth publicly turned a blind eye to such affronts to the Spanish pride and purse, but privately profited by them.

Philip II of Spain. Philip saw himself as a protector of Catholicism and resolved to restore the religion to England.

NO ORDINARY FLEET

The huge Spanish fleet that entered the Channel on July 29 was 125 ships and 30,000 men strong. About twenty-five of the ships were mighty fighting galleons, the rest armed merchantmen, transport ships and pinnacles for swift scouting and message-bearing between the larger ships. The Armada was commanded by the Duke of Medina-Sidonia aboard his flagship, the *San Martín de Portugal*. Philip had appointed Medina-Sidonia to the job after the previous commander, the Marquess de Santa Cruz, had died unexpectedly. Medina-Sidonia had a high social standing in Spain and was a brilliant administrator, but he was not an experienced sea admiral, although he had very able advisers.

As the Spanish ships passed by, the English fleet left Plymouth and deliberately fell in at the rear of the Armada so that it had the wind behind it and therefore an advantage if the Spanish turned to fight. Lord Admiral Howard was aboard his flagship, the *Ark Royal*, Drake on his ship, the *Revenge*. Their much lighter and more nimble fleet contained thirty-four royal warships and almost two hundred other vessels. However, most of these were small, privately owned and lightly armed pinnacles. In fact, although the English fleet was sizable, it was in a desperate position. For the Armada was no ordinary fleet of warships, but rather the most potent invasion force that had ever been pointed at England. Of its thirty thousand men, only seven thousand were sailors, the rest soldiers. The ships contained powerful land artillery, siege equipment, six months' worth of food and wine, and tons of ammunition. At this point, however, the immediate objective of the Armada was not to fight the English fleet, but to head north and rendezvous with a second Spanish force in the Netherlands.

"GOD'S OBVIOUS DESIGN"

The Netherlands, or Low Countries, as it was also known, was the flashpoint in the feud between Philip and Elizabeth, a place where their contrasting cultures and religions clashed. It had been under Spanish rule for some time, and the Dutch Protestants there had been persecuted for their religion and forced into the role of second-class citizens. Under William of Orange, the northern provinces revolted. When the southern provinces declared their loyalty to Philip by signing the Union of Arras on January 6, 1579, seven of the northern provinces declared their independence a few weeks later with the Union of Utrecht, regarded as the founding document of the modern Netherlands.

In response, Philip had William of Orange assassinated in 1584, and, thereafter, Spanish control of the region began to increase once more. But in the following year, Elizabeth, alarmed at the Spanish presence so close to her northern shores, openly sent an army to the Netherlands after years of covert aid to the Dutch rebels. This helped the Dutch force a stalemate between rebel forces and those of the Duke of Parma — and enraged Philip.

Then, in 1587, Elizabeth's execution of her cousin, the Catholic Mary, Queen of Scots, who was plotting against her, greatly heightened religious and political tension. In her will, Mary left her accession rights to the English throne to Philip, formerly her brother-in-law. Philip and his advisers subsequently convinced themselves that the security of Spain relied upon the destruction of Elizabeth's regime and the restoration of a Catholic monarch to the throne of England. Even the Pope agreed. It was, as one Spanish noble put it, "God's obvious design" that Spain rule England.

PACKING FOR AN INVASION

The invasion strategy had been cobbled together from two separate plans. The aggressive and strategically astute Duke of Parma had suggested placing thirty thousand men in seagoing barges in the Netherlands and making a surprise assault across the Channel. The Marquess de Santa Cruz, who commanded Philip's Atlantic fleet, wanted instead to take a huge invasion force of some fifty-five thousand men from Spain and land in England or possibly southern Ireland.

It was Philip who decided to merge the two plans. The Armada was to sail up the Channel with part of the invasion force. When it reached Flanders, it would protect Parma's men as they crossed to Kent, then unload its own forces. In total, some fifty

. . . .

Bowling While the Armada Approaches?

Was Sir Francis Drake playing the English game of lawn bowls in Plymouth on the afternoon of July 29 when he heard of the news of the approaching Spanish Armada, as has long been reported? And did he say, "We have time enough to finish the game and beat the Spaniards, too?"

Possibly, although not probably. Drake did like to bowl, as did most English gentlemen at the time, and Plymouth Hoe, the grassy open space by Plymouth harbor, was perfect for the game. Such a statement also sounds like something that Drake, who was renowned for his

irreverence and impetuosity, might have said. But no one reported the statement at the time (the first record of it comes forty years later).

In any event, every English seaman present that day knew that the unfavorable tides would prevent the royal fleet leaving Plymouth Harbour until about ten o'clock at night. That left plenty of time for several games of bowls, not just one. So, if Drake did utter his famous statement, it simply reflected the reality of navigating against an ebb tide, rather than braggadocio.

This painting of the clash of the Spanish and English fleets captures the tumult of the battle, albeit in a fanciful composition.

thousand well-provisioned Spanish troops would then find themselves ashore in England, a force that Elizabeth would be hard pushed to resist. Many in Philip's court envisioned a slaughter of the English. Some of the Spanish commanders even brought their finest china with them, thinking they would need it once they settled comfortably into English castles.

The only problem was, the massive build-up of the Armada had become the worst-kept secret in Europe. The English had already delayed the action once in the previous year when Sir Francis Drake had wreaked havoc among the Spanish ships at Cadiz, and Drake had sortied out twice in the summer of 1588 to attack the Spanish fleet on its own coast, only to be forced back by storms.

So when the sails appeared off Plymouth, the English, refitting in port, knew what

was afoot. They also knew that if they did not stop the Armada before it reached the Netherlands, an invasion of England would almost certainly occur.

NEW RULES OF BATTLE

When the Spanish fleet saw the English coming out for them, they formed with startling precision into a crescent, something that had obviously been practiced, with the heaviest warships on the two horns of the crescent, and the slower ships within.

The English attacked at about nine in the morning of July 31, just off Plymouth. Divided into two groups, one headed by Lord Howard, the other commanded by Drake, they struck at the flanks of the Spanish in single file, discharging their cannon at long distance.

This cannonade may be thought of as the opening blow of modern naval warfare. Traditionally, ships tried to get close to each other, attach themselves to the enemy with grappling hooks, and fight what were essentially mini-infantry battles at sea. But the English, under the influence of a radical naval thinker named John Hawkins (who was in Drake's group at the battle), had recently overhauled their strategy, tailoring their ships to move fast, and so avoid being boarded, and to cannonade with accuracy. An English innovation helped greatly here – the replacement of fixed gun mountings by moveable carriages, which allowed cannon to be reloaded more rapidly.

On July 31, however, the cannonading had little effect initially. The English were skittish, perhaps overawed by what must have looked like an extraordinary

their next move. In the meantime, Queen Elizabeth, needing to stir her people, famously appeared in front of her troops at Tilbury, telling them, "I know I have the body but of a weak and feeble woman, but I have the heart and stomach of a King, and a King of England, too! And I think it foul scorn that Spain or Parma or any prince of Europe should dare invade the borders of my realm!"

FLUSHING OUT THE ENEMY

Unfortunately, despite the months of planning, the Duke of Parma had been slow in putting together his own invasion force,

Victory over the Spanish Armada provided the English with an enduring patriotic myth.

metropolis of ships, a veritable city on the sea. One powerful Spanish galleon came out almost tauntingly and challenged three English ships – Drake's *Revenge*, Martin Frobisher's *Triumph*, and John Hawkins's *Victory* – to close and do battle. The English declined the invitation, preferring to lob shots from a distance.

As the engagement continued, the Spanish remained in control, outmaneuvering Howard and Drake. On August 6, after a week of running battle, Medina-Sidonia anchored his fleet off the port of Calais, waiting now for word from the Duke of Parma that he was ready to invade. The English, who were nearly out of ammunition, waited offshore, plotting

and his twenty thousand men were now being blockaded in their ports by Dutch rebels. To make matters darker for the Spanish, the water along the Flanders coast was so shallow that the deeper-draft Armada vessels could not strike close enough to shore to breach the blockade – something that the Spanish planners should have foreseen.

Around midnight on August 7–8, as Medina-Sidonia pondered his next move, the English sent eight fire ships into the anchored Spanish fleet. These vessels were not just drifting old pinnacles filled with pitch and tar, but warships running at full sail, holds full of gunpowder, ready to be set alight by their suicidally courageous crews, who leaped off at the last possible moment. Two of the English fire ships penetrated the Spanish defenses, wreaking havoc. The Spanish ships were forced to cut their anchor cables to escape and move to the open ocean – exactly where the English wanted them.

THE BATTLE OF GRAVELINES

On August 9, the English closed in for a pitched, decisive battle off Gravelines, a town in the far southwest of the Spanish Netherlands. The engagement lasted eight hours, with English and Spanish ships engaged in ferocious cannon duels, tacking back and forth in the shallow waters. Finally, the effect of the cannonading took its toll on the confused and scattered Spanish fleet. Four vessels were lost to English gunfire and the entire fleet was very nearly stranded on the sandbanks off Flanders.

When the wind turned to the west, pushing the ships off the sandbars, Medina-Sidonia was faced with a choice: cross to invade England on his own, return south through the channel, or head north and west, around the British Isles. With the prevailing winds against him, he chose this last course. Unfortunately for the Spanish, he did not know two things: one, Howard's English fleet was out of ammunition and could not have withstood a Spanish attack; and two, horrible gales would face the Spanish on the west coasts of Ireland and Scotland.

During the long return voyage, thousands of Spanish sailors drowned in storms, and hundreds were killed by scavengers along the British coastlines. By the time it returned to Spain, the Armada had lost about half its invasion fleet, as well as fourteen thousand soldiers and seamen. During the battle, the English had lost only seven ships.

A PATRIOTIC MYTH

In the short run, the victory saved England from a Spanish invasion and a Roman Catholic monarch on its throne. It also helped preserve an independent Netherlands. Of the two royal adversaries, Elizabeth was to live longer, until 1604, while Philip, blinded by cataracts and with a crippled arm (probably from a stroke), died in 1598.

Eventually, the defeat of the Spanish Armada was seen as marking the beginning of English supremacy over the seas, which reached its full fruition after Admiral Lord Nelson's victory at Trafalgar in 1805, as well as the demise of Spain as a great naval power. But more recently, historians have concluded that Spain's demise did not really begin until the end of the Thirty Years' War in the middle of the next century, and that England achieved its preeminence on the high seas only after a long period when the Dutch – whom they had saved – ruled the oceans.

Regardless of this, victory over the Spanish Armada provided the English with an enduring patriotic myth – much like Washington's victory at Trenton or the French storming of the Bastille – that would be summoned back into the public consciousness again and again when the country faced dark days in the future.

The Great Fire of London

How London's Architectural Splendors arose from the Ashes of an Apocalyptic Conflagration

LONDON IN THE MID-SEVENTEENTH century, with a population of about half a million, was a great and thriving metropolis, one of the most important urban centers in the world, and yet it covered an area so small it represents only a tiny semicircle on a map of the present-day city. Old London — essentially medieval London — was surrounded by walls thirty feet high, a vestige of the days when outlying highwaymen often raided the city. Within the walls, rich and poor lived closely together in startling contrasts. The poor inhabited tumble-down garrets made of wood, while across the street might be the home of a wealthy and mighty banker. (Another quarter of a million people lived in wooden shanties in the out-parishes or suburbs that had sprung up outside the city walls.) Most people ate bread or grains or whatever they could steal, yet the wealthy feasted daily on rich fare almost beyond our imagining — everything from pheasant's tongue to salads of selected flowers to huge sides of beef and pork.

Yet the great leveller was the London streets. They were so narrow that houses on either side seemed to lean over, lending a strange darkness to the byways below. This was not a planned city, with squares and parks and grids, but a haphazard one, with side streets ending in blind alleys without names. Open sewers ran down the middle of the roads. There were no sidewalks. Not only did pedestrians have to beware of fast-moving horses and carriages, but they had to keep a sharp eye out lest a window open above and a chamber pot of "night soil" be emptied on their heads. The streets were in general so foul that many people wore small metal platforms that fitted to the bottoms of their shoes, which they would then remove before entering their homes.

In 1664, a writer named John Evelyn published a pamphlet called *Fumifugium*, dedicated to King Charles II, in which he warned of the dangers of so many open fires and furnaces in such a "wooden ... and inartificial congestion of Houses." A few days later, on September 2, 1666, when a great fire rose up from a baker's oven and smote London a blow of "infinite mischief," Evelyn was there to watch his warnings gain the status of prophecy.

WARNINGS IN THE SKY?

Actually, there were other signs and portents in the year before the fire, celestial events, which, it was decided, portended momentous things. In December of 1664, and yet again in March of 1665, comets were seen in the night sky over London and there was much debate over what they meant. Samuel Pepys, the famous diarist and then Secretary of the Admiralty, went out one night to view one of these heavenly visitors, noted how close it seemed to London's rooftops, and reported that people felt "it imported something very peculiar to the city alone."

To Puritans and other supporters of Oliver Cromwell, until recently head of state, the comets were a sign that God himself was unhappy with the return of the Stuart monarchy in the form of King Charles II. But to many astrologers, the comets predicted a return of the plague, the deadly disease that had sporadically appeared in London since the Black Death of the fourteenth century, most recently in 1625. Each reoccurrence, the astrologers said, had been presaged by a comet.

Of course, this was sheer poppycock, but the plague did return, and with a vengeance. Beginning in about April of 1665, London was stricken by a horrible outbreak of bubonic plague. The Great Visitation, as it became known, killed perhaps seventy-five thousand to one hundred thousand people, causing horrible scenes of suffering. The rich and prominent, including Parliament and the king, fled the city. The poor died in droves, to be dragged out and dumped on carts and buried in mass graves. People driven insane by the final stages of the disease accosted others on the street, trying to infect them.

The plague raged until the winter of 1665–66, then seemed to subside. By the summer of 1666, plague deaths were still averaging about thirty or so a month, but they seemed to be mainly confined to outlying suburbs. Merchants returned, warehouses filled up again with goods, commerce restarted. By September of 1666, London was breathing a wary sigh of relief.

And then the king's baker forgot to douse his fire.

THE BAKER'S HOUSE

Thomas Farynor, baker to King Charles II, usually doused the fire in his oven before going to bed at night, but on Saturday September 1, he appears to have forgotten to perform this basic task. At about two o'clock on Sunday morning, he was awakened by a fire that was already engulfing the first floor of his house. Reacting quickly, he was able to get himself, his daughter Hannah, and a manservant onto the roof, but a maid, afraid of heights, refused to accompany them, and thus became the first victim of the fire.

Farynor lived on Pudding Lane, about one hundred feet or so from Thames Street, a busy thoroughfare lined with warehouses,

A Prospect of LO

THAMESIS FLVVIVS.

London before the fire. Old St. Paul's Cathedral stands out on the north bank. London Bridge and the Tower of London are on the right.

which ran along the river wharves. Pudding Lane was typical of hundreds of London side streets, so narrow a hand barrow could barely fit through it, according to one contemporary observer. The houses were all of timber that had been weatherproofed with pitch. It had been a hot, dry summer and it did not take long for the blaze to spread. Farynor and his companions were able to escape, scrambling over rooftops, but the blaze ate the houses behind them as a fresh wind blew up. The next street west, Fish Street Hill, ignited as piles of straw in the yard of an inn exploded into fire.

BLUDDER'S BLUNDER

At about four o'clock in the morning, after bucket brigades had failed to douse the blaze, local constables woke the Lord Mayor of London, Sir Thomas Bludworth (known to those who didn't like him much as "Bludder"), and warned him that a fire

was spreading. Apparently, Bludworth had been out carousing the night before and didn't much like being dragged down to the scene of what was, to his eye, merely another London blaze. He took a quick look around Pudding Lane, and then made the remark for which his name was to live on in notoriety. "Pish," the hungover Mayor said. "A woman might pisse it out!"

And then he went back to bed. But by 7 a.m. on Sunday, when Samuel Pepys climbed the Tower of London to get a better view, an east wind that he described as a "gale" had stirred the fires into one "lamentable" conflagration. Tongues of flame had sped down Pudding Lane and Fish Street Hill and devoured warehouses full of oil, brandy, pitch, and tar, and

mounds of coal and piles of lumber. Explosions rang out as the flames engulfed the ancient church of St. Magnus Martyr.

FIREFIGHTING, LONDON-STYLE

There were fire engines in mid-seventeenth-century London, but they were rudimentary ones – essentially large pumps mounted on carriages, which could shoot out relatively strong streams of water. Moreover, there was no London fire brigade; instead, the vehicles were privately owned or sponsored by local parishes.

In all the chaos, contacting the owners and obtaining permission to use the pumps proved almost impossible. And any pump companies that did get into action found themselves hampered by large crowds wandering the narrow streets, which were also clogged with furniture people had dragged from their burning homes in the hope of salvaging something from the blaze.

The normal strategy for fighting fires in London was to create fire breaks – empty areas over which a fire cannot travel, for lack of fuel. This was done by pulling down buildings with fire-hooks – huge iron hooks attached to long poles or ropes, which were routinely kept in public buildings. Fire workers would frantically sink the hooks into the top beams of houses and pull them down, collapsing the house. The next step was to clear the debris, creating a barren stretch.

Unfortunately, by the time Bludworth finally ordered this to be done, he had the demolition started too close to the fire, so that the flames either ate up the buildings as they were being torn down, or blazed through debris that had not yet been cleared. Consequently, as Samuel Pepys observed, "an infinite great fire" was soon headed right at London Bridge.

OLD LONDON BRIDGE

The London Bridge that spanned the Thames at the time of the Great Fire was an extraordinary structure, lined with houses and shops separated by a passageway only a few yards wide. The fire attacked the bridge greedily, leaping from rooftop to rooftop, as people fled the span in panic. Onlookers thought the entire bridge would collapse. Indeed, the fire seemed intent on heading for the south

command the Lord Mayor to spare no effort in demolishing huge swaths of the city to halt the fire, but when Pepys returned and found Bludworth, the mayor was practically hysterical and of little use to anyone.

By Sunday evening, boats carrying families and their belongings swarmed across the river to the south bank, where onlookers lined the shore, watching the extraordinary blaze. It was, as one observer remarked, like seeing "a foretaste of the Last Judgment."

> It was, as one observer remarked, like seeing "a foretaste of the Last Judgment."

shore of the Thames, but was slowed by an empty area. A few sparks reached the south side of the river, causing several houses to go up in flame, but the blaze was ultimately checked there.

Seeing the fire speed across the bridge was enough for Pepys, who, taking advantage of his status as a senior naval official, urgently requested an audience with the king to advise him of the dire seriousness of the situation. Flames were now roaring to the north and west through London, leaping high into the air, sucking oxygen out of the atmosphere – Pepys even noticed pigeons simply dying where they stood, like canaries in a coal mine. King Charles told Pepys to

The Great Fire of London, by the Dutch artist Lieve Verschuier (1630-86), shows the city blazing out of control while residents flee.

DEVOURING A CITY

Monday dawned a hot, dry, sunny day, and as a powerful east wind drove the fire on through London, houses, churches, and buildings went up in explosions of flame. A firestorm had been created, with oxygen from the high winds feeding the flames. The dark cloud rising above London could be seen in Oxford, sixty miles away. Citizens no longer made any attempt to fight the fire, but now fought fiercely to get away. The rich were willing to pay the poor almost any sum to help cart their belongings from the city, which engendered the line in John Dryden's later poem "Annus Mirabilis," about the events of 1666: "The rich grow suppliant, and the poor grow proud."

It was essentially every man for himself. With no one in charge of the firefighting – Bludworth seems to have fled – the king stepped in and put his brother, the Duke of York, in charge. He created fire posts around the city, and the men at these posts tried to create fire breaks by pulling down houses. But the blaze moved too fast, and eventually gunpowder was used to blast out fire breaks.

It was a time like no other. An East India Company warehouse full of spices blew up into smoke and the smell of incense drifted across the city. The king himself rode with his guards through the blazing ruins, carrying with him a bag of silver coin to pass out to heroes.

CONSPIRACY THEORIES

As the fire continued to consume London on the Tuesday, rumors of arson spread through the town. The smell of incense proved to some that the blaze was the work of the Catholic Church. Others blamed the Dutch, with whom the British had fought a war for naval supremacy, or England's perennial enemies, the French. "Many Citizens, having lost their houses and almost all that they had, are fired with rage and fury," wrote one chronicler. "Arm, Arm, Arm doth resound the Fields and

Suburbs with a dreadful voice." Mobs roamed the streets, attacking anyone who appeared to be Dutch or French. King Charles sent armed troops out to save the foreigners from such attacks. Later, the government was forced to go through a lengthy investigation of the causes of the fire, just to prove there was no conspiracy.

Finally, by Wednesday, the wind had died down and, with it, the fires. Two hundred thousand homeless Londoners looked in astonishment at their great city, now turned to ash and charred wood. About 13,000 houses, 87 parish churches, St. Paul's Cathedral, the Royal Exchange, the Custom House, all the city prisons, and the General Post Office had been destroyed.

Charles II by the studio of Pieter Nason (1612-90). At the height of the fire, Charles took to the streets to rally firefighters.

John Evelyn walked the ruined streets of the city he had tried to save from fire and noticed that those around him, wandering in shock, looked like "men in some dismal desert." The official death toll, amazingly, stood at four, but no one really believed this — you could smell the death in the smoldering ruins — and today it is thought that thousands must have died.

A NEW LONDON

If the Great Fire had a silver lining, it was that, from then on, far more attention would be paid to fire safety. In 1667, a Rebuilding Act was passed, and Londoners set about with a will to make their new city a shining one. Ten thousand houses were built in less than eight years — and by ordinance, they were made of brick. The old pestilential open drains disappeared. Streets were widened and provided with sidewalks for the first time.

Insurance companies, which had lost heavily in the fire, now realized that it would be to their benefit to hire and train competent fire-fighters. When the new London arose, it was not only a far more beautiful city — the great architect Christopher Wren designed forty-nine new churches, as well as a new St. Paul's Cathedral — but also a far safer one.

There were some who felt that getting rid of the old wooden houses also helped get rid of the plague, which disappeared at about this time. More likely, rats died fast enough, trapped in the fire, to reduce the incidence of the disease. Despite these benefits, however, the Great Fire of London remained a feared and almost apocalyptic event, one that fulfilled earlier warnings: "All astrologers did use to say Rome would have an end and Antichrist come, [in] 1666," said mystic Anthony à Wood, "but the prophecie fell upon London."

The Death Toll

Could it be true, as the official version had it at the time, that only four people had died in the massive conflagration that was the Great Fire of London? It seemed impossible, but for many years this remained the official death toll. In part, this was due to the fact that the hall of the Parish Clerk's Company, which under normal circumstances published a weekly "Bill of Mortality," listing all deaths in London and their causes, was one of the buildings that burned to the ground.

But it was also due to the intensity of the firestorm. It created such fierce heat that it melted steel lying on the docks and even the iron locks of the city gates. With this degree of heat (possibly reaching as high as 2,700 degrees Fahrenheit), there would have been no bodies left, and probably not even any bone fragments.

A more realistic estimate of the deaths caused by the fire might be several thousand, but no one will ever know for sure.

The Battle of Quebec

The Daring Gamble That Dashed French Hopes of a New Empire and Brought Britain Control of North America

ON THE NIGHT OF SEPTEMBER 12, 1759, a flotilla carrying the cream of the British army in Canada floated up the St. Lawrence River, under the noses of the watchful French guarding the citadel city of Quebec. A quarter-moon had arisen around ten o'clock, which provided enough light for the fleet to steer by, but not so much that it might be clearly seen. Moving under the towering cliffs of Quebec, the British continued west to a cove called the Anse au Foulon, landing in the dark perhaps two hours before dawn. They looked up from the beach to see a sheer rock face some 175 feet high, with a narrow path winding across its face. The path had been pointed out to the British a few weeks earlier, probably by a French deserter.

With haste, yet trying to be as quiet as possible, the detachment of perhaps two hundred Light Infantry crept up the path; when a French sentry challenged them, a French-speaking Highlander told him with some indignation that they were reinforcements sent from up the river. This fooled the French soldier long enough for the British to reach the top of the cliff and overwhelm the French garrison on guard duty.

One of the officers who accompanied the first companies to the top of the cliff was their brilliant, cold commander in chief, General James Wolfe. He had donned a new uniform for what he was certain would be the defining moment of his military career. Plagued by illness and possessed of a dark soul and temperament, he had convinced himself that he would die in the coming battle, and had hinted as much when he gave his personal effects and a picture of his fiancée to a Royal Navy officer for safekeeping. Yet now, as thousands more British troops climbed the cliff, following those who had so easily taken the guardpost, he may have thought for a moment that he might yet escape the fate he had foreseen for himself.

A PIVOTAL MOMENT

The battle for Quebec – which controlled the St. Lawrence River, the water highway by which the interior of the North American continent and its rich fur trade could be

An idealized view of Quebec in the late eighteenth century, depicting the settlement as a typical European city.

accessed – came three years into the Seven Years' War, as France and Great Britain, age-old rivals, engaged in a global struggle for supremacy. Beginning in 1753, the war was fought on two fronts. In Western Europe, Great Britain and Prussia were pitted against France, Austria, Russia, and Sweden. Britain and France continued the battle on the second front, in North America. Known as the French and Indian War due to the French use of Indian allies, it was fought mainly in what would become New York, New England, and Canada.

The French had had the best of it up until Wolfe's arrival at the Anse au Foulon. They and their Huron and Abenaki allies had destroyed a force under General Braddock at Fort Duquesne, on the

Pennsylvania frontier in 1755. The next year they had made inroads into what would become northern New York State, capturing Forts Ontario, George, and Otswego. And in August of 1757 they had captured Fort William Henry on Lake George.

The commander of the victorious French forces at Fort William Henry was a man named Louis-Joseph, the Marquis de Montcalm. He guaranteed the safety of the British troops and civilians inside the fort after they surrendered. But as soon as the British were allowed to begin their journey to British lines, the Abenakis set upon them,

killing 180 in cold blood and taking perhaps 500 as slaves. When he heard about this, Montcalm raced out on horseback to restore order. Montcalm's brave and judicious actions were the only bright spot in an ugly episode that became a rallying cry for British and Americans.

ON THE PLAINS OF ABRAHAM

After the advance company of the British had scaled the cliffs and neutralized the small French outpost, the rest of the British force — about five thousand men — made its way up and marched to the Plains of Abraham, southwest of the city. The Plains of Abraham were named, not after the biblical figure, but after a farmer named Abraham Martin, who had been given this long piece of land west

of Quebec in the 1650s. On September 13, as the sun rose over these plains, the French beheld an astonishing sight: thousands of red-coated troops who had formed up in a line two deep that extended all the way across the thousand-yard-wide plains. These men were five hundred yards from Quebec's western wall. On their right were cornfields and then the cliff-edge over the St. Lawrence. On their left was a forest.

The French leader, the Marquis de Montcalm — the same Montcalm who had tried to stop the massacre at Fort William Henry — was stunned when he rode his horse out in front of the French lines. He kept staring at the seven battalions of British troops as though, one observer noted, "his fate was upon him." Despite the fact that Canadian irregulars and French Indians sped to the cornfield and the forests to begin picking off British troops, Montcalm seemed frozen.

Far across the plain, his counterpart, General Wolfe, with little regard for his own safety and perhaps deliberately tempting fate, strode up and down behind his men, whom he had ordered to lie down.

devoted. Montcalm, however, was away much of the time, fighting wars. He was wounded on several occasions and showed such conspicuous gallantry that he was promoted to major general. In 1756, he arrived in North America and led French troops to a series of stunning successes before being placed in charge of the all-important fortress of Quebec.

Major General James Wolfe was a more complex, more troubled man, and had had a far more mercurial rise than Montcalm. Thirty-two years old, he was the son of an

Montcalm kept staring at the seven battalions of British troops as though "his fate was upon him."

Montcalm and Wolfe could almost certainly not see each other, but their lives and deaths would be forever intertwined on that day.

In some ways, they presented a study in opposites. Montcalm was a decent man; not a brilliant commander, but a strong and intelligent one. Born in 1712 (which made him fifteen years older than Wolfe), he was the product of wealthy royal French parents and a classical education. His father died when he was a young man, leaving him a fortune, which, unfortunately, was riddled with debts. Friends arranged a marriage for the young marquis to a rich heiress named Angelique Louise Talon du Boulay; surprisingly, the union of convenience turned into a happy marriage, producing ten children to whom both parents were

undistinguished army general. His looks were the first thing most people commented on: he was tall and gangly, with a pinched face, pale skin, and a mop of red hair, which he refused to cover with a wig. He had made his reputation with the British army in Scotland in 1746, fighting the Jacobite rebellion, and a cruel reputation it was — Wolfe thought nothing of burning villages or executing civilians. Cold and egotistical, unable to connect with men or women, and prone to maladies that left him ill much of the time, Wolfe was bad-tempered, but a powerful fighter, which he had proved during the successful siege of the French fortress of Louisbourg, Nova Scotia, in 1758, a victory that opened up the approaches to the St. Lawrence for the British Royal Navy.

Despite protests from rivals, some of whom thought Wolfe mad, King George II put him in charge of the invasion force that was to attack Quebec. "Mad, is he?" the king famously said. "Then I hope he will bite some others of my generals."

DILEMMAS ON BOTH SIDES

Wolfe had been besieging Quebec for three long months – "burning and laying waste the countryside," as his orders to his scouts read, blockading the St. Lawrence and hoping to starve the French garrison out. But his forces had not been quite strong enough to do this, and so he had settled on a last gambit before winter set in: all-out attack on Quebec.

Mad or not, Wolfe had taken an extraordinary chance. As the French cannon lobbed shots at his lines, he knew that somewhere west of him was a French force of some three thousand troops commanded by Louis-Antoine de Bougainville, a man who would later become one of the most brilliant explorers in French history, and who now, Wolfe assumed, was on his way to reinforce the French garrison. If so, British forces would be caught between the cliffs, the French in Quebec, the snipers in the woods, and Bougainville approaching from the rear. To avoid this trap, he was going to have to order his 4,500 troops to attack soon, charging directly at Quebec's defenses.

Montcalm, too, was having his anxieties. His forces equalled Wolfe's, but he had far fewer regular army troops, being dependent on unreliable militia as well as scouts and

What Happened to Bougainville?

Louis-Antoine de Bougainville did finally show up with his force on the battlefield, but only after Montcalm had been wounded and the French forces were in flight. His force outnumbered the British force, which turned to face him, by a two-to-one margin, but he inexplicably chose not to fight, instead veering away from the battlefield.

Bougainville later went on to become a famous explorer – he circumnavigated the globe from 1766-69, explored the South Pacific (where a Solomon island is named after him) and wrote a well-known book detailing his adventures and natural observations, *Voyage autour du monde,* which became influential in portraying South Pacific people as "noble savages" living in an earthly paradise. But his performance at Quebec continued to dog him.

He always claimed that he had simply not had enough time to turn his force around and bring it back to Quebec to attack Wolfe from the rear. Most of his contemporaries disagreed, however, and history does, too. The historian C. P. Stacey writes: "Bougainville botched the task of guarding Quebec ... He failed to observe what was happening and to march to counter Wolfe's actions ... His inefficiency had much to do with the French disaster."

Indians. It seemed that his best move would be to retire behind Quebec's walls to await the coming of Bougainville and his relief forces, but there were two problems with this strategy. Quebec's defenses at this point in the city walls were weak, since it had been assumed no one would be able to scale the cliffs. Secondly, where was Bougainville? No one knew. Montcalm paced up and down impatiently. "Is it possible Bougainville doesn't hear all that noise?" he asked an aide.

A PERFECT VOLLEY

Bougainville later claimed he received too little notice to muster his forces for an attack on Wolfe. Whatever the case, by 10 a.m., he had still not shown up. Montcalm thus made a decision which, while understandable, was almost certainly the wrong one. Instead of retreating within the walls of the city, he chose to attack Wolfe's forces.

When Montcalm gave the order to attack, the French forces, cheering and whooping, charged at the British lines. But here the lack of discipline among the militia showed, for they were either ahead of or behind the regular forces, and they did not fire in volleys at the British lines a few hundred yards away, instead kneeling and snapping off single shots whenever they could. The regular British troops simply waited for the French to get within thirty yards and then fired what one British officer later called: "the most perfect volley ever fired on a battlefield."

The effect on the French was devastating. The British then moved forward and fired yet another volley and this became the pattern of the battle. Steadily, the French withered under such a terrible onslaught of lead at such close range, and those who survived turned tail and ran. The British gave fixed bayonets and charged, chasing the French back toward the city.

But Quebec was temporarily saved by the fifteen hundred or so French irregulars and Indians in the woods off the British left flank, who poured fierce fire into the British and forced them to stop and re-form several times. This allowed the French army in the field to escape, for the time being, to a fort upriver. Quebec remained strongly garrisoned, however, and for the moment, the British, still concerned about the threat from Bougainville, did not attack.

TWO LEADERS IMMORTALIZED

Probably just as the British charge was beginning, James Wolfe, who had continued to recklessly expose himself, was shot in the chest and bled to death. However, he lived long enough to hear an aide cry, "They run!" Wolfe asked who ran, and the aide said: "The enemy sir. Egad! They give way everywhere!" Wolfe, ever the commander, gave orders to cut off the enemy's retreat, then said, "Now, God be praised, I can die in peace." A few moments later, he was gone. His was and remains one of the most famous last moments in British military history, immortalized in art and literature, most notably in Benjamin West's famous painting, *The Death of General Wolfe*.

Remarkably, at about the time Wolfe was hit, Montcalm also suffered a mortal wound, either from sniper bullets or grape-shot, and had to be helped back into the city. He died the next day and was buried in the yard of an Ursuline convent. He, too, passed into legend, staring fixedly at the sky in numerous French paintings, the most famous being Jean-Antoine Watteau's *The Death of Montcalm*, which has the General dying on the battlefield, flanked by Indians, instead of at the convent. Ironically, although the battle was one of the most pivotal in North American history, its prominence in the public imagination derives mainly from these stirring but inaccurate portrayals.

The British did not enter the city that day, but the French finally surrendered. The British lost 650 men, the French a few less, but the British triumph was great. Although the French would try in vain to retake Quebec in 1760, after Wolfe's posthumous triumph the French empire in North America was as good as lost. Wolfe's great gamble at the Anse au Foulon had paid off. The British now had complete control of Canada and would soon gain control of New England and New York. The battle of Quebec had determined that North America would be a British, not a French, continent.

Benjamin West's *The Death of General Wolfe* (c. 1771), a romanticized version of the British leader's demise, helped immortalize the event.

Washington Crosses the Delaware

The High-risk Strategy That Ensured American Independence

GEORGE WASHINGTON'S crossing of the Delaware River to attack British forces at Trenton, in what is now the state of New Jersey, on Christmas Day of 1776, is a legendary event in U.S. history. And Emanuel Leutze's 1850 painting *Washington Crossing the Delaware*, which now resides at the Metropolitan Museum of Art in New York, is one of the most famous pieces of art in America.

However, for some Americans, Leutze's painting is infamous for the number of factual errors it contains. Leutze has the crossing happening as the horizon glows with light, when in fact it took place in the middle of a dark and sleety night. Washington is standing at the prow of a rowboat; he probably was standing, but in a high-sided, flat-bottomed ore-transport barge. The American flag depicted is wrong: the Stars and Stripes did not exist at the time of Washington's crossing. Poor Leutze was even mistaken about the *ice*, some historians quibble: the sharp floes he depicts are more akin to those found on the German-born Leutze's native Rhine than to the flat sheet ice of the Delaware.

With all these errors — and many more — why in the world is the painting so famous? Because, details aside, Leutze captures the *spirit* of the whole affair, the determination, desperation, and dignity of these men as they rowed into the fight of their lives. For had George Washington failed in his crossing of the Delaware, it is entirely possible that America's fight for independence could have failed, as well.

ON THE RETREAT

The American Revolution, in which Great Britain's thirteen North American colonies sought to push off the rule of the motherland and govern themselves, had begun in the spring of 1775 with armed skirmishing between American irregular troops and the British army near Boston. Full-scale war soon followed, with New York State becoming a key battleground. In a campaign beginning in August 1776, George Washington and his rebel force, the Continental Army, were pushed out of Long Island and New York, and harried southward, first into New Jersey and then into Pennsylvania, toward their base at Philadelphia, by aggressive British forces under General Sir William Howe. By December, half of Washington's army had been killed, wounded, or captured, or deserted, leaving him with perhaps five to six thousand men, many of them injured. On December 13, the British even captured one of the rebels' top commanders, General Charles Lee – whom they believed in every way to be George Washington's superior in military thinking and tactics.

As soon as the Delaware River – the borderline between New Jersey and Pennsylvania – froze, Howe planned to brush aside the ragamuffin army in front of him and easily sweep down the river to take the rebel capital, from which the

Jean-Antoine Houdon's bust of Washington (1786–93) was based on casts and sketches made during a visit to Washington's home in 1785.

Continental Congress had already fled. After this, the war would be over.

Washington had yet another problem: most of the men in his volunteer army had enlisted for only a year, meaning that they could legally leave on December 31, just a week away. If he was going to strike at the British, he had to do it at once. Not only Washington but all of his men understood this, which is why the password for the Christmas mission Leutze later depicted would be "Victory or Death."

A BLOODY TRAIL

Just before the crossing, George Washington readied to mount his horse and inspect the 2,400 shivering men forming on the Pennsylvania side of the Delaware River, near McKonkey's Ferry, approximately eight miles upriver from Trenton. At that moment, a Continental officer from Philadelphia rode into camp with a letter for Washington. How on earth had the man found them, Washington asked? Easy, he replied; he

had followed the bloody footprints left in the snow by Washington's soldiers.

Bloody footprints pretty much seemed to sum up the situation George Washington and the Continental Army were now in. Before heading with his men to the transports that would take them across the Delaware, Washington sent a notification to the head surgeon of the Continental Army, telling him to expect heavy casualties. At six o'clock, it was already dark and sleeting heavily, and the men standing on the banks of the river, which was fast-moving and swollen, were freezing. Still, there were a few lighter moments. One soldier noticed how red Washington's nose looked in the cold and later wrote: "[His nose] was scarlet in the wind … He was not what ladies would call a pretty man." Washington himself, watching his thee-hundred-pound artillery commander, Colonel Henry Knox, enter one of the boats and try to sit down, joked: "Shift your tail, Knox, and trim the boat."

The width of the Delaware at this point was only 300 yards, but the fast-moving water, filled with ice (and, in Leutze's defense, some of it may have been craggy, since it may have washed into the Delaware from streams along its banks), crashed into the boats, and freezing rain and snow blew hard into the men's faces. The plan was for the entire force of 2,400 (plus horses and 18 cannon) to cross by midnight. But, despite the best efforts of the Massachusetts soldiers (fishermen in civilian life) to whom Washington had assigned this task, each

Previous page: Washington Crossing the Delaware (1851) by Emanuel Leutze: the details are wrong but the spirit is captured brilliantly.

separate crossing took much longer than expected, and the operation was not completed until three o'clock in the morning of December 26.

Washington stood on the banks of the Jersey shore, supervising the landing, his cloak wrapped around him. He seemed to onlookers to be extraordinarily determined. He may have been thinking about certain lines from the patriot writer Tom Paine's *The American Crisis*, the first issue of which had just been published. "These are the times that try men's souls. The summer soldier and the sunshine patriot will, in this crisis, shrink from the service of their country, but he that stands it now, deserves the love and thanks of man and woman." Just over two days before, on December 23, Washington had formed the very troops now crossing the Delaware into ranks, and had these soon-to-be famous sentences read to them.

There were no summer patriots with Washington on that freezing night. And, despite the desperation of his crossing, it had sound military strategy behind it.

VITAL INTELLIGENCE

The British, having chased Washington into Pennsylvania, had formed a line of outposts nearly eighty miles long, extending all the way from Burlington, New Jersey, to the Hackensack River in New York. The deeper the British forward lines were placed in New Jersey, the farther away they were from their supply base in New York.

When Washington had first crossed into Pennsylvania that fall, he had used his network of spies and scouts to carefully survey the British positions. They had noted that the British had placed 1,500 German mercenaries in Trenton under the command of Colonel Johann Rall (sometimes spelled Rahl), and that these Hessians, as they were known, were so confident that they had not bothered to dig or erect barricades. Washington's spies had also told him that Rall, although a soldier who had served with some distinction in previous battles, was given to drinking and lax discipline when away from the direct gaze of his supervisors. Washington also noted that Trenton was at least a half-day's march from the nearest

British outpost, leaving it relatively isolated. So, as well as his own force, he planned to have two smaller forces cross the river downstream, one to engage the British at Bordentown as a diversion and stop them coming to Rall's aid, the other to block the retreat of the Hessian forces from Trenton.

MOVING ON TRENTON

In normal conditions, an eight-mile march would have been nothing to a hardened Continental soldier, but on this freezing cold night, the trek to Trenton was extremely difficult. Moving through a forest of black oak and hickory, the soldiers followed a path that was rutted and crisscrossed with tree roots, as an ice storm raged. Bringing up the rear of the line were cannon, which had small torches stuck in their touch-holes for guidance; one

The Hessian Factor

At the beginning of the war, the British hired professional mercenaries from Germany to help defeat the Americans, and, in all, about thirty thousand German mercenaries would eventually fight in the American Revolution. They were called Hessians because most of them were from the German principality of Hesse-Kassel. While hiring mercenaries was standard practice in European wars, Americans were outraged by it — in part because it seemed to them that the king had brought outsiders into what they

considered to be a sort of family quarrel. Washington's troops viewed the captured Hessian soldiers at Trenton with great curiosity, describing them as diminutive, muscular men with short pigtails that "stuck straight back like the handle of an iron skillet." They even had, according to one Continental private, "a bluish tinge" to their extremely pale complexions. The Hessians themselves were quite leery — they had been told by their commanding officers that the savage Americans killed and ate prisoners.

Connecticut private later remembered how these lights "sparkled and blazed in the storm of the night." At one point, messengers brought news from one of Washington's officers that the rain and sleet had ruined their powder. Washington merely said, "You have nothing for it but to push on and use the bayonet."

By coincidence, this march on Trenton was populated with men who would later become important figures in U.S. history. Along with Washington were a future president, James Monroe; a future Chief Justice of the United States, John Marshall; Aaron Burr, a future vice president; and

The sound of shots and yells awoke Colonel Rall from what most sources state was an alcohol-induced stupor. The good colonel had spent much of Christmas night drinking, and so had missed a chance to discover Washington's plans. For a Tory farmer — loyal to the Crown — had come to Rall's quarters that night to tell him about the attack, but Rall had refused to see him. Frustrated, the man had written what he knew on a piece of paper and passed it to Rall via a guard, but (much like Caesar ignoring a similar note handed to him on the Ides of March) Rall had stuck it in his pocket and forgotten about it.

Trenton was a pivotal victory, achieved at the darkest hour for the American rebels.

the man Burr would later famously kill in a duel, Alexander Hamilton, later the Secretary of the Treasury.

THE BATTLE BEGINS

At about eight in the morning, having divided his troops into two columns and sent one to attack from the north, Washington arrived at Trenton. He was at least two hours off schedule, having planned to attack before dawn, but the storm had worsened and the only guards standing duty were pickets posted in small houses perhaps a half-mile from town. Washington's men drove the pickets in with a clatter of musketry, and the battle for Trenton began.

Now it was too late. Some of the Hessian troops began firing from the windows of their quarters, as others raced half-dressed into the streets, only to be cut down by disciplined Continental fire. Hundreds more Hessians were rallied by their officers and began forming near a church, but Henry Knox lined six of his artillery pieces up on King and Queen Streets, and fired at them with devastating effect. American infantry seized most enemy cannon before they could be fired, or shot their crews as they lined up and tried to fire them (Lieutenant Alexander Hamilton led a brave charge which destroyed one Hessian battery).

Washington's other column moved in from the north, boxing the Hessians in. Rall tried to lead a charge of his panicked men, yelling, "All who are my grenadiers, forward!" He started to ride his horse at Continental lines, but his men would not move from cover, and Rall was shot twice and knocked onto the snowy streets of Trenton. Mortally wounded, he was carried into a church and placed on a pew.

DUMBFOUNDED BY VICTORY

Everywhere, groups of Hessians, surrounded by Continental troops with bayonets drawn, were surrendering. Washington at first seemed almost dumbfounded by his victory. He ordered a battery of guns to fire upon a Hessian position, and the gunner said to him, "Sir, they have struck." "Struck?" Washington replied, as if he could not assign a meaning to the word. "Yes. Their colors are down." At last, Washington understood. He turned to one of his young officers, Major Wilkinson, and shook his hand: "This is a glorious day for our country."

Four hundred Hessians had escaped before the Continental noose tightened, but more than nine hundred were captured, while about fifty had been killed or wounded. Washington's losses were amazingly light: three dead (one of whom had frozen to death along the line of march) and six wounded. Along with the prisoners, Washington had captured six artillery pieces and a thousand badly needed muskets, and seven wagonloads of powder and ammunition. And this had been achieved without the support of Washington's two other contingents, which had been unable to cross the Delaware and create diversions downstream.

Colonel Rall, dying in a nearby house, was visited by Washington, who spoke with him through an interpreter. Rall had by this time seen the note that he had failed to read, and thus knew that he had given away his command, and his life, because he had been so careless.

"THAT UNHAPPY AFFAIR"

Crossing the Delaware and defeating the Hessian forces at Trenton gave Washington and his Continental Army an all-important victory at a time when the American forces were at a low ebb. Following it up with triumphs at Trenton, when British forces counterattacked on January 1, and at nearby Princeton on January 2 and 3, Washington was able to save Philadelphia. "The enemy was within fifteen miles of Philadelphia," Henry Knox wrote his wife, "They are now sixty miles [away]."

Though the triumph at Trenton was followed by other, greater, battles, it was a pivotal victory, achieved at the darkest hour of the American Revolution. Washington himself, with modesty, called the strike at Trenton "a lucky blow." But the disgruntled British Secretary of State, Lord George Germain, later summed up the British view of the battle: "All our hopes were dashed by that unhappy affair at Trenton."

The Storming of the Bastille

The Downfall of a Notorious Symbol of Tyranny
Triggers a Momentous Revolution

THE STORMING OF THE BASTILLE on July 14, 1789, is renowned and celebrated as the heroic uprising that started the French Revolution by conquering an infamous symbol of oppression and liberating many of the French Crown's most hard-done-by and mistreated vicitms. But as with many legends of the French Revolution and other uprisings, the reality was somewhat different, and nothing highlights this better than the scenes that immediately followed the liberation.

When the mob broke through the gates of the infamous fourteenth-century jail and the garrison had capitulated and was dragged off to its fate, the prison was discovered to be almost empty. Unknown to the attackers, the government had scheduled the building for demolition and only six prisoners were left in all of its many cells and chambers. (There would have been seven, but the Marquis de Sade, its most famous inhabitant, had been transferred elsewhere a week before.) Four of the prisoners were forgers. Two were insane. Of these, one, the Comte de Solages, had

been committed by his family for libertinism and incest. The other was a deranged Irishman known to history as Major Whyte.

Of the six inmates, only this lunatic fitted the picture most people had of prisoners in the Bastille: men or women who had been wronged by the Crown and sentenced to a living death in the great prison's dungeon. Unlike the other inmates, who had been in the prison but a short time, Whyte had languished for decades and was gaunt, white-haired and had a beard down to his waist. So he was paraded in a cart through the streets while crowds gathered and cheered at this symbol of the oppression of the King of France. And because it was Major Whyte's particular delusion that he was Julius Caesar, this suited him perfectly: thinking the crowds were applauding the dictator of Rome, he smiled broadly and waved his hands in grateful thanks wherever he was taken.

INEVITABLE BUT UNFORESEEN

The French Revolution was, as Alexis de Tocqueville later wrote, both "inevitable yet

... completely unforeseen." Arising in a France wracked by extreme poverty, the Revolution was to change the face, not only of France, but of Europe. When the revolutionaries subsequently came to power, established a constitutional democracy, and executed France's formerly untouchable monarchs, it sent shock waves through nearby nations, which feared such progressive ideas might be exported. And not just ideas. As the French Revolution went careening out of control and thousands of nobles and alleged counterrevolutionaries were executed, it seemed to observers that such change must inevitably be accompanied by violent bloodshed.

Later, Revolutionary France would fight wars with England, the Netherlands, Austria, and Italy and, ironically, its success in these wars would see its great general, Napoleon Bonaparte, ultimately become a dictator, thus subverting the ideas of the Republic. But the French Revolution, like most revolutions, began out of a genuine desire to reduce hunger and injustice.

"RAVENOUS SCARECROWS"

In the early spring of 1789, France, a country of about twenty-six million people, suffered from a level of poverty that horrified even hardened foreign observers. One English writer, traveling through the countryside, described seeing everywhere starving peasants who looked like "ravenous scarecrows." There were numerous reasons for this level of poverty, but heavy taxes were chief among them. These taxes were almost universally borne by the peasantry and poor urban workers, rather than by nobles (who could take advantage of any number of loophole exclusions) or the rich and powerful Catholic Church, which owned ten percent of the land, yet paid no taxes at all. The taxes were particularly onerous in the city of Paris, where every foodstuff, dried good, barrel of wine, or mooing, baaing, clucking head of livestock coming into the city for sale was stopped at a "customs barrier" and its owner forced to pay an excise tax.

With a staggering national debt of around forty-six million *livres* and a struggling and uncertain tax base, France was in terrible shape. King Louis XVI had inherited this situation when he ascended the throne in 1774, but had been unable to do much about it. Although not the beast he was later made out to be, he was an uncertain king who was not by inclination sympathetic to the needs of the common people.

Prior to 1789, France already had a constituent assembly — made up of the First Estate (the clergy), the Second Estate (the aristocracy) and the Third Estate (the middle class and the peasants) — but it hadn't met since 1614. Under pressure, Louis XVI called together this Estates-General to deal with the crisis of the worsening economy and starving peasantry. The Third Estate clamored for reform, but was stifled by the clergy and the nobility. On June 17, 1789, led by a group of radical Parisians, it broke off and formed the National Assembly, whose purpose was to create a French constitution. An increasingly powerless Louis was forced to accept this development.

Soon, liberty was in the air in Paris. Fiery debates took place on street corners and ordinary people — merchants, students, farmers from the countryside — began to sense that they now might have a say in their own futures.

A 1786 portrait of King Louis XVI. After trying unsuccessfully to flee the country in 1791, Louis was guillotined in January 1793.

CITIZENS TAKE UP ARMS

The incident that sparked the storming of the Bastille was the dismissal of Jacques Necker, Louis XVI's finance minister. The king's conservative advisers had urged him to fire Necker, who had shown sympathy for the plight of the French people and had approved of the formation of the National Assembly, and Louis did so on July 11.

By July 13, crowds carrying wax busts of Necker (who had fled to Belgium) were demonstrating in the streets of central Paris. Rumors spread that Louis XVI was about to unleash his Swiss and German mercenaries on the crowd, since his own French-born army could not be trusted to fire on their compatriots. Inflamed by this and intoxicated with the sudden feel of freedom in the air, the demonstrators – the citizens' army, as they called themselves – became desperate for arms to defend themselves. Shortly after dawn on Tuesday July 14, they gathered in front of the Hôtel des Invalides, a military complex and hospital, demanding weapons. With the guards standing by, they then broke into the basement and took over twenty-eight thousand muskets and ten cannon.

The only problem was they had very little powder and ball with which to fire their weapons. Fearing that the ammunition crimes, real or imagined, against the Crown. Along with de Sade, famous prisoners had included the writer and philosopher Voltaire; the journalist Simon Linguet, whose writings had been published in 1782 and helped inflame the mobs gathering on July 14; and a prisoner who wore a velvet mask and whose identity was never discovered, though he was subsequently immortalized in literature and film as the "Man in the Iron Mask."

THE NERVOUS GOVERNOR

The governor of the Bastille was Bernard Jordan, the Marquis de Launay, who had actually been born in the prison – his father

Liberty was in the air. Ordinary people began to sense that they might finally have a say in their future.

might be used by the rebels, the commander of the Invalides had sent it to be stored protectively in the stark fortress of the Bastille – all twenty thousand pounds of it.

To the mob, the Bastille was not only a source of powder and ammunition, but also a symbol of the longstanding aristocratic political and social system, the so-called *ancien régime*. An enormous building with eight rounded towers and walls eighty feet high, the Bastille (from a French word meaning "castle" or "fortress") had been built in the fourteenth century as a military stronghold and used as a state prison thereafter. It had more recently gained a sinister reputation as a place that housed those who had committed political was the previous governor. His forces in the prison amounted to eighty-two pensioned-off soldiers, or *invalides*, who could not be counted on to fight a pitched battle in the best of circumstances, let alone against many of those who were their friends and neighbors. But Launay also had a command of thirty-two professional Swiss soldiers, who would become the core of any defense he could offer, as well as thirty or so cannon, many aimed out the upper embrasures at the crowd now approaching.

The Bastille was entered through a small gate that opened into an outer courtyard, the Cour de Passage, which was lined with shops. Here, in more peaceful times,

A reasonably accurate depiction of the taking of the Bastille. Note the prison's enormous rounded towers, which stood eighty feet high.

prisoners were allowed to mingle with their relatives and walk or smoke. The thick gate to the inner courtyard of the prison lay across a drawbridge over a dry moat. Once through that, any attackers would have to brave still another moat and drawbridge before arriving in the Bastille proper.

In an attempt to avert confrontation, certain Electors – members of the new National Assembly – raced ahead of the mob to speak with Launay, at about ten o'clock in the morning. Pointing out that the cannon poking out of the upper embrasures could be seen as an act of aggression, they asked him to withdraw the guns, which he did. While these negotiations were going on, however, a crowd of about a thousand arrived outside the walls of the Bastille, crying "We want [the] Bastille! Out with the troops!"

Impatient with the pace of the negotiations going on inside the prison, a few of the demonstrators leaped onto the roofs of the shops lining the Cour de Passage, climbed up onto the undefended lower ramparts and jumped to the ground inside the inner courtyard. There, they grabbed sledge-hammers and smashed the chains holding the drawbridge up. It came crashing down across the moat – killing one rioter who could not get out of the way in time – and the mob surged into the inner courtyard.

At this point, about 2 p.m., someone opened fire. It has never been discovered who it was – some in the mob, unaware of how the drawbridge had been let down, were certain that the Swiss soldiers had lured them into the courtyard to be slaughtered, while the Swiss troops later swore that the first fire had come from the rebels, who had aimed at the guards on top of the towers. In any event, bullets and cannon shot began to fly, as the demonstrators scattered to the side of the courtyard.

Some of the Electors tried to effect a ceasefire over the sound of battle, but could not make themselves heard. Makeshift pallets carrying the wounded began to emerge onto the streets from the smoky courtyards. Inside, Launay was frantic. Despite there being numerous French troops stationed nearby, none had come to his aid – both because many within the ranks of the infantry sympathized with the rebels and because of the curious vacuum of power that had opened up in central Paris, which had been virtually abandoned to the mob.

THE FORTRESS FALLS

Finally, reinforcements came – but not to Launay. At about 3:30 p.m., the mob was joined by about a few hundred *gardes français*, soldiers of the rebellion's "new militia," formed from any man or woman who could acquire a gun, as well as deserters from Louis XVI's forces. They brought with them not only more muskets, but also two cannon, including, ironically enough, a silver gun given to the king by the Raj of Siam, which Louis had largely used as a sort of toy. It had been looted from the royal warehouse and now stood ready to bring down the Bastille.

Led by two veteran officers, the militia members set up the guns in the inner courtyard, aiming them directly at the wooden bottom of the raised drawbridge (the walls of the prison were too thick for cannon shot to penetrate). On the other side of the gate, Launay lined up his own cannon. Perhaps one hundred feet apart, the forces of old and new faced each other.

Shortly thereafter, convinced of the hopelessness of his situation, Launay decided to concede defeat. At first, the crowds would not accept his terms (which would have guaranteed safe passage for the defenders) and kept on firing. Desperate, Launay wrote a note, which he had passed out to the crowd: "We have twenty thousand pounds of powder. We shall blow up the garrison and the whole neighborhood unless you accept our capitulation." But when the officer in charge of the rebel guns made as if to fire them into the gates, Launay gave up without condition. The drawbridge was opened and the mob poured into the Bastille.

A SYMBOL OF FREEDOM

The rebels disarmed the Swiss soldiers and led them through the streets, stoning them and screaming at them. The soldiers survived, however, unlike some of the *invalides*, who were mistaken for prison wardens and hung or beaten to death. Launay, too, suffered a horrible fate when the mob stabbed and shot him to death and then carved off his head to put on a pike.

Eighty-three members of the mob died, but the victory of the crowd was great. On the evening after the fall of the prison, huge crowds thronged Paris, shouting, celebrating, and firing their guns in the air. Thereafter, those who had taken part in the assault were given the title *Vainqueur de la Bastille* and marched on every anniversary of the event for as long as they lived.

The king announced that he would recall Jacques Necker. Louis even wore a tricolor cockade, the symbol of the Revolution, as he approved a new government. However, many nobles were appalled at the violence (which would later claim the king's life, as well as that of his wife, Marie Antoinette), and began fleeing the country.

During the next decade, France would be radically transformed. More widespread mob violence would turn the Revolution very ugly, very soon. The Reign of Terror that began in 1792, in which thousands of those suspected of "counterrevolutionary" sympathies were killed — a terror that foreshadowed similar bloodlettings after the successful rebellions in Russia and China in the twentieth century — was to forever besmirch the ideals of the Revolution. Not only that; the Terror pushed away countries (especially America, which had just undergone its own successful revolution) that might otherwise have been sympathetic.

But on July 14, 1789, it was truly the common people who took the first step toward a republic. And ever since, Bastille Day has been celebrated annually in France as the day when the French people, at least symbolically speaking, won their freedom.

Demolishing the Bastille

The Bastille did not long survive its garrison. It at once became an attraction for visitors of all stripes hoping to see some signs of the horrors of bygone days (a few old bones and some chains were produced, but by and large nothing grotesque was found within the old fortress's walls). Then, in 1790, a French entrepreneur and showman named Pierre-François Palloy bid for and won the rights to demolish the structure, so that he could sell pieces of it to eager souvenir hunters. Palloy personally knocked the first stone off with a pickax. Demolition then continued, involving as many as a thousand workers, and was finished by November. As well as selling off much of the structure, Palloy created a masonry model of the prison and held festivals amid the ruins. Today, the former site of the prison is occupied by a broad square, the Place de la Bastille, and the Bastille Opera.

The Battle of Waterloo

*How Napoleon Finally Met His Match, and
Europe Turned Its Back on Revolution*

I T'S JUST POSSIBLE THAT THE Battle of Waterloo is the most famous battle in the history of the world. Sure, it has a few strong competitors – Cannae, Gettysburg, the Somme, D-Day. But Waterloo is one of the very few battles in world history that decided the outcome of a war on a single day. Had Coalition forces not stopped Napoleon at Waterloo, the map of Europe would have been drastically redrawn, with, just possibly, Napoleon presiding over a French empire on the Continent. The mighty clash at Waterloo also encouraged war planners for years to come to plot massive set-piece battles that might end conflicts at a single, bold stroke. This shining chimera was to cause much carnage when World War I began.

To this day, the very name of the battle is synonymous with crushing defeat and personal downfall – with overreaching ambition being thwarted. But things could have gone quite differently on that June day of 1815 in Belgium, as even the victorious British commander would acknowledge. If it had, we might be sitting in a very different world today.

A QUIET MORNING

On the morning of June 18, a few miles outside the Belgian village of Waterloo, 140,000 men faced each other over a piece of land two miles wide and about two-thirds of a mile across. On the north side, drawn up along and behind a ridge, was the Army of the Seventh Coalition, which contained forces from Great Britain, the Netherlands, Belgium, and Germany, totaling about sixty-seven thousand men. Their commander was the Duke of Wellington, the most successful British general of his generation. An allied Prussian army under Field Marshal Gebhard von Blücher was not far away. To the south across the field were seventy-three thousand French troops commanded by Napoleon Bonaparte.

Napoleon Crossing the Alps (1801), one of five versions of the same portrait painted by the French artist Jacques-Louis David.

It had rained heavily and both armies had spent the night miserable and cold in the open fields around Waterloo. The land separating the two armies had become a morass of mud. After dawn, the skies cleared and the sun came out. The British readied themselves, certain that the notably aggressive Napoleon would attack their positions. And then … nothing happened.

As the hours wore on without action, soldiers relaxed, wrote letters, tried to catnap. Among the French forces, word went around that Napoleon was waiting for the fields to dry, in case the mud slowed any attack, particularly one made by artillery or cavalry. This was a perfectly reasonable assumption, except that it wasn't really like Napoleon. Those who knew him had never seen him slowed by inconveniences like muddy fields. And the longer the delay, the greater chance that von Blücher's Prussian forces would be able to reinforce Wellington's troops – the very thing Napoleon wanted to avoid. Many in the French ranks began to ask, what was the matter with the emperor?

THE THREAT TO EUROPE

This confrontation in Belgium represented the culmination of almost two decades of conflict in Europe. War had broken out between France and most of Europe after the French Revolution in 1789. These hostilities had briefly ended in 1802, but under Napoleon, who had seized power in 1799 and had himself proclaimed emperor in 1804, the fighting continued, with most of Europe attempting to check Bonaparte's attempts to seize more and more territory.

Wellington was later to say "France has not enemies. We are the enemies of one man only," and there is some truth to this. The wars had been fought against Napoleon, not against France.

Wellington was notably successful in his early encounters with the legendary general. Taking control of British, Portuguese, and Spanish forces in the Peninsular War, he ousted Napoleon from Spain and Portugal. Then, in 1814, after Napoleon's disastrous attack on Russia left the French army at fewer than one hundred thousand men, Coalition armies occupied Paris, and Napoleon was forced to abdicate and surrender unconditionally, on April 11. The Treaty of Fontainebleau exiled him to the tiny Mediterranean isle of Elba. In the wake of Napoleon's resignation, royalists grabbed power in France and Louis XVIII, brother of Louis XVI, was restored to power, supported by Coalition powers that wanted a stable monarchy in France. Europe breathed a sigh of relief, and most of the armies disbanded.

Escape from Elba

In 1814, Napoleon was exiled by Coalition powers to the island of Elba, off the west coast of Italy. He was not, literally, a prisoner. He had a personal guard of six hundred or so men, was ruler of Elba's population of around 120,000 and was also allowed, perhaps cruelly, to keep the title of "Emperor." British ships guarded the island around the clock, but, even so,

Napoleon was not isolated from the outside world and received thousands of letters from supporters all over Europe, which stoked his still simmering ambitions. On February 26, 1815, around midnight, he was fairly easily able to board a ship, elude the British vessels guarding Elba, and then make his way to France, and eventually to Waterloo.

But not for long. After escaping from Elba on February 26, 1815, Napoleon landed in France, where he was met by a regiment of soldiers sent by Louis XVIII to capture or kill him. These men had previously been Napoleon's Fifth Regiment and were led by his former subordinate, Marshal Ney. In true Napoleonic fashion, the general leaped off his horse, approached the regiment and cried out: "Soldiers of the Fifth, you recognize me, if any man will shoot his emperor, he may do so now!" The soldiers spontaneously rallied to Napoleon and marched on Paris with him. Louis XVIII fled, and Napoleon, using the same charisma that had brought the Fifth Regiment to his side, raised an army consisting of many of his old imperial soldiers.

It was a time of profound fear and distress among the Coalition powers in Europe, probably not rivaled until the ascendancy of Hitler in the late 1930s. Here was a man many considered a dangerous megalomaniac, returned from what was supposed to be permanent exile, who had, with astonishing swiftness, raised an army of 140,000 men. He needed to be stopped, and immediately, or the very future of Europe was at risk.

As it happened, representatives of Britain, Austria, Prussia, and Russia were meeting in Vienna when the news came that Napoleon had escaped. The swift response of these countries was to assemble another coalition — the seventh to fight Napoleon — and declare war on France on March 25. The intention of the Seventh Coalition was to surround France on all sides, march on Paris, and destroy Napoleon once and for all. But the only force ready to fight was Wellington's Anglo-allied army in Belgium, although the Prussian force commanded by von Blücher would soon be on its way to join the British commander.

Napoleon, meanwhile, decided to strike at Belgium and capture the port of Brussels. He deployed his army along the French border and sent Marshal Ney to attack the Prussians. After fierce fighting, the French forced von Blücher's army to retreat — but did not destroy them — and Napoleon brought his army, on the evening of June 17, to the village of Waterloo.

PAINFULLY AFFLICTED

Forty-five years old as the engagement began (just a few months younger than the Duke of Wellington), Napoleon was in a state of odd indecision on the morning of the battle. He arose quite early, having spent the night in a farmhouse, and conferred with his generals over maps. "We have ninety chances in our favor," he said, "and not ten against us. I tell you Wellington is a bad general, the English are bad troops and the whole affair is nothing more than a picnic."

But his behavior belied such confident words. After reviewing his troops, he did not give any order to attack and simply brushed off every commander who suggested he do so, giving as his only excuse the fact that the ground was still too muddy to maneuver.

Finally, he asked his aides to take him to a small inn at the rear of the lines, where he dismounted his horse and sat on a chair, at one point putting his elbows on his knees and placing his face in his hands. One of his staff officers later wrote that he seemed to be in a stupor.

It began to dawn on those around him that Napoleon was ill, although no one dared ask if he was and he never said so. But years after his death, his brother, Prince Jérôme, and his personal physician, Baron Larrey, revealed that the emperor suffered fiercely from an affliction he found embarrassing to admit to — hemorrhoids, which if aggravated by long periods of sitting on a hard surface, such as a saddle, can became painfully prolapsed. He may have also suffered from cystitis, a bladder infection that makes urinating painful and causes high fevers, and is aggravated by cold, wet conditions. It had struck him before, most notably at the battle of Borodino.

Historians have also speculated that Napoleon, whose formerly taught physique had suddenly become pudgy, suffered from a pituitary disorder, which can cause weight gain, as well as indecisiveness and blurry thinking. Whatever was happening, it wasn't until around 11:30 a.m. that Napoleon roused himself from his lethargy and ordered that the attack begin with a cannonade.

Denis Dighton's *The Battle of Waterloo 18th June 1815* depicts the Duke of Wellington amid the chaos and tumult of the battle.

THE THUNDER OF ARTILLERY

Some Coalition troops later claimed they were relieved that hostilities had finally begun. This was their moment to oust Napoleon, who, to some of the younger troops, had been a *bête noire* from infancy, a figment of evil used by nursemaids to frighten them. The relief of the troops to finally get the action underway turned to horror, however, as eight- and twelve-pound French cannonballs flew through their ranks, wreaking havoc. One raw British recruit watched his sergeant major literally cut in half by a ball.

But here is where the Duke of Wellington's foresight came into play. He had personally suggested the ridge amid the farmers' fields near Waterloo as a place to make a stand against the French, and one of the reasons was the protection offered by its reverse slope. Now, he ordered that all of his men lie down behind it. To the watching French, it looked like the Coalition line, mainly British at its center, had simply disappeared. Although the artillery assault was the worst many British veteran could remember, the ridge was their savior. Most of the cannonballs flew over the men, who tucked themselves as close as possible to the back of the ridgeline, and landed well to the rear. The balls that did most damage were those that hit the top of the ridge and bounced across the supine soldiers.

When the barrage ended, after perhaps half an hour, the Coalition infantry raised their heads.

HALTING THE CHARGE

Even to men half-deaf from gunfire, the sound of the charge was recognizable. First, the *rat-tat-rat-tat* of drums, then bugles, ragged shouting, and finally, stronger and more unified, the cry "Vive l'Empereur!" – "Long live the Emperor!" When the Coalition forces rushed to reoccupy their lines at the center of the ridge, they saw, coming directly at their left center, three columns of French infantry, each 24 ranks deep and 150 soldiers wide. These were flanked by cavalry on either side. This was the classic and deadly formation of the French Grand Army, the one that had won battles all across Europe: for Napoleon used these shock columns to punch rapidly through enemy lines, destroying all cohesion in a moment.

The French soldiers marched, as one British officer said admiringly, "as if on parade," directly at the Belgian division commanded by Sir Thomas Picton. Unnerved, the Belgians turned and ran, leaving a great hole in the center of the Coalition lines. But all was not as it seemed in the French ranks. Because of the deafening noise, men could not hear their leaders, and when the other British ranks opened fire, the columns started veering to the right and into a row of double hedges. Here, Picton had stationed the only men he had left, a troop of Scottish infantry, and he ordered them to attack just as a French bullet struck him and killed him instantly.

The Scots opened up from in front of the hedges, three thousand rifles pouring a volley into the French columns at close range. The French outnumbered the Scots many times over, but because of their column formation could not bring as many rifles to bear in reply. Next, the two forces hit each other, hard, and the combat turned into hundreds of deadly hand-to-hand melees in the swirling smoke, fought with rifle butt, saber, pike, and fists. Then, as the French wavered, there came an amazing sight: leaping the hedges, as if in a steeple-chase, the British cavalry arrived, led by the Scots Greys, in a charge that utterly destroyed the French advance.

ON THE RUN

Heavy fighting now swirled around three isolated farmhouses and their outbuildings – Hougoumont, La Haye Sainte, and Papelotte – which were ready-made defensive positions. At about three in the afternoon, Napoleon sent Marshal Ney to capture La Haye Sainte and after a bloody fight, the French infantry managed to tear it from British hands. French artillery was then emplaced there, aiming directly at the Coalition-held ridge. But when Ney asked for backup, Napoleon said he had none to spare. For arriving on the French right were the Prussian forces under von Blücher. These were the reinforcements Wellington had needed and prayed for. Napoleon was appalled, for a force under one of his commanders, the Marquis de Grouchy, was supposed to have blocked these troops; but Grouchy had failed, allowing himself to be held up by other Prussians in a pitched battle at nearby Wavre while von Blücher made his way to Wellington.

Napoleon sent one last roaring attack of his elite forces, the Imperial Guard, against the Coalition-held ridge. But while some managed to break through, the rest were overwhelmed and began to flee. Seeing this elite corps on the run, the French lines broke, pursued by the Coalition cavalry. Napoleon's army was now in flight and Napoleon himself, bitter, broken, and ill, retreated with it to Paris.

They knew that Napoleon had finally been defeated here, this time for good, and that therefore history had been made.

Napoleon managed to escape from the battlefield, pursued by Coalition forces. With defeat inevitable, he abdicated, then tried to flee to the United States, but was captured by the British and forced to surrender aboard a British warship on July 15. The ailing general was exiled once again, this time far away, to the tiny South Atlantic island of St. Helena, where he was to die in 1821, possibly poisoned, possibly, finally, a victim of the many ailments that had begun to plague him at Waterloo.

The Duke of Wellington later said of the battle that it was "the nearest-run thing you ever saw in your life."

FINAL EXILE

On the battlefield that night lay forty thousand men, dead and horribly wounded. The subsequent looting has passed into legend. Ghoulish Belgian peasants stripped thousands of dead men bare, while Coalition soldiers wandered through the night, sometimes even robbing and killing their own. Officers, with their purses and gilded swords, were especially good sources of booty. The French wounded could expect no aid, and died, screaming for water.

The very next day, Belgian civilian sightseers came out to wander the battlefield, holding handkerchiefs over their noses against the unpleasant smell.

Europe had been saved, but the political effects of the battle of Waterloo would be long-lasting. Horrified by the way in which Napoleon's reemergence from Elba had once more stoked the fires of rebellion, Europe's leading powers became fiercely conservative. Signs of social change and moves toward democracy were quickly stamped out. Traditional monarchies were restored and bolstered across the continent, nationalist and republican movements quashed.

Supporters of the old order well knew how close they had come to catastrophe. As the Duke of Wellington said of the battle of Waterloo itself, it was "the nearest-run thing you ever saw in your life."

The Irish
Potato Famine

*How Nineteenth-century Europe's Greatest Disaster Accelerated One of
the Largest Diasporas in History and Fueled the Rise of Irish Nationalism*

DURING THE COOL, WET summer of 1846, those Irish peasants who had managed to stave off starvation since the fall of 1845, mainly by selling their livestock and eating corn imported from America, waited anxiously for their potato crops to come in on fields and garden patches all over the country. Surely the potato would not fail again, would not turn black and stinking on its vine due to some unknown disease, as it had done the previous year?

At first, the crop seemed healthy and the people rejoiced that the blight would not continue. But by September, potatoes began to die in the west of Ireland; then, the malevolent disease moved across the country, at the rate of fifty miles a week, until no potato remained untouched. One parish priest wrote: "In many places the wretched people were seated on the fences of their decaying gardens, wringing their hands and weeping bitterly." Government officials estimated that there were only enough potatoes left in Ireland to feed people for one month. Black '47, as the Irish would later refer to the year of 1847, was about to begin.

A DRAMATIC IMPACT

It is almost impossible to overestimate the importance of the so-called Great Famine or Great Hunger in Irish history, but the following statistics convey the magnitude of its impact. In 1845, the population of Ireland was about eight million. Six years later, it was five and a half million. About one million died of starvation and disease. The other million and a half emigrated – mainly to Britain, Australia, and America.

The effect of this population loss was extreme. It left Ireland an impoverished country for generations to come – indeed, it would take until the beginning of the twenty-first century for a resurgent Ireland to build its population levels back to those of 1845. It also began the rise to prominence of Irish communities in countries around the world, most notably the United States and Australia. In addition, it precipitated the growth of Irish nationalist movements such as the

Fenian Brotherhood and the Land League of the late nineteenth century. The latter, notably, would preach that the only way to avoid another dire famine was to wrest Irish land from corrupt English lords.

KING POTATO

As the Irish consumed their last supplies of potatoes and the winter of 1846–47 began, they started to eat nettles, turnips, rotten cabbages, seaweed, even grass. Those who lived along the west coast could stare out at a sea teeming with fish, but they had no way to harvest them – their tiny round boats, or coracles, were too flimsy for the deep water the fish inhabited.

Few countries were as vulnerable to famine as Ireland. It had been dependent on the single crop of the potato since the 1590s, when this marvelous, life-giving tuber was imported from South America, where it had first been cultivated in the highlands of Peru. In the cool, wet climate of Ireland, it thrived. Indeed, potatoes grew so easily there, and with so little labor, that they were planted in what were called "lazy beds." One acre of the very scarce farmland in Ireland could bring up to twelve tons of potatoes a year, enough to feed a large Irish family easily.

It has been estimated that by the mid-nineteenth century three million Irish survived on potatoes alone, with perhaps a little cabbage and buttermilk added. One adult Irish person would generally eat up to fourteen pounds of potatoes a day.

Potatoes were rich in protein, carbohydrates, and Vitamin C – if poverty forces you to eat just one food, the potato is not the worst choice you can make.

Unfortunately, not only did the Irish cultivate only one food source, but they grew only one variety of potato, called Lumpers. It produced a high yield but was vulnerable to being completely destroyed by blights; and since it was not genetically diverse, a single blight could wipe it out.

The cause of the blight that began at harvest time in September of 1845 was a killer fungus called *Phytophthora infestans*, which had been brought from America on ships to England, and then blown on an ill wind across the Irish Sea. This fungus not only killed the potatoes, it turned them black and rotten, leaving them putrefying in their beds. What's more, it returned with a vengeance the following year.

The winter of 1846–47 was the worst anyone could remember: freezing cold, with one blizzard and sleet storm after another, very unlike the usual mild Irish winter. People began pouring into government poorhouses, but these places were hellholes, rife with disease and desperation. In one poorhouse in Skibbereen, in Cork, fifty percent of the children admitted in late 1846 died. The chief magistrate of Cork, a man named Nicholas Cummins, wrote in horror of a visit to one poorhouse: "Six famished and ghastly skeletons to all appearances dead were huddled in a corner on some filthy straw. Their sole covering what seemed a ragged horse cloth. Their wretched legs hanging about naked above the knees. I approached with horror and found by a low moaning that they were still alive. They were in fever. Four children, a woman, and what had once been a man ... in a few minutes I was surrounded by at least two hundred such phantoms ... Their demoniacal yells are still ringing in my ear and the horrible images are fixed upon my brain." Stories like this had been coming out of Ireland for a year — and now people were dying, truly, by the thousands. Why wasn't anyone doing anything about it?

"THE ENGLISH GAVE US THE FAMINE"

The Irish had been fighting the English occupiers of their country on and off for two centuries before the famine. As recently as 1798, an army of Irish peasants under an Anglo-Irish lawyer named Wolfe Tone had risen up against the English. Forty thousand of them were killed before Britain put down the rebellion. Even after the 1801 Act of Union integrated Ireland into Great Britain, the Irish were still considered poor cousins. Catholic Ireland remained under the control of an Anglo-Protestant landlord class which owned vast tracts of land. These were divided into tiny parcels by middlemen and sublet to tenant farmers. It has been estimated that over ninety percent of land in Ireland in 1845 was split up into plots of thirty acres or less, and that perhaps four hundred thousand Irish peasants lived on plots of five acres or smaller.

There is a saying among the Irish that "God gave us the potato blight, but the English gave us the famine."

Sir Charles Edward Trevelyan, who pronounced himself unmoved by the sufferings of the starving Irish.

The prevailing stereotype of the Irish among British landlords (most of whom seldom visited their holdings) was that they were superstitious, cunning, lazy, and dishonest. When the famine first hit, the British Prime Minister Sir Robert Peel attempted to help those in need by repealing the duties on imported corn, paying for Indian corn (maize) to be imported to feed the hungry, and setting up other relief efforts. But even this mild and inadequate response met with opposition in Britain, and Peel was voted out of office in the summer of 1846.

A CRUEL AND BIGOTED RESPONSE

Without Peel's leavening hand, control of the Irish was left entirely up to the Assistant Secretary of the British Treasury, Charles Edward Trevelyan, who visited Ireland only once during the famine. He claimed that, unlike the majority of those who witnessed the suffering at firsthand, he was unmoved by the experience – and that this made him better able to make decisions. One of his first was to halt shipments of government food, for fear that the Irish would become "habitually dependent." The only option left to the bulk of famine victims was public works relief. In the winter of 1846–47, seven hundred thousand Irish – men, women, and children – found work breaking stones with hammers, transporting the pieces in baskets, and laying roads. But the pay was so poor that not enough food could be bought to assuage hunger pangs, and so, in turn, the people grew too weak for such hard labor.

The cruel and bigoted response of Trevelyan and others like him infinitely worsened the suffering. As 1847 wore on, there were scenes, especially in the west, that were comparable to those of the plague years of the fourteenth century. Villages were depopulated, with survivors too weak to bury the dead, who lay on the roadways. There were reports of cannibalism. There were outbreaks of typhus, dysentery, and something called famine dropsy (hunger edema), which causes the limbs and the body to swell and ends with the victim dropping dead suddenly. And the situation didn't just affect the peasantry: over two hundred Irish doctors died in 1847 alone.

As all this occurred, the Irish watched while shiploads of Irish grain and livestock were sent to ports all over Europe. For while one crop had failed, others had thrived, and the British needed to turn a profit, "thus inflicting upon the Irish people," as one Irish politician wrote at the time, "the abject misery of having their own provisions carried away to feed others, while they themselves are left contemptuously to starve."

There were food riots in ports in Cork, where mobs tried to storm warehouses and take grain. In County Waterford, British troops guarding a food shipment were stoned; in return, they fired indiscriminately into a crowd, killing two people and wounding numerous others. Six landlords were shot and killed, murdered along dark roads. The British responded by sending more and more troops to Ireland.

KEEPING THE PEOPLE ALIVE

In June of 1847, the British government, influenced by outrage at home and abroad, decided to "keep the people alive," as Trevelyan put it. While still not providing any direct aid, it passed the Temporary Relief of Destitute Persons (Ireland) Act, also known as the Soup Kitchen Act, whereby soup kitchens were set up to feed the starving for free, but only through the auspices of international groups like the Quakers or the private British Relief Organisation.

The demand for soup far exceeded the ability of these groups to provide it, but by the summer of 1847, as another potato crop was anxiously awaited, three million people were kept alive in this way, on a pound of "stirabout" and a four-ounce slice of bread per day. In September, the potato crop appeared – and this time was without blight. But so few farmers had been able to afford

Previous page: A nineteenth-century painting of an all-too common scene during the famine – the eviction of an Irish family.

seed to plant the previous years (or had been to busy doing public works projects) that the crop was comparatively tiny. Consequently, landlords decided that they needed to turn to other sources of income – wheat or livestock. But to create the larger fields needed, they had to destroy the dozens of tiny farms and potato plots on their lands – farms to which the starving Irish were desperately clinging.

The solution for the landlords was to evict their Irish tenants on grounds of nonpayment of rent and send them out to wander the roads or knock on the doors of the poorhouses. Some paid to send their peasants on ships to North America. These "coffin ships," as they were known, were overcrowded and pestilential. In the summer

Success Stories – and Lasting Scars

One and a half million Irish emigrated during the course of the Great Famine. They became workers, policemen, and politicians in the United States, and gold miners, farmers, and judges in Australia, most notably in the state of Victoria, where one out of every four people by 1871 was an Irish immigrant. It was not an easy transition. The Irish who arrived in other countries were in sorry shape – malnourished, illiterate, usually toothless (as a result of scurvy or starvation), and,

more often than not, disease-ridden. And something else distinguished them from other immigrants. Customs officials in Liverpool, from where many Irish emigrated, used adjectives like "passive," "resigned," "stunned," and "mute" to describe them in official records. From today's perspective, one can see that these men and women were suffering from post-traumatic stress disorder. They had survived, but just barely, and the psychological scars would remain forever.

of 1847, forty ships containing fourteen thousand Irish waited under quarantine on the St. Lawrence River to enter Canada at Quebec; hundreds died of typhus, their bodies thrown overboard to float past the horrified eyes of the Canadians.

FLIGHT AND REBELLION

Ultimately, during Black '47, about one hundred thousand Irish went to Canada. Half of them walked across the border to the United States (which had more stringent immigration regulations and would not allow disease-carrying ships to enter). There, they paved the way for a great wave of Irish

Others, tired of the oppressive rule of the British and their inhumane response to the famine, proposed drastic action. In the middle of the Great Hunger, in 1848, a group of rebellious young Irish nationalists formed the Irish Confederation and plotted throughout the summer of 1848 to rise against the British. But, heavily infiltrated by the British secret police, unable to secure arms, and also underestimating an exhausted populace's willingness to revolt, the rebels were quickly overcome after a few minor skirmishes. Their leaders were arrested and sentenced to transportation to Australia. However, their writings would influence a future generation

Desperate Irishmen got themselves arrested in the hope of being transported to Australia.

emigration to America, consisting of hundreds of thousands of men and women anxious to leave anything to do with Great Britain behind and find work in a new and bustling country. By the 1870s, Irish immigrants would control the inner political workings of some of America's largest cities, including New York, Boston, and Chicago.

Black '47 was the worst year of the Famine, but when it was over the Irish continued to suffer. In 1849, after another failed potato crop, things became so bad that young Irishmen got themselves arrested in the hope of being transported to Australia, where at least they would be fed. Still more waves of Irish left the country for America.

of rebels, both in Ireland and in America, who would fight to cast off British rule.

The 1850s brought normal harvests of potatoes, and, with the diversification of crops, the expansion of railroads for transporting food, and the politicization of the working class, the specter of famine was gradually diminished. Politicization led to agitation for land reform, notably by the Land League movement in the late 1870s, and gave the Irish a greater awareness of the importance of controling their own destinies. In this sense, a line can be traced from the Great Hunger to the events that brought about independence in 1921 and the creation of the Republic of Ireland in 1949.

The Charge of the Light Brigade

*The Military Debacle That Inspired an Immortal Verse —
and an Overhaul of the British Army*

Theirs not to reason why,
Theirs but to do or die:
Into the valley of Death
Rode the six hundred.
Alfred, Lord Tennyson,
"The Charge of the Light Brigade"

THERE ARE MONUMENTS aplenty to meaningful deaths in war, but Tennyson's poem "The Charge of the Light Brigade" provides history with a dramatic recounting of the opposite: the sacrifice of hundreds of good men by criminally stupid officers in a futile, meaningless attack. Most people today would know nothing about the Charge of the Light Brigade were it not for Tennyson's poem. It brilliantly depicts the bravery of the "six hundred" — to be precise, 673 — cavalrymen of the British Light Brigade as they galloped for a mile down a valley near Balaklava, on the Crimean Peninsula (now in the Ukraine), under murderous fire from their Russian adversaries. Even so, although the poem also says "not tho' the soldiers knew, someone had blundered," it doesn't come close to capturing the true nature of this debacle.

THE THIN RED LINE

Beginning in 1853, the Crimean War pitted the Imperial Russia of Czar Nicholas I against Great Britain, France, and the Ottoman Empire, which aimed to block Russia's attempts to expand its sphere of influence into the Middle East. Most of the fighting centered on the Crimean Peninsula, which thrusts southward from the Ukraine, then part of the Russian Empire, into the Black Sea. In 1854, Great Britain, France, and Turkey invaded Crimea with an allied expeditionary force intent on besieging the Russian port of Sevastopol. On October 25, the Russians attempted to break the siege by attacking the nearby port of Balaklava, from which the allied forces got their supplies.

These attacks were repulsed by remarkably brave actions on the part of the British army and cavalry. The Ninety-third Highlanders stood their ground against the

Russian onslaught, earning the famous nickname "the thin red line" from William Howard Russell – often called the first war correspondent – who was on the scene reporting for *The Times*. (Actually, Russell, watching from nearby heights, depicted the Ninety-third as "a thin red streak tipped with a line of steel," the red referring to their uniforms, the steel to their bayonets, but the phrase was at once condensed into "thin red line" and is still used to describe valiant stands.) In addition, in an extraordinary uphill charge, the so-called Heavy Brigade of about five hundred dragoons, or mounted infantry, attacked a charging Russian cavalry formation of three thousand horses, engaging them in ferocious hand-to-hand combat.

"UNUSUALLY STUPID"

At that moment, about five hundred yards away from this desperate see-saw battle, stood an extraordinary figure – James Thomas Brudenell, the Seventh Earl of Cardigan, commander of the Light Brigade – so-called because its members were true cavalry, less heavily armed than the Heavy Brigade. He turned to a fellow officer and said, "Those damn Heavies will have the laugh on us this day." But it never occurred to him to leap on his horse and lead his men to join the battle. As he explained later, he had not received orders to do so.

This was typical of Cardigan. Fifty-seven years old in 1854, an immensely wealthy aristocrat, he has been described by the British historian Cecil Woodham-Smith as "tall, handsome, opulently dressed, carrying himself with a mixture of arrogance and self-importance said to make one lose one's temper just to look at him." Cardigan – who wore, at casual moments, the sweater that he popularized – was also, as Woodham-Smith puts it,

The imposing but witless Seventh Earl of Cardigan, James Thomas Brudenell, led the disastrous Charge of the Light Brigade.

"unusually stupid ... The melancholy truth was that his gorgeous head had nothing in it."

Cardigan had had a checkered career in the British Army (which had not fought a war since the battle of Waterloo). He had been publicly reviled for such excesses as fighting duels and having a man under his command flogged on Easter Sunday. But, despite this, he had steadily advanced himself, by dint of the perfectly legal practice of buying commissions, and was by this time a major general. After each day's campaigning, he retired to his private yacht on the Black Sea, there to drink champagne and have his uniforms freshly pressed.

WHOSE SIDE ARE THEY ON?

While Cardigan leaned on his horse and made comments about the fight between the Heavies and the Russians, as if he were at a sporting event, sixty-six-year-old Fitzroy Somerset, Lord Raglan, watched from the Sapoune Heights, an imposing escarpment high above the raging battle. A career officer, Raglan was the commander of the British forces in the Crimea and he had seen action – forty years before at the battle of Waterloo, where he had lost his right arm serving under his hero, the Duke of Wellington. Unfortunately, Raglan had little command experience and also possessed the embarrassing habit of referring to France (Britain's ally in the Crimea, but a foe in earlier wars including the Napoleonic Wars) as "the enemy," for which he had to be corrected time and again by his staff.

From his bird's-eye viewpoint, Raglan could see the Heavy Brigade breaking the will of the Russian cavalry and forcing them into a retreat. The Russians subsequently streamed back along the Causeway Heights, a low line of ridges stretching above the beaches of the Black Sea. On their advance, the Russians had captured British redoubts complete with artillery that had been emplaced there; now, Raglan and his staff could see them attempting to remove these guns as they fell back. Anxious to stop the Russians from retreating with British artillery, Raglan issued orders to Lord Lucan, commander of the British cavalry division, to attack.

PLODDING AND UNIMAGINATIVE

Fifty-four-year-old George Bingham, the Third Earl of Lucan, was the third sorry figure in the trio of British aristocratic officer dunces at Balaklava. Lucan had been retired from the army for nearly twenty years before being called to duty in the Crimea; he had paid twenty-five thousand pounds to purchase a colonelcy, much of which had been extracted penny by penny from the peasants who farmed his vast Irish estates. Plodding and unimaginative, he was the polar opposite of Lord Cardigan, who was his direct subordinate. The two men happened to be brothers-in-law. They also hated each other passionately and had done so for thirty years.

Lucan's cavalry division was positioned at the mouth of what was known as the North Valley, which was about a thousand yards wide. On his right were the Causeway Heights, from where the Russians were removing the British guns. On his left were the Fedioukine Hills, where there were more Russian guns emplaced. About a mile away, at the far end of the valley, were heavy Russian guns and Russian troops. Lucan now received a series of confusing orders from Raglan ordering an attack by his light cavalry against the Russian guns, but could not understand them and asked for clarification – why would Raglan order an attack by cavalry along a mile of open ground exposed to Russian fire on three sides?

failure to pursue the retreating Russians and he blamed this failure squarely on Lucan, Cardigan's commander. Arriving with frothing horse at Lucan's position, he verbally and with some impatience delivered Raglan's order for Lucan to attack the Russian guns.

Angered by this junior officer's air of insolence, Lucan replied: "Attack sir? Attack what? What guns, sir?" And Nolan, instead of pointing at the Causeway Heights, flung his arm in the direction of the Russian emplacements at the end of the North Valley: "There, my lord, is your enemy, there are your guns!"

Cardigan was "unusually stupid ... The melancholy truth was that his gorgeous head had nothing in it."

TRAGIC CONFUSION

The answer was, he had not. Raglan wanted Lucan to attack to his right, against the gun emplacements on Causeway Heights. But because Lucan did not have Raglan's bird's-eye view of the land, he could not understand what his commander was talking about.

After repeated delays and requests for clarification from Lucan, an impatient Raglan finally sent an officer by horse to speak directly to Lucan. This man was a key figure in the whole affair, thirty-six-year-old Captain Louis Nolan, an aide de camp with a wide knowledge of cavalry tactics. He had been enraged by Cardigan's

Nolan's words and tone were so insubordinate that members of Lucan's staff felt that he should be placed under arrest. To this day, no one knows quite what Nolan was referring to when he pointed. He certainly knew that Raglan did not intend for Lucan to charge his men right down the valley, but those present, along with Lucan, took his gesture to mean just that. It is possible that his arm-waving was simply gesticulating, meaning nothing at all. But the men on the ground could not see the Russians with their captured guns on the heights, so it is easy to understand why they might have assumed that he was directing them to the far end of North Valley.

In any event, Lucan accepted that he was being forced to make a suicidal charge, and spurred his horse over to see his hated brother-in-law, Lord Cardigan.

INTO THE VALLEY OF DEATH

Had Cardigan and Lucan been on better terms, it is possible that together they might have made some sense of these puzzling orders. Instead, they spoke stiffly, in military formalities. Lucan told Cardigan of Raglan's orders and instructed him to lead the charge with the Light Brigade while Lucan followed with the Heavies. Taken aback, Cardigan remonstrated: "Certainly sir, but allow me to point out that the Russians have a battery in the valley at our front and batteries and riflemen on both sides."

Lucan replied, "I know it, but Lord Raglan will have it. We have no choice but to obey." At this, Cardigan saluted, wheeled his horse around and ordered his brigade to make ready to attack. An aide heard him mutter: "Well, here goes the last of the Brudenells."

Cardigan next divided his brigade of 673 men into two lines, but then Lucan, countermanding Cardigan's orders, stepped in to divide it into three. When the lines were ready, Cardigan marched about five horse-lengths out in front of his men and

This romanticized illustration of the charge shows the moment when the survivors reached the Russian gun emplacements.

raised his sword. He said, quite calmly: "The brigade will advance. Walk, march, trot." A trumpet blew, and they were off.

NO LOOKING BACK

While Cardigan's intelligence and leadership skills can be fairly impugned, his bravery cannot. Erect in his saddle, wearing a resplendent (and freshly pressed) uniform of red, blue, and gold, riding a beautiful chestnut mare, he led his men down the valley, never once looking back.

Shells began bursting among the lines, shattering men and horses. Whenever a man fell, the ranks parted around him and then closed again. The Russians, who were able to bring about fifty guns to bear on the charging British horses, were astonished when the attacking cavalry did not wheel into the hills, but instead kept going straight down the valley.

During this early stage of the charge, an inexplicable thing happened. Captain Nolan, Raglan's aide de camp, rode his horse out in front of Lord Cardigan (an unforgivable breach of etiquette) and, crossing the British line of advance, turned in his saddle, waved his sword, and began shouting something. Was he trying to lead the charge, as the enraged Cardigan thought? Or was he finally urging the British to veer off to the right to attack the Causeway Heights?

No one will ever know, for in the very first volley of shells, Nolan became the first casualty of the charge, as a hot metal fragment tore into his heart. In a scene of sheer horror, his sword fell to the earth, but, with the right hand frozen in an upright position, his body was carried by his horse back through the ranks of the brigade while issuing a bone-chilling and

Tennyson and the Light Brigade

Alfred Lord Tennyson's appointment as Poet Laureate of Britain in 1850 saw him move away from early mythical poems of great beauty, like his medieval tale "The Lady of Shallot," to verse he considered of more importance to Britain, both politically and militarily, such as "Ode on the Death of the Duke of Wellington" (1852). "The Charge of the Light Brigade" was also in this vein. It spoke mainly to the bravery and sense of duty of the soldiers, and included little criticism of the officers in charge. Interestingly, although Tennyson had inserted the line "not tho' the soldiers knew, someone had blundered" when the poem was first published in 1854, he took it out in a subsequent version, apparently feeling its criticism of command officers, thought by some to be mild under the circumstances, was inappropriate coming from the Poet Laureate. It took no less a personage than the English writer and critic John Ruskin to convince him to reinsert it.

seemingly endless shriek. This caused the ever-empathetic Cardigan to declare: "Imagine that fellow screaming like a woman when he was hit."

GONE IN A CLOUD OF SMOKE

Despite this distraction, Cardigan led his men on. Shells and bullets whizzed by, but he was not touched, despite the fact that he was weirdly alone, out in front of everyone. His men were now being hit by the guns at the end of the valley, as well as from the sides. As more and more men fell, those who came behind were forced to trample their bodies to keep going. After eight minutes that must have seemed like an eternity for the attackers, and with the first line about eighty yards from the guns at the end of the valley, Cardigan raised his sword to lead the final attack. Then, all at once, the guns blazed in unison, and the first line of the Light Brigade seemed to simply disappear.

Cardigan later claimed that he felt the flames of the cannon singe his legs. In any event, he picked a gap between two guns, kept on going through a cloud of smoke, and found himself on the other side of the Russian guns, face to face with a troop of Cossack cavalry. As extraordinary coincidence would have it, one of the Russian officers, Prince Radzivil, recognized Cardigan from the social circles of London, and ordered his men to capture the earl, not harm him. Cardigan evaded them and galloped back the way he had come. On the way, he passed some of his soldiers clashing with Russian troops. Their position was precarious and they were soon forced to retreat, however, back through the curtain of fire and steel that constituted the "Valley of Death." Cardigan never seems to have felt any duty to his men to rally them or help lead them back. In fact, he arrived at British lines well before most of the stragglers — only 195 men survived — leading to rumors that he had not even made the famous charge at all.

THE CHARGE IMMORTALIZED

After Russell's report in *The Times* and others that followed, the Charge of the Light Brigade became a major point of controversy and public debate. Blame was variously assigned: to Lord Raglan for giving confusing orders, to Lord Lucan for not clarifying them, to Lord Cardigan for not communicating with his commanding officer.

But ultimate blame lay with an official system that allowed unqualified aristocrats to purchase officer ranks and be placed in charge of the lives of thousands. In fact, this system was abolished after the Crimean War, as a direct result of the debacle of the Light Brigade. And while the stupidity of senior officers was highlighted, the bravery of the men of the Light Brigade did not go unnoticed, and the British public began to demand better treatment for the ranks, in terms of food, medicine, and nursing care. So, in the end, some good did come out of one of the most famous military disasters in history.

The Gettysburg Address

Rallying the Union, Abraham Lincoln Defines for All Nations the Sacrifices Necessary to Achieve and Uphold Democracy

THE SPEECH WAS JUST 272 words long – ten sentences – and it took Abraham Lincoln at most three minutes to deliver it. Yet it became and remains a rallying call for Americans, and one of the most eloquent, powerful, and influential expressions of the value of freedom and democracy ever made.

The date was November 19, 1863, the place a once-sleepy hamlet called Gettysburg in the rolling farmland of southern Pennsylvania. About twenty-three thousand people were in attendance, but only fifteen thousand of these were alive. The rest were some of the dead of the ferocious battle of Gettysburg fought the previous July, who were in the process of being transferred from their hasty battlefield graves to more suitable accommodation in the new cemetery the President of the United States had come to help dedicate.

As Lincoln sat on the dais at the new cemetery, waiting literally for hours to speak, he had, on two sheets of paper tucked in his inside jacket pocket, what amounted to a prophecy. The Gettysburg Address spoke to a country that Lincoln envisioned rising like a phoenix from fire, blood, and ashes. It would be a country that was no longer merely a union of disparate states, but a nation. There was no surety in the summer of 1863 that this nation would come into being – quite the opposite possibility, that the Union would shatter into pieces, was the one many people contemplated. Such an outcome could have had a dramatic effect on world history and the global balance of power, even to this day.

"A NEW NATION"

Fought in high, hot summer, the battle of Gettysburg pitted the invading Southern forces of General Robert E. Lee (approximately seventy thousand in all) against the defending Union Army of

President Abraham Lincoln, whose address at Gettysburg has proved one of the most influential speeches in history.

about ninety thousand, led by the newly appointed General George Gordon Meade, the latest in a string of commanders that Abraham Lincoln had turned to in increasing desperation. The war had begun in 1860, but the conflict had been coming for decades.

Upon freeing themselves from British rule in 1776, America's first thirteen states had asserted in the Declaration of Independence that all men – including the slaves used in America since the seventeenth century – were born equal and should be free. In the industrialized North, this goal was embraced. But in the agrarian South, where cotton was the main crop and

Confederate dead, swollen by the heat, lie unburied on the battlefield at Gettysburg, as Union troops and sightseers stand by.

enslaved Africans did much of the work, the institution of slavery was retained and defended. Northern antagonism to slavery steadily increased, and things came to a head as America expanded westward in the 1850s. Were the new territories, as they became states, to be "free" or slave states? When no agreement on this issue could be reached, the Southern states seceded from the American Union and formed the Confederate States of America. Soon after, war began.

"A GREAT CIVIL WAR"

At the battle of Chancellorsville in Virginia, early in May of 1863, a badly outnumbered Lee had defeated the Union forces. Thereafter, the Confederate general invaded Pennsylvania, planning on capturing the state capital of Harrisburg or even the major urban center of Philadelphia. With Philadelphia, which was only about 150 miles from the Union capital of Washington D.C., in hand, Lee could cut off Union supply lines and even surround Washington, ending the war at a stroke.

But the Union, with its back against the wall, blocked Lee at Gettysburg, fighting well and desperately over three days and finally inflicting casualties on the South of twenty-three thousand killed, wounded, or captured. Although Meade's forces lost even more, Lee could ill afford these casualties in the manpower-poor South, and he was forced to retreat on July 4. Although the over-cautious Meade missed an extraordinary opportunity to follow and finish off his opponent, the North had won a great victory.

"A GREAT BATTLE-FIELD OF THAT WAR"

When Meade finally moved south after Lee, he told Lincoln: "I cannot delay to pick up the debris of the battlefield." And quite a debris it was. Eight thousand human bodies and the corpses of three thousand horses still lay unburied, rendering the ridges and farmlands of Gettysburg a wretched, stinking mess. Burial parties were hastily recruited from civilians and Confederate prisoners, but with few resources available and time pressing, the most they could do for the human dead was to lightly cover them with earth. (The horses were burned in great piles south of the town.) Soon, relatives of Union soldiers who had fallen began to scavenge through the shallow graves, looking to identify their loved ones or at least find mementos. In the process, bodies became unburied, and arms and legs and even heads protruded from the ground, becoming food for pigs, crows, and masses of buzzing flies.

Obviously something had to be done about this, for even then everyone knew that Gettysburg was a major turning point – a "Waterloo," as the *New York Times* called it. You could not have the semiburied corpses of Union heroes littering the landscape.

So an interstate commission was set up (for the cost of burying these dead would fall on all the northern states whose soldiers had died there), seventeen acres of land were bought for a cemetery, and William Saunders, cemetery landscape architect, was chosen to design the plots. The time-consuming process of digging up the dead (some already twice buried), identifying what states they were from, and placing them in the thousands of coffins provided by the Federal Government, now began. (The Confederate dead stayed in their field burial plots, until their bodies were repatriated to the South some ten years later.)

"WE HAVE COME TO DEDICATE"

So it was that when the principal speaker came to the podium on November 19, he looked out over a brilliantly landscaped cemetery. Saunders had shaped the Soldier's National Cemetery at Gettysburg (now called the Gettysburg National Cemetery) so that the dead were arranged in a series of semicircles around a central monument to their valor. The reburial process was still in progress and would not be completed until the following spring.

The principal speaker was not, however, Abraham Lincoln, but the orator, former senator, cabinet member, and Harvard president Edward Everett. Indeed, not only was he the principal speaker, but he was allowed to deliver thirteen thousand words over two hours. His prominence at the event fueled one of the many myths about Gettysburg: that Abraham Lincoln was deliberately snubbed by its organizers, many of whom were from an opposing political party, the Democrats. In fact, at this time presidents had little involvement in state affairs and the organizers weren't even sure that Lincoln would turn up for a ceremony managed by a state government.

In any case, Everett was a famous orator who specialized in battlefield topics and had previously dedicated monuments at such Revolutionary War sites as Lexington, Concord, and Bunker Hill. At Gettysburg, he provided what the historian Garry Wills has called a kind of "docudrama" for his listeners — a sort of reenactment of what happened on the battlefield, the fruit of his careful study of the events of early July. His speech was well received. When he finally sat down, Abraham Lincoln stood up.

"ALTOGETHER FITTING AND PROPER"

Lincoln may have been casually invited to make a "few appropriate remarks," as the dedication organizers had put it to him, but he was not about to let this opportunity pass by. Here, at last, was a major victory for his administration that he was keen to exploit for propaganda purposes. People, in America and in Europe, needed to be reminded that the Union would be victorious. But moving beyond the immediate political implications, Lincoln carefully wrote his short speech to expound upon a glorious vision of an America with a bright future ahead of it beyond these dark days.

The care that went into the writing of the Gettysburg Address puts to rest another myth that has since arisen — that Lincoln scrawled it on the back on an envelope on his train ride from Washington to Pennsylvania. On any number of levels, this is highly unlikely. Lincoln was a careful organizer who understood the power of words better than almost any U.S. president before or since. It seems highly improbable that he would have left such an important task to the last moment, let alone until a train ride that would have involved meeting and greeting any number of politicians and well-wishers traveling to Gettysburg.

B-4975

The best evidence has Lincoln working on his speech for several days at the White House before he set off. In crafting it, he drew upon broad but not formal learning. Unlike Edward Everett, Lincoln had not had a university education. Far from it. He had had perhaps one year of grammar school, put together a few months at a time while he worked on various farms in Kentucky, Indiana, and Illinois, and he was essentially self-taught. But what an education he had

A photograph of the crowd, which ultimately swelled to fifteen thousand, gathering at Gettysburg to hear the dedication ceremony.

given himself: large doses of the Bible, Shakespeare, history, literature, and the law.

Arriving the night before the speech was due to be given, Lincoln stayed at the house of David Wills, prime mover behind the cemetery and its dedication, and there he may have added a few finishing touches.

"FOUR SCORE AND SEVEN YEARS AGO"

Another myth that surrounds the Gettysburg Address is that Lincoln spoke hurriedly and essentially mumbled his address, so that few present could hear it. In fact, Lincoln (a former amateur actor who loved to recite Shakespeare) was known for his ability to project. True, he did not have Everett's stentorian tones – Lincoln had a high-pitched, twangy, backwoods Kentucky drawl, but it apparently carried quite clearly to all areas of the great crowd.

Everett's speech, though finely written and topical, was of the moment, whereas Lincoln's address was for the future. He began by harking back to a time eighty-seven years earlier – deliberately using biblical language ("four score and seven years ago") to provide a timelessness and importance to

Two Hundred and Seventy-two Words That Made History

No one really knows exactly which text Lincoln used at Gettysburg, because at least five known copies of the address exist, in Lincoln's hand, each with minor differences. However, the version below is the one most widely accepted and used, since it was the last copy written out by Lincoln personally, to be lithographed for sale and distribution in February 1864, to benefit a charity.

Four score and seven years ago our fathers brought forth on this continent a new nation, conceived in Liberty, and dedicated to the proposition that all men are created equal.

Now we are engaged in a great civil war, testing whether that nation, or any nation, so conceived and so dedicated, can long endure. We are met on a great battle-field of that war. We have come to dedicate a portion of that field, as a final resting place for those who here gave their lives that that nation might live. It is altogether fitting and proper that we should do this.

But, in a larger sense, we can not dedicate – we can not consecrate – we can not hallow – this ground. The brave men, living and dead, who struggled here, have consecrated it, far above our poor power to add or detract. The world will little note, nor long remember what we say here, but it can never forget what they did here. It is for us the living, rather, to be dedicated here to the unfinished work which they who fought here have thus far so nobly advanced. It is rather for us to be here dedicated to the great task remaining before us – that from these honored dead we take increased devotion to that cause for which they gave the last full measure of devotion – that we here highly resolve that these dead shall not have died in vain – that this nation, under God, shall have a new birth of freedom – and that government of the people, by the people, for the people, shall not perish from the earth.

his counting of the years — when America was born with the idea, put forth in the Declaration of Independence, that "all men are created equal." Now, Lincoln went on, this basic premise, important not just for Americans, but for "any nation" that desired freedom, was being put to the test. Through the extraordinary sacrifices of those who had died at Gettysburg, American ideals had been, for now, defended, but this cemetery dedication, this "consecration" (with its sense of the sacred, of hallowed ground), would be of little use, unless the living carried on with the sacrifices necessary for a "new birth of freedom": a unified nation that was truly "of the people, by the people, for the people."

Summarizing his nation's history, from first birth through a painful struggle to an envisioned rebirth, Lincoln made every one of his few words count.

"THE GREAT TASK"

Yet another myth that has arisen around the events at Gettysburg was that Lincoln left the dais disappointed with both his speech and its reception. This was promulgated in part by his friend and bodyguard Ward Lamon, who claimed Lincoln had muttered to him afterward that the speech was a "flat failure" and "fell upon the audience like a wet blanket." In fact, most historians consider the memories of the dramatic and self-aggrandizing Lamon suspect. Contemporary newspaper reports show that Lincoln was interrupted five times for applause in only three minutes. These accounts were mainly

quite laudatory — *The Chicago Tribune* said, "The dedicatory remarks by President Lincoln will live among the annals of man." Indeed, Edward Everett wrote Lincoln the very next day to say: "I should be glad, if I could flatter myself, that I came as near to the central idea of the occasion, in two hours, as you did in two minutes."

Everett had it exactly right. Lincoln's prophetic speech not only focused the minds of Americans on the purpose behind this horrible war, but was a text future Americans would return to again and again, to find meaning in the struggles they found themselves engaged in. Moreover, the Gettysburg Address would soon be adopted internationally as a symbol of freedom and equality. As early as 1865, in an address before an international conference of workers, Karl Marx praised the Gettysburg Address and Abraham Lincoln as being instrumental in defeating "the slave driver" of the South. When Winston Churchill addressed a special meeting of the U.S. Congress on December 26, 1941, just after America had declared war on Japan and Germany, he said: "I have been in full harmony all my life with the tides which have flowed on both sides of the Atlantic against privilege and monopoly and I have steered confidently towards the Gettysburg ideal of government, of the people, by the people, for the people." And even today, the Gettysburg Address, which has been translated into more than thirty languages, continues to inspire people around the world.

Custer's Last Stand

The Massacre That Created an Unlikely Martyr and Spelled the Beginning of the End for America's Indian Peoples

Oh, what a slaughter how Manny [sic] *homes are Made desolate by the Sad disaster eavery* [sic] *one of them were Scalped and otherwise Mutilated but the General he lay with a smile on his face …*
– Private Thomas Coleman, B Company, Seventh Cavalry, U.S. Army

IT TOOK PLACE ON A HOT, DUSTY Sunday morning near an obscure river in a remote part of the American West 130 years ago – and yet we still can't forget Custer's last stand. Why? The name may have something to do with it. "Last stand" has an epic ring to it, although many think it implies that Custer was the last man standing on the battlefield, which was certainly not so. Perhaps it's because everyone on one side of the battle – General George Armstrong Custer and 210 members of his Seventh Cavalry – was massacred. Battles where nobody among the defeated survives to tell the tale have a way of capturing the human imagination; only half the story is brought home, the rest resides with ghosts.

Had Custer been defeated, but with much of his command left alive, would we remember the Battle of the Little Bighorn in the same way?

Almost certainly, the battle's fame has something to do with the fact that it marked the beginning of the end for the thousands of Sioux warriors who surrounded Custer that day – in fact, for all the Indian peoples of America. Following the defeat, public outcry turned George Armstrong Custer into a martyr whose spilt blood had to be revenged. An expanded American army fiercely hounded the great Sioux leader Sitting Bull and his people afterward; although Sitting Bull escaped to Canada with a small band, most of the Sioux were forced to surrender and ended up on reservations. And within fifteen years of Custer's death, the battles had faded into legend.

General George Armstrong Custer, in a pose that captures some of the self-confidence and hautiness for which he became renowned.

MOVING WEST

In the late 1860s, America's westward expansion, slowed considerably by the Civil War (1861–65), had begun again in earnest. The new drive west was fuelled by gold strikes in Colorado and Montana, but also by white settlers hungry for the rich farmland of the Great Plains, which spread from the Mississippi River all the way to the foot of the Rocky Mountains.

The tribes that ranged the northern Great Plains were called the Lakota, although the whites and the tribe's other foes referred to them as the *Sioux*, from an Ojibwa word meaning "serpent" or "enemy." The Sioux were a close-knit, wandering tribe, which followed the herds of buffalo and worshipped *Wakan Tanka*, the Great Spirit. By the 1860s, however, the Sioux found a formidable foe swarming into their lands – white men, whom they called *wasichus*, meaning, literally, "you can't get rid of him." The *wasichus*, the Indians felt, simply didn't listen very well. So they tried to underscore the point that white people were not welcome on the land they were trying to preserve – by slaughtering miners and other incomers, sometimes by broiling them over open fires.

In 1868, the U.S. government and the Sioux signed the Second Treaty of Fort Laramie. In return for a cessation of attacks against whites, the government would cede the Sioux much of western South Dakota and eastern Wyoming, and keep settlers and miners away from the Sioux's sacred *Paha Sapa*, or Black Hills. By 1876, however, after the discovery of gold in the Black Hills, fifteen thousand white miners swarmed through Sioux territory. Using Sioux attacks on settlers as a pretext, the administration, under President Grant, sent troops to the region with orders to push the Indian tribes farther west. This put the Sioux on a collision course with one of the most controversial military figures in American history: George Armstrong Custer.

DARING AND DASHING

In June of 1876, Lieutenant Colonel George Custer's regiment of the Seventh Cavalry set off as one arm of a three-pronged expedition to find the Sioux, who were rumored to be encamped along the Little Bighorn River in present-day Montana. Brigadier George Crook's command would move up from the south, Colonel John Gibbon's regiment would approach from the west, and Brigadier General Alfred H. Terry's group, which included the 31 officers and 566 men of Custer's Seventh Cavalry, would approach from the east. But Crook was delayed by a battle with the Sioux, and it was only Terry and Gibbon who rendezvoused late in June. They decided to send Custer down the Rosebud River with his regiment, while they traveled along the Bighorn and Little Bighorn Rivers, hoping to trap the Sioux between them.

Before the Seventh Cavalry galloped off, swallowtail flags snapping in the breeze, Gibbon called out jokingly to Custer,

"Custer don't be greedy! Wait for us!" Custer wheeled his horse and waved, replying in the same vein, "No, I will not!"

This kind of comment was characteristic of George Armstrong Custer, who was born in 1839, in a small Ohio town, one of five children of a blacksmith father. Custer graduated from West Point in 1861, last in his class. But the Civil War was starting and every man was needed, so he was hurried into combat as a raw young cavalry officer. Despite his poor performance at the academy, Custer was a revelation on the battlefield. He quickly earned a reputation as a fierce fighter in the Union Army; from

Custer's contempt for danger also made him controversial. His cavalry units suffered extraordinarily high casualty rates, even by the bloody standards of the Civil War, because he was known to charge into situations where another commander might proceed more cautiously. Despite this, he was offered another commission after the war ended, as Lieutenant Colonel of the newly created Michigan Seventh Cavalry.

ON THE TRAIL OF THE SIOUX

After parting from the army regiments at Yellowstone River, Custer moved his Seventh Cavalry up Rosebud Creek in

Custer's contempt for danger made him controversial. His units suffered extraordinarily high casualty rates.

the First Battle of Bull Run and the Battle of Gettysburg to the denouement of the war at Appomattox, Custer played a critical role in defeating the enemy. During the war, he was promoted from first lieutenant to brigadier general (the youngest in the Union Army) — an unheard-of rise in rank.

Not only was Custer brave, but he also had dashing style. His long, curling blonde hair and fair, youthful complexion caused some troops to snicker, "Who is this child? Where is his nurse?" But Custer ignored them and even added to the controversy by designing his own uniform made of black velvet with a brilliant crimson scarf tied round his throat.

the direction of the Bighorn Mountains, scouting out Indian trails as they went. All trails seemed to point in the same direction — to the valley of the Little Bighorn River, which the Indians called the Greasy Grass. Custer assumed there was a village there, but he had no idea of its size.

On the morning of June 25 – a bright, hot, clear Sunday – he took his command over the Wolf Mountains and down into the valley of the Little Bighorn, about fifteen miles from the Indian base. Since he still wasn't completely sure of the location of the village, Custer chose to divide his command into three sections, headed by himself and two other officers, Major

Marcus Reno, a nervous, excitable soldier, and Captain Frederick Benteen, an indisputably brave fighter who, however, hated Custer with a passion because of what he considered to be Custer's vanity and posturing.

Custer put three companies (about 140 men) under Reno and three under Benteen. Five companies, about 210 men, he kept with himself. The plan was for Custer to approach the village from the north, and Reno from the south. Benteen, trailing, with

Custer blazes away with two pistols in this somewhat fanciful nineteenth-century lithograph of the battle of Little Big Horn.

months. Now, spread out across a plain on the west bank of the Little Bighorn was a large mass of Indians, an estimated two thousand of whom were warriors. And they knew Custer was coming.

FIRST SKIRMISHES

Reno's men, advancing in three long columns, crossed the Little Bighorn River and then spread out into a line abreast and moved to a gallop. When they neared the village, they were horrified by what they saw: instead of just one village, it was a huge conglomeration of Indian tents extending for three miles along the banks of the river — six villages in all, set up in large, interlocking circles.

At once, a swarm of Indian warriors rose up to meet the advance. Reno, whose conduct on this day would later be the subject of much speculation and of an official inquiry, led a panicked retreat back across the river and up the banks of a steep bluff. His men finally reached the top and formed a defensive line, where they were joined by Captain Benteen's contingent. Together, their two commands made a stand on the bluff.

Meanwhile, Custer led his five companies to a place that was parallel to the village and across the river from it, in a shallow depression that bisected the small ridges that rose from the water's edge. Indians in

pack mules laden with ammunition, would be available to either column, as needed.

What Custer did not know was that the Sioux chiefs had decided to band together for protection against the *wasichu* soldiers and had been gathering in the area for the village could not see his horses at first, just a rising cloud of dust moving across the river. Turning left and heading toward the water, Custer's men saw Reno's first skirmish with the Indians and heard the sounds of shots popping. The raw recruits began shouting and cheering. Most of them were poorly trained German or Irish immigrants, fighting not for love of country but for thirteen dollars a month, a bed and three square meals a day.

TOTAL ANNIHILATION

There is still some question about Custer's exact movements, but it appears that, after sending a messenger to tell Benteen to reinforce him, he wheeled his command away from the river and ended up crossing it further north, leading his force onto a ridge above the village, about four miles from where Reno and Benteen were locked in battle. More and more Indians now flocked in Custer's direction, like "bees swarming out of a hive," as one Sioux later described it. They fired arcing showers of arrows or made quick, rushing attacks on the cavalry, most of whom had dismounted and shot their own horses to use for cover. A cloud of grey dust and black gunpowder began to obscure the battlefield as the charging Indians gradually divided Custer's forces. Figures dashed in and out of the cloud as if through artificial night, and gun barrels blazed yellow in the dimness.

The squads and platoons of the Seventh Cavalry disintegrated quickly under the

onslaught, with perhaps six or seven "last stands" occurring at various ridge tops. Individuals were then cut down by Indian warriors, who appeared like wraiths out of the smoke and dust. Indian veterans of the battle later told how many of the soldiers did not appear to know how to fight. In their panic, some of these raw recruits even began shooting themselves.

The total annihilation of Custer's force probably took no longer than two hours. One last Indian charge, led by the famous war chief Crazy Horse, swept over the battlefield, and the last survivors went down, shot or speared or clubbed. After that, there was silence and drifting smoke.

At the bluff, Reno's and Benteen's men continued to fight for their lives. They managed to hold off the Sioux attack for the rest of that day and into Monday afternoon, June 26, when the Sioux, fearing the approach of more soldiers, packed up their tents and moved off to the south in a massive cloud of dust.

"THERE HE IS, GOD DAMN HIM"

On the morning of Tuesday June 27, a forward unit of Brigadier General Terry's cavalry, comprised of one lieutenant and his Crow Indian scouts, rode cautiously through the valley of the Little Bighorn River and saw on a distant hillside numerous objects. At first they thought they were buffalo carcasses and skins drying in the sun. But soon they realized with horror that the objects were the stripped bodies of Custer's entire command, along with their horses.

At the site, in the hot June sun, the stench was terrible. Sioux squaws, who had swarmed over the battlefield soon after hostilities had ceased, had horribly mutilated the bodies of the slain. Five companies lay dead, a total of 210 men in all (plus another 53 members of Reno's command had died during his desperate fight). Custer's body was discovered near the crest of a hill, surrounded by the slaughtered members of his staff. The corpse was reclined, semi-upright against the bodies of two slain soldiers. He had been shot in the left side near the heart and in the left temple.

Captain Frederick Benteen rode down from what would become known as Reno's Hill to examine the body of his old commander, and decided that the killing shot near the heart had been fired from a rifle at fairly long range. The shot in the temple had been a Sioux coup de grace later. Although the public was told afterward that the Indians had not mutilated Custer's body as a sign of respect, in fact, after death, his left thigh had been gashed, a finger cut off, and an arrow had been driven through his penis. In 1927, a Cheyenne woman named Kate Bighead, who had been present on the field after the battle, told a researcher that the Indian squaws had also punctured Custer's ears with a sewing awl, in order to make him hear better the next time.

But, of course, there would be no next time. An onlooker recalled Captain Benteen rising from Custer's recumbent form and exclaiming, "There he is, God Damn him, he will never fight anymore."

Where Was Custer's Support?

Did Major Reno and Captain Benteen fail their commander? Almost certainly, yes. Reno's panic in withdrawing to Reno Hill allowed the Indians to corner him, and then concentrate on wiping out Custer. And despite receiving Custer's desperate message begging the captain to come to his aid, Benteen made a decision not to assist, later claiming there were too many hostile Sioux between his position and Custer's. He may have been right. But, never a loyal fan of his commander, he was certainly not likely to go to extraordinary lengths to save him or die in the attempt.

Benteen redeemed himself in some eyes by a courageous performance on Reno Hill, bravely organizing the fight against the Sioux with little regard for his own safety. Reno's performance, on the other hand, was said to have had a tinge of hysteria to it — some thought he was drunk — and he was later made the subject of a court of inquiry, although eventually the army dropped all charges against him.

A World at War

1900–1950

The Battle of Gallipoli

*The Catastrophic Allied Invasion That Helped Forge
the National Identities of Three Fledgling States*

THE ALLIED INVASION OF THE the Gallipoli Peninsula in Turkey during World War I, which began in February 1915, is little known to most Americans. In Britain, it is regarded as an embarrassing military debacle and remembered chiefly for the fact that it almost cost the young Winston Churchill his career — Churchill was forced to resign from his job as First Lord of the Admiralty in May 1915 as a result of the failure of the campaign. However, for the peoples of Australia, New Zealand, and Turkey, the intense, eight-month-long struggle at Gallipoli was, despite the carnage that occurred on the peninsula, something quite different, something much more positive. It was the event that forged their national identities.

In Australia and New Zealand, whose soldiers were so pivotal to the battle, Gallipoli acquired enormous importance as the place where the courage and spirit of the "Anzac" (a term deriving from the acronym for the Australian and New Zealand Army Corps) fighting man was demonstrated on a world stage for the first time. And for the triumphant Turks, Gallipoli was a glorious victory that helped spur the nationalist fervor that would lead to the founding of the Turkish Republic, some eight years later.

METHOD IN THE MADNESS

Despite the campaign's later reputation, there was some sound reasoning behind the original plan for an attack at Gallipoli. By early 1915, the war that had begun only the previous August was stalemated, with long lines of trenches running from the North Sea all the way to the Swiss Alps. It was, furthermore, a horrendously violent stalemate: by November 1914, the Allies had suffered nearly a million casualties. Seeking to staunch this epic bloodletting, British strategists, and in particular Winston Churchill, the forty-year-old First Lord of the Admiralty, looked for ways to relieve the pressure on the western front. Soon, they turned their eyes to Asia Minor, and specifically to the Dardanelles Strait, part of

the Ottoman Empire, an ally of the Central Powers – Germany and Austria-Hungary.

The Dardanelles is the narrow neck of water that connects the Aegean Sea to the Black Sea, via the Sea of Marmara and the Bosporus Strait, site of the city of Istanbul, formerly known as Constantinople. The British planners saw clearly that if they could gain control of the Dardanelles and thence Istanbul, they could not only neutralize the Ottoman Empire, but also funnel munitions to their ally Russia. This, in turn, could draw German troops away from the western front, allow the Allies to

Allied troops bathe during a rare moment of calm at Anzac Cove, while others move weaponry and assess the terrain above.

make a decisive breakthrough there and help achieve ultimate victory.

There were a couple of significant problems, however. The narrow strait of the Dardanelles, only three-quarters of a mile to four miles wide, has a strong current that makes naval maneuvers difficult. At the time it was also heavily guarded. The Turks had forts along both the Gallipoli Peninsula on the western, European side, and the Turkish mainland on the eastern, "Asiatic" side, and had mined the waters of the strait. There was nowhere in the entire forty-mile trip up the Dardanelles that a vessel could not be easily reached and sunk by shellfire.

ATTACK BY SEA

In the early winter of 1914–15, Winston Churchill managed to push through a plan to try to attack the Turkish forts along the Dardanelles using naval power alone. Like most British planners, Churchill considered the Turks to be inferior opponents with old munitions and guns that could not stand up to British firepower. In February 1915 and then again in March, a combined British and French force – the largest yet seen in the Mediterranean – sailed up the Dardanelles to bombard the Turkish defenses, only to be pushed back, with heavy losses that included seven

hundred dead, three battleships sunk, and three others badly damaged.

Having lost to these "inferior" Turkish fighters, the British now pulled back to lick their wounds. The vice admiral in charge of the sea assault told Churchill that he could not silence the forts without the help of an infantry assault. And so the Gallipoli campaign began – as so many other disastrous campaigns have begun – as an escalation after a galling failure.

REDIRECTING RESOURCES

Right at the start, there was a dispute over resources. The British commander of the campaign, General Ian Hamilton, asked Lord Kitchener, British Secretary of War, for 150,000 men. Kitchener, faced with competing demands for men and supplies from his commanders in France, would only allow half that number.

Fraternizing with the Enemy

Going into combat against the Turks, many soldiers of the British Commonwealth held prejudiced attitudes toward them: they were said to be lazy, shiftless cowards, who would run away as soon as fight. These stereotypes gradually evaporated during the months of warfare against the tough and hardened Turkish fighters, who suffered enormous casualties in their defense of Gallipoli. At Anzac Cove, in particular, a mutual respect developed between the adversaries. New Zealand and Australian troops even refused to wear gas masks, asserting that "the Turks won't use gas. They're clean fighters." Trading went on between the lines, with Allied tinned beef and cigarettes being exchanged for candy and grapes. These fighting men even accorded each other the greatest compliment: sometimes private contests were fought between just two men, who, while the others watched, would blaze away at each other with rifles until one or the other fell.

And while he sent the veteran British Twenty-ninth Division to take part in the assault, a significant proportion of the Allied force was to be made up of the green and untried volunteer soldiers of Australia and New Zealand, who were currently seven hundred miles away, in Egypt, being trained to fight in France. Their units were subsequently combined into the Australian and New Zealand Army Corps (ANZAC), which consisted of the Australian First Australian Division and the Australian and New Zealand Division. Together with the British Royal Naval Division and the French Oriental Expeditionary Corps (which included four Senegalese regiments), these units made up the Mediterranean Expeditionary Force.

The British Twenty-ninth Division was to land at Cape Helles, at the tip of the Gallipoli Peninsula, where it was expected to advance inland and attack the Turkish strongpoints that guarded the Dardanelles. The job of the Anzac troops was to land further north on the west, or Aegean coast, of Gallipoli, at Gaba Tepe, move inland to block the expected Turkish retreat from Cape Helles or Turkish reinforcements moving down the peninsula, and assist with the attack on the Dardanelles narrows. The French corps would provide a diversionary landing on the south side of the Dardanelles to draw off Turkish forces and keep them pinned down; the British Royal Naval Division would also make a feint near the top of the Gallipoli Peninsula at Bulair.

A RECIPE FOR DISASTER

The Allied landings took place in the pre-dawn darkness of April 25. Amphibious landings were poorly understood at the time and the rugged, hilly landscape of much of Gallipoli, with its short, shallow gravel beaches overlooked by heights, was a recipe for disaster. The British took so long to plan their attacks that the German commander of the eighty-four thousand Turkish troops, Limon Von Sanders, was able to carefully dig in his men.

At Helles, the British landing was delayed and it was not until 8 a.m., in broad daylight, that the British soldiers arrived on shore. They approached on motor launches and on a transport ship, the *River Clyde*, which deliberately grounded itself and, through a special opening carved in its hull, debouched two thousand troops.

The Helles landing was a bloody mess, with the Turks bringing heavy firepower to bear on the invaders from only 50 yards away, blowing the men to bits in their boats. And as the soldiers left the *River Clyde* along gangplanks, they provided easy targets for Turkish gunners who shot them down one by one. A British commander flying overhead in a small biplane was horrified to see the clear, bright blue water "absolutely red with blood" for 50 yards from the beach. Of the first two hundred soldiers who disembarked from the *River Clyde*, only twenty-one actually made it to the beach.

At other landing spots along Cape Helles, at beaches designated X, Y, and S,

The view from the *River Clyde* as it neared V Beach. British soldiers can be seen huddling on the beach at the center of the picture.

the British had more luck, and found themselves landing almost entirely unopposed. By nightfall, thirty thousand soldiers were ashore. But at V and W beaches, heavily defended by Turks, the reception was hot. On W, 950 Lancashire Fusiliers landed; five hundred were killed or wounded that morning. Six Victoria Crosses (the highest British award for valor) were later handed out as a result of actions on W and V, and the Cape Helles landings in general were marked by extreme bravery. But a total of two thousand casualties were incurred by the British. The slaughter was horrific, and the Allied forces that did get ashore were left clinging desperately to the beachheads.

BIRTHPLACE OF THE ANZAC MYTH

The Australian and New Zealand troops were supposed to land at the somewhat wider beaches of the Gaba Tepe headland, but in the inky black of the predawn attack, their boats landed a mile farther up the coast at what would soon be immortalized as Anzac Cove. (Exactly why is still debated: it may have been human error, or possibly a last-minute change in plans that was not properly communicated.) Above the beach here towered the Sari Bair range of hills, which was creased with dead-end gullies and sharp ravines and covered with thick scrub brush, and almost impassable. Even so, the Anzac forces made inroads of fifteen hundred yards. However, they were stopped by the quick work of the Turkish commander Mustafa Kemal Ataturk, who ordered a counterattack that drove the Anzacs back, forcing them to dig in on the hillsides, under unremitting fire and blazing sun. Here, too, the Allied forces suffered heavy casualties, with an additional two thousand killed and wounded that day.

To protect themselves against naval shellfire, the Turks built their trenches very close to the Anzac lines, in some cases only ten yards away. To raise one's head above the parapets was suicide for either side, and thus much of the fighting was done by lobbing grenades over the tops of the trenches. The only defense against this was catching them and hurling them back before they exploded, which some Anzacs became extremely good at.

STRETCHED TO BREAKING POINT

As the summer months wore on, they brought disease, thirst, and privation. Every possible surface was covered by swarms of flies, which had been feeding on the corpses that abounded everywhere – in fact, corpses

being the most readily available raw material, both sides built them into their defenses, as parapets at the tops of the trenches. The Turks attacked numerous times, and each time were thrown back with great losses, yet still they kept coming. After a final Turkish attack failed on May 4, the Turks dug in again all around the Anzac defenses. By then, the Turks had lost fourteen thousand men, the Anzacs almost ten thousand.

Three thousand miles away from Britain, the Allied force was at the end of the food and supply chain, and was in danger of being forgotten by the public, whose attention was focused on the western front. Meanwhile, members of the British government fought with each other over the course of the campaign – two of its architects, including Winston Churchill, were soon forced to resign.

In Turkey, in contrast, the British threat reinforced the unity of the government of "Young Turks" (Mehmed Talat Pasha, Ismail Enver, and Ahmed Djemal) who had taken control of the crumbling Ottoman Empire in a coup in 1913. For the Turks, a stalemate could be seen as a success. For the British, with their supply lines stretched thin, a breakthrough was essential; nothing less than victory would do.

THE AUGUST OFFENSIVE

On August 6, the British made one last-gasp attempt to break the increasingly stagnant and bloody stalemate at Gallipoli with a landing farther north, at Suvla Bay.

A group of Turkish senior officers observes the fighting at Gallipoli from a vantage point on a high ridge behind the front lines.

Two infantry divisions embarked and the Turks were caught completely by surprise. But unfortunately, Lieutenant General Frederick Stopford, in charge of the operation, moved far too slowly to exploit this advantage. Turkish reinforcements made it to the high ground, which the British troops were never able to take from them, despite repeated efforts.

At Suvla and at Anzac Cove, the fighting up and down each hillside and ridgetop was hand-to-hand and bayonet-to-bayonet. Often the scrub brush would catch fire from the munitions being expended, incinerating the attacking Anzac and British troops. But the Turks, inspired by the courageous leadership of Ataturk, continued to hold the high ground along the peninsula. With the stalemate enduring, the Allied campaign was effectively over — except for more bitter slaughter.

A SKILFUL RETREAT

A war of attrition continued over the next few months. At the beginning of September, it was suggested that the troops be pulled out. General Ian Hamilton resisted this, but was finally removed from command in October and replaced by Lieutenant General Sir Charles Monro, who began planning an evacuation. Meanwhile, in November, a terrible rain and snow storm hit the battlefields, the worst in forty years. While the well-dug-in men at Helles and

Anzac Cove had some protection, those in more exposed positions, at Suvla Bay, for example, suffered mightily – many drowned in shallow trenches that caved in and flooded. So horrible was the disaster that the two sides almost forgot about fighting each other – the Turks and British hanging onto their parapets for dear life. By the time the storm finally blew itself out, two hundred troops had died of drowning and exposure, and thousands more were suffering from frostbite and illness.

This natural disaster, even more than the fighting, showed how precarious the Allied positions were. In December, the evacuation

was a triumph for the Ottoman Empire and personally for Mustafa Kemal Ataturk. His heroic performance saw him rise rapidly through the ranks during the battle and greatly expand his influence in military and government circles. After the Young Turks fled the country at war's end, he began an ascent to power that saw him become the founder of the modern state of Turkey in 1923, following the collapse of the Ottoman Empire and a war of independence.

But it is among Australians and New Zealanders, whose forces had performed so impressively and whose reputation as ferocious fighters was now undisputed, that

At Suvla Bay and Anzac Cove, the fighting was hand-to-hand and bayonet-to-bayonet.

began. It turned out that nothing quite became the Allies at Gallipoli like their manner of leaving it. In a departure that salvaged some honor from the debacle, they were able to evacuate 105,000 men right out from under the noses of the Turks, and had everyone gone from the shambles of the battlefield by January 9, 1916.

A FOUNDING MYTH

The Gallipoli campaign became an inspiration for the peoples of Australia and New Zealand, and, in a different way, for the Turks. Known in Turkey as the battle of Canakkale after the port where the initial Allied sea invasion was blocked, Gallipoli

the event had and continues to have its greatest influence. From the horrors of the peninsula, these former colonies, newly separated from their mother country of Great Britain, emerged as fully fledged nations. The pride that Australians and New Zealanders took from Gallipoli and their reverence for their soldiers continue to be manifested as strongly as ever today. Not only is the landing commemorated solemnly in both countries every April 25 – Anzac Day – but in recent years thousands have made pilgrimages, ninety years after the event, to the Dardanelles. There they pay their respects on the hallowed ground where their heroes shed so much blood, even if it was for a lost cause.

The Battle of the Somme

Britain's Bloodiest Day Reveals the Reality of
Warfare to a Bewildered Nation

FROM JUNE 24 TO JULY 1, 1916, a total of 3,000 British and French guns bombarded the German lines along the Somme River valley with such ferocity that many of the 750,000 allied troops facing west from their trenches were quite certain that there could be no opposition when they went over the top to attack. At 7:20 on the broiling hot morning of July 1, ten huge mines went off in quick succession right under the German lines — mines that contained hundreds of tons of explosives. Then, as the poet John Masefield, who was present, later wrote, "the time drew near, [the British soldiers] ... saw the flash of our shells, breaking a little further off as the gunners 'lifted,' and knew that the moment had come."

So certain was the Allied High Command that the Germans had been pulveriszed that they ordered the British troops to advance in waves, at a walk, behind one last rolling barrage — artillery fire that crept forward ahead of the troops, clearing their way and concealing their approach. The soldiers' job would be merely to mop up, after which British cavalry would break through and finish off the retreating Germans.

Then, as Masefield wrote, "There came a whistling and a crying. The men of the first wave climbed up the parapets, in tumult, darkness, and the presence of death, and having done with all pleasant things, advanced across no-man's-land."

It took just a few moments for the slaughter to begin, but when it did, it changed British history, and attitudes to war, forever.

GRISLY RECORDS

The battle of the Somme lasted from July 1 to November 13, 1916, and was the costliest battle in the history of the world, with a combined total of 1,265,000 British, French, and German dead and wounded. The Somme also holds the record for the heaviest loss suffered in one day (July 1) by any British army: 57,450, with 20,000 of these dead.

It was at the Somme that the new British volunteer army of the Secretary of War,

Lord Kitchener, was violently blooded. This army consisted for the most part of so-called "Pals Battalions" – ranks of volunteers recruited from the same rugby clubs, soccer teams, and neighborhoods. The Pals had left their homes to bands playing and flags waving. It was as if they were marching off, not to war, but to a big game. At the time, Arthur Conan Doyle, author of the Sherlock Holmes stories, spoke for many patriotic Britons when he said: "If the cricketer [has] a straight eye, let him look along the barrel of a rifle." The enthusiasm of the Pals Battalions was overwhelming, and matched only by their naivety about war. The first day of the Somme would end all that.

The Somme was by no means the first bloody battle of World War I – the war had, after all, been going on for two years, and the terrible battle of Verdun was still being waged. But the *way* in which the British fell on the first day, steady wave after wave of eager Tommies tumbling like ninepins to the chattering German machine guns ("so many we didn't even need to aim," wrote one German soldier later),

The bemedaled British commander in chief, General Douglas Haig, who planned the disastrous offensive at the Somme.

horrified all who saw it. The observers and participants included influential writers such as Masefield, Siegfried Sassoon, Robert Graves, and Liddell Hart. Historian Hart, who was gassed during the battle, later made the Somme a cornerstone of his influential argument that direct attacks against an enemy holding a fixed position almost never work.

OVERWHELMING FORCE?

The Somme is a river in northern France whose name, in Celtic, means "tranquillity." It travels east through a gentle valley for about 150 miles, from the forested highlands of the Aisne to the Bay of the Somme in the English Channel.

In 1916, northern France was a prime battleground, where the Fourth and Fifth British Armies north of the Somme and the Sixth and Tenth French Armies south of the river faced off against the Second German Army. With superiority in numbers, French Field Marshal Joseph Joffre planned on attacking the Germans in a battle of attrition, ten miles south of the river. Massively powerful, this offensive should have made mincemeat out of the outnumbered sixteen German divisions. But Haig and Joffre made the crucial error of depending too much on their artillery. Not only did it destroy any semblance of surprise, but it barely damaged the Germans at all.

STOPPED IN THEIR TRACKS

The first day at the Somme stands as a microcosm of the dreadful cauldron that was World War I. As the artillery barrage entered its final moments, the British waited in their trenches carrying their heavy packs,

One British division suffered eighty percent casualties in the first ten minutes of the advance.

to force them to commit and bleed their reserves. But the massive German attack at Verdun, beginning in February, had tied down most of the French Army, so the British, under their commander in chief Sir Douglas Haig, took over the planning and provided most of the manpower. Under pressure from the French, the start date of the attack was brought forward to take place on July 1 rather than August 1, and the goal now became to divert German resources from Verdun to relieve the pressure on the French.

The plan was for twenty British divisions to launch an attack on a fifteen-mile front north of the Somme, while seven French divisions charged along a ten-mile-wide line smoking cigarettes. Some of them shook hands with each other. When the order was given to fix bayonets, the sound could be heard up and down the line, a metal clinking under the roaring of the shells and mines going off.

Officers blew their whistles, and the men then "stepped off." The British battalions attacked in four to seven successive lines, separated by perhaps a hundred or so yards, with the men instructed to walk almost shoulder to shoulder and upright, with their rifles held diagonally across their bodies. Officers wore different uniforms from those of the enlisted men and carried only pistols, which made them perfect targets for German snipers. Some of the men from the Pals Battalions went into battle that morning with puppies gamboling ahead of them as mascots. One company commander suggested his troops kick a soccer ball in front of them as they went, to mark their distance; they would "score a goal" by kicking it across enemy lines.

Sergeant Richard Tawney, a thirty-six-year-old writer and teacher in civilian life, jumped off with the first wave of British troops, following the rolling barrage. Initially, things seemed to be going swimmingly, as Tawney and his unit maneuvered over four enemy trenches without a hitch. But then "when we'd topped a little fold in the ground, we walked straight into a zone of machine-gun fire. The whole line dropped like one man." The sights Tawney saw in that split second haunted him for the rest of his life. "My platoon officer lay on his back. His face and hands were as white as marble. His lungs were laboring like a bellows worked by machinery. But his soul was gone. He was really dead already; in a minute or two he was what the doctors called 'dead.'"

Tawney was wounded twice but survived the day. Out of 850 in his company, there were only 24 left on the line by July 3. The Germans were supposed to have been pulverized. What had happened?

PERFECT POSITIONING

During the initial advance soldiers like Tawney were astonished to see Germans leaping from their trenches and setting up machine guns in still-smoking shell holes. While the bombardment had been stunning in its ferocity, the Germans' ability to fight had not been eroded. This was mainly because the Germans at the Somme had built not just trenches, but heavy dirt-and-concrete bunkers, some up to twelve yards deep, which no amount of shelling could destroy. Underground passages connected the bunkers (which had amenities such as electricity and wood-paneling). There were also field hospitals underground, and German reserves waited behind the lines in old caves that the French had used for years to mine chalk.

Adding to this, the German defensive positioning was nearly perfect. Their divisions were aligned along the miles-long crest of a low ridge, which reached out in numerous spurs toward the British lines. Most of the spurs had forests or villages situated on them, and each of these had been turned into an armed strongpoint. The Germans had two forward lines and one line in reserve, each separated by heavy coils of barbed wire approximately twenty to thirty yards thick. Because the German troops were at an elevation, they could easily see what the British were doing, while the British could only observe the Germans' front line.

Not that the offensive was a surprise, of course. The shelling had given it away, but, even before that, French newspapers, read avidly by German spies, had bragged of the coming offensive. And, at 2:45 on

the morning of July 1, German forward listening posts picked up a message from the British commander of the Fourth Army, wishing his soldiers "Good luck." It was all the confirmation Berlin needed that the big attack was about to take place.

"THIS WAY TO ETERNITY!"

In a few places along the line, the soldiers were able to get as far as Tawney did before the machine guns opened up, but mainly the guns caught them only a few steps from their trenches, causing bodies to tumble

backward onto those who were climbing up behind. Since thousands and thousands of men were moving forward, the dead and injured were trampled and the line kept moving, beyond the British wire, into no-man's-land. One battalion commander

British troops step off into no-man's-land, on the first day of the Somme, July 1, 1916.

described "heaped-up masses of British corpses suspended on the German [barbed] wire while live men rushed forward in orderly procession ... human corn-stalks falling before the reaper. 'This way to eternity!' shouts a wag behind."

The poet Siegfried Sassoon was in reserve that day (after earning the Military Cross the day before for a daring mission). He sat on a hill behind the lines and watched the British advance through field glasses. "I am staring at a sunlight picture of Hell," he wrote.

By three o'clock in the afternoon, up and down the line, there was no one moving in no-man's-land except the crawling, moaning wounded, still exposed to machine-gun fire, – particularly from the elevated spurs – begging for water as the sun tormented them. Most of the others were dead or had stumbled back into their own trenches.

One fairly typical British division – Eighth Division of III Corps – suffered eighty percent casualties in the first ten minutes of the advance. It lost 218 out of 300 officers, 5,200 out of 8,500 soldiers. The German battalions on the opposite side of the wire from Eighth Division lost 8 officers and 273 men.

A few companies of the British managed to reach the German lines. But they became isolated survivors, who had, as one put it, been "playing leapfrog with death" and were generally unable to hold their positions. One exception was XV Corps, which was able to advance over three-quarters of a mile and seize its target, the village of Mametz. The cost was eight thousand dead and wounded; but on a horrible day for the British Army, this was viewed as a considerable success.

A BLOODY STALEMATE

By nightfall of July 1, the British High Command had realized that the attacks of the first day had failed miserably. While some British officers, including Haig himself, refused to accept the blame for their failed planning – for attacking a well-entrenched enemy in broad daylight after giving ample warning that they were coming – the ordinary soldier knew what had happened. Sassoon's simple listing in his journal captures the state of affairs on the evening of July 1 succinctly: "C Company now reduced to six runners, two stretcher-bearers, Company Sergeant Major, signallers, and Barton's servant. Sky cloudy westward. Heavy gunfire on the left."

Most British soldiers now felt the attack would be called off, but Haig, despite the British army having suffered its worst-ever single-day casualty rate, decided to press on. In the next two weeks or so, he ordered dozens of "small-scale" attacks against the Germans, which nonetheless cost another twenty-five thousand casualties.

The British were finally able, on July 11, to capture the first line of German trenches. But then the Germans brought in reinforcements from Verdun and the contest degenerated into a bloody stalemate, as so many battles did in this slogging war of attrition, drawn out over the next four months. In November, the British began to make a slow, but steady advance, but then bad weather brought the entire campaign to a halt. By then the casualty figure had reached 1,250,000 for both sides. And the total amount of ground gained since July 1? Seven miles.

DREAMS OF GLORY DASHED

In one respect, it could be said that the Somme had achieved its purpose: the fighting at Verdun shifted to the Somme and the Germans certainly lost irreplaceable manpower. Yet the battle will forever go down in history as a slaughter that shows what happens when inflexible and unimaginative planning meets rapid-fire automatic weapons.

More than that, the Somme was a turning point in British public opinion about the war. Never again would ordinary people look at the British government, specifically the British high command, in the same way. After all, it was the Pals Battalions from working-class towns who were decimated at the

Somme. Half the British population saw a silent documentary film of the battle, which was made by the War Office as patriotic propaganda, but had an entirely different effect: viewers were left wondering why these working-class men had been sacrificed in what was evidently a pointless slaughter. Where was the glory of war now? Ever since, the Somme has represented the callousness of upper-class leaders prepared to turn soldiers into cannon fodder.

The transformation of mood, among British troops and among the public at home, was reflected in the diary of a nineteen-year-old British lieutenant named Edwin Campion Vaughan. He had entered the war with dreams of glory and had fought on the front lines for eight months. By the time of the Somme, his attitude had changed completely: "I sat on the floor and drank whisky after whisky as I gazed into a black and empty future."

The Advent of the Tank

Tanks were first used in warfare during the Battle of the Somme in an attack by the British Fourth Army on September 15, 1915. The British had fifty of these top-secret weapons, which, unlike modern tanks, were oblong, with huge treads. They could only make about two miles an hour, but could easily roll over barbed wire, trenches, and machine-gun nests. Shocked German troops retreated at the onslaught of these metal behemoths, but soon learned that they were vulnerable to artillery and also to breaking down at crucial moments. While British tanks did achieve some notable successes later in the war (most particularly in their massed attack at Cambrai in November of 1917, which punched a hole five miles deep in German lines), they were not a decisive factor in World War I. Within twenty-five years or so, however, tank warfare would play a crucial part in another war between the same combatants.

The October Revolution

The Uprising That Created Capitalism's Strongest Rival

ON THE MORNING OF OCTOBER 25, 1917, the U.S. journalist John Reed and his wife, Louise Bryant, were staying at the Hotel Astoria in Petrograd — the former St. Petersburg, grand city of the czars. They awoke about 10 a.m. to the sounds of bells ringing and trucks racing up and down the street. Reed and Bryant dressed and went downstairs to find that the trucks belonged to the Bolsheviks, the small, leftist revolutionary party headed by Vladimir Ilich Lenin. They carried soldiers, who stopped at every street corner to plaster up a proclamation written by Lenin just that morning. It stated, in ringing tones: "To the Citizens of Russia! The Provisional Government has been deposed. State power has passed into the hands of the organ of the Petrograd Soviet of Workers' and Soldier's Deputies ... Long live the revolution of workers, soldiers, and peasants!"

Actually, the provisional government of the moderate Alexander Kerensky not been deposed at all, but Lenin, ever impatient for action, had decided it wouldn't hurt to stretch the truth a little. And in one important respect, at least, he was right. That morning in Petrograd, the revolution that would change the face of a century — the revolution that "shook the world," as Reed would write in his famous book on the October Uprising — had truly begun.

The events of those ten days set in motion a seismic upheaval. Spreading out from the epicenter of this old imperial city, the earthquake of the Russian Revolution created a massive Communist empire. Ultimately, it would represent the strongest challenge ever to Western capitalism — a challenge that the West has only recently faced down.

CHANGE LONG OVERDUE

Could anyone have doubted that Russia was in need of a revolution as the twentieth century began? While serfdom had been officially abolished in 1861, peasants still worked twelve-hour days six days a week for the small number of wealthy landowners who owned most of the land in Russia. The

country had been ruled for centuries by omnipotent czars, and was mainly governed by a corrupt and crumbling bureaucracy. Common people were treated as little better than animals. Thousands of people existed on the edge of starvation.

Czar Nicholas II – the "little father" of the country – was, even as czars went, autocratic and conservative. Beginning his reign in 1894, he was unable to see that Russia was changing. The Industrial Revolution had transformed the landscape. Factories had drawn peasants to the cities, in turn bringing them into contact with radical theories. One of the most attractive was the idea that all men should be equal, that all should have a share of the Earth's bounty and no man have to work for an unjust wage or be a serf.

The country underwent a major upheaval in 1905, when thousands of unarmed Russian workers, carrying religious banners and pictures of the czar, marched to the Winter Palace in St. Petersburg to present a petition to Nicholas, telling him of their grievances. In response, the czar's soldiers opened fire on this peaceful group, killing hundreds. The mass strikes that followed shut down the country's railroads and businesses, and forced Nicholas to issue what was called his October Manifesto, which promised a democratic parliament. But the October Manifesto was merely an empty promise, as the czar subsequently undermined almost any effort at participatory government. Workers and radicals came to realize that yet more drastic action would be required.

BOLSHEVIKS AND MENSHEVIKS

The two men who would lead the revolution in 1917, Vladimir Lenin and Leon Trotsky, both spent years in exile as a result of earlier subversive activities. Born Vladimir Ulyanov in 1870, the son of a school inspector, Lenin worked as a lawyer in St. Petersburg and became radicalized after joining a Marxist group. In 1895, he was arrested for his activities, jailed for fourteen months, and sent into exile in Siberia. After his release in 1900, he lectured on the socialist cause throughout Europe. During this time, he took on his revolutionary nom de plume.

At the Second Social Democratic Congress, a convention of Russian socialist groups that met in 1903 in London (for fear of being targeted by czarist forces), Lenin led attempts to create a socialist political party. But the delegates split into two groups: the more radical and more numerous Bolsheviks (from the Russian for "one of the majority"), and the more moderate Mensheviks ("those of the minority"). Prominent on the Menshevik side was Leon Trotsky. Born Lev Davidovich Bronshtein in the Ukraine, Trotsky had become involved in Marxism while at school. In 1898, he was arrested for his activities, imprisoned, and exiled to Siberia. He escaped to London in 1902 and then moved from country to country.

Both the Bolsheviks and Mensheviks played a part in the 1905 uprisings and their popularity increased steadily thereafter. Soon, all that was needed to fan the flame of revolution was social upheaval – and World War I provided that.

DEFEAT SPARKS REBELLION

The bloodletting of World War I became the catalyst for the Russian Revolution. Russia's entry into the war against Germany was an attempt by Czar Nicholas to regain the prestige the country had lost in its disastrous defeat in the Russo-Japanese War of 1904–05, and to try to unite his increasingly fractious people in a common cause. But the attempt backfired as the Russian army took hundreds of thousands of casualties. By the winter of 1917, Russia had lost millions of soldiers – as casualties and prisoners of war, but also to desertion. These deserters, in no mood to knuckle down under the rule of the czar, returned to their home villages and began seizing land from the wealthy.

In the meantime, food shortages were rampant in the country. In St. Petersburg, people were forced to wait in line a total of forty hours a week, just for bread. They began to riot, and this time the troops did not shoot them, as they had done in 1905, but instead joined them, tying red ribbons around their bayonets. With mounting losses from the war, and a complete lack of support from his own government and army, Nicholas II was forced to abdicate in

March 1917, ending the three-hundred-year rule of the Romanov dynasty. He and his family were sent into exile in Siberia. A moderate provisional government took over, and a Constitutional Assembly was set up. The government was led by a thirty-six-year-old lawyer and politician, Alexander Kerensky.

Young, eloquent, and charismatic, Kerensky was a threat to the more radical groups like the Bolsheviks, whose exiled leaders began making plans to return to Russia. In early April, Lenin was given safe passage homeward from Zurich through Europe in a "sealed" train (meaning it could not be stopped or searched) by the German government. Under pressure from Britain and France, Kerensky was then preparing for another Russian offensive against Germany (one that would result in failure and heavy losses for the Russians). The Germans hoped that a Bolshevik revolt would unseat Kerensky before he could mobilize his troops, and force Russia to sue for peace.

When he arrived at Petrograd's Finland Station, Lenin was met by a cheering crowd; he then began planning a revolution that would result in a government run by groups of workers, known as soviets. In May, Leon Trotsky also returned to Petrograd, to agitate on behalf of the Mensheviks.

FIGHTING IN THE STREETS

In June, Kerensky, pushed farther to the right by criticisms from leftist groups like the Bolsheviks, launched his offensive against

The American Revolutionary

John Reed, the journalist who famously described the seminal stages of the Russian Revolution in his 1919 book *Ten Days that Shook the World*, was an extraordinarily controversial figure in his day. Born the son of a wealthy Oregon minister in 1887, he went to Harvard, but then moved to New York and became a socialist, traveling to Mexico in 1913 to witness the Mexican Revolution. With his feminist wife Louise Bryant and funded by a wealthy American radical, he made his way to Russia, where he reported on the revolution. It was very clear from his writings that he was by no means an unbiased observer – in fact, some felt him to be a pawn of Lenin and Trotsky, who certainly saw him as a valuable propaganda tool in getting their version of the revolution out to the world at large.

Later, Reed was charged with treason in the United States under the wartime Sedition Act because he had spoken out against U.S. involvement in World War I. Before his trial, he fled the country and returned to Russia. There is some evidence that he later became disillusioned with the totalitarian nature of the revolution. However, when he died in Russia of typhus in 1920, he became (and still is) the only American to be buried in the Kremlin.

Germany – with disastrous results. As the summer progressed, conditions at the front deteriorated. Rebellious troops commandeered trains and forced the engineers to drive them to the rear of the lines. Returning to their farms, they murdered landlords and pillaged the bounty of the great estates. Factories in major cities such as Petrograd and Moscow ground to a halt as workers abandoned their machines and joined the Bolsheviks. There were food shortages everywhere.

Generally, Kerensky could do very little about the breakdown of law and order, but in July, when Bolsheviks and anarchists launched violent street demonstrations in Petrograd (possibly instigated by Lenin), Kerensky was able not only to quell the uprisings but also to discredit Lenin by claiming he was a German agent. As a result, Lenin was forced to flee back to Finland.

With Lenin discredited, Kerensky might have moved forward, but in August he suffered a disastrous setback. His army commander in chief, General Lavr Kornilov, led an attempted coup in Petrograd. Kerensky was forced to ask the Bolsheviks for help; Kornilov was defeated, but not before the Bolsheviks gained large stores of arms and ammunition. Meanwhile, Trotsky was briefly jailed by the government and while there joined the Bolsheviks. His practical leadership complemented Lenin's theorizing perfectly

In this early twentieth-century painting, the searchlights of the cruiser *Aurora* light up the Winter Palace as the Bolsheviks approach.

and the combination created a forceful partnership at the head of a movement that now had tremendous momentum.

THE REVOLUTION BEGINS

On October 24, Kerensky gave Lenin and Trotsky the opening they were looking for. In an attempt to nip the Bolshevik insurrection in the bud, Kerensky cut off the telephone service to the Bolshevik headquarters, raided the offices of the Bolshevik newspaper *Pravda*, and sent troops to patrol the streets. He then appeared before a meeting of certain members of the Constituent Assembly, promising to pass reforms (such as turning over land to the peasants) immediately. At the same time, he claimed that he would defend his provisional government to the last.

But Kerensky received little support from the assembly. Sensing the true weakness of Kerensky's government, Lenin launched his revolution the next day.

By noon on October 25, Kerensky (who had awoken to find his own telephone lines cut) had decided that it would be dangerous to stay in Petrograd any longer. The Bolsheviks had seized key bridges, and his own troops, mainly inexperienced cadets, were deserting. He was almost certain to be captured and executed. Commandeering a car, he fled the city to attempt to find loyal troops to support him.

"NO MORE GOVERNMENT"

As John Reed and Louise Bryant walked the streets of Petrograd on October 25, trying to find out how events were unfolding, they found themselves surrounded by excited crowds and saw posters everywhere. "A whole crop of new appeals against insurrection had blossomed out on the walls during the night – to the peasants, to the soldiers at the front, to the workmen of Petrograd," Reed wrote. He and his wife came to the State Bank and queried the soldiers standing in front of it.

"What side do you belong to?" I asked. "The government?"

"No more government," one answered with a grin. "Slava Bogu! Glory to God!"

Kerensky's loyal ministers remained in the fifteen-hundred-room Winter Palace, which was by then surrounded by Bolshevik troops. The subsequent siege became one of the strangest in history, with an almost farcical air. Reed and Bryant were able to stroll through the porous Bolshevik lines into the palace, which was guarded by Kerensky's cadets, whom Bryant called "poor, uncomfortable, unhappy boys." There were also old czarist retainers there, wearing their royal blue coats. Many of the defenders were drunk.

In the afternoon, two Bolsheviks came by on bicycles, demanding that the ministers give up by seven that evening. The ministers refused, thinking Kerensky might return with reinforcements. Then they sat down to a dinner of soup, fish, and artichokes, although in the dark, since they had put all the lights out to hide their presence.

The Bolsheviks had seized a cruiser on the Neva River, the *Aurora*, and it was ordered to open fire on the Winter Palace. But because it was a training vessel it was equipped only with blanks, which it dutifully hurled at the defenders. The cadets responded with machine-gun fire until they realized the shells weren't hitting them. At about 11 p.m., the Bolsheviks fired on the palace using the guns of the Peter and Paul Fortress, an old czarist fortress built on a small island in the Neva. Only two shots managed to hit the palace, however, the rest falling harmlessly into the river. They did little more, as Leon Trotsky put it in disgust, than "injure the plaster."

Finally, at about 1.30 a.m., the Bolsheviks rushed the palace. The first to notice they

murdered, as well as other prominent Romanovs. He quickly made peace with the Germans, so that he could turn his attention to the civil war that was spreading across the nation, a vicious, take-no-prisoners battle between the newly formed Red Army and the "Whites," a coalition of czarist supporters and other conservatives backed by the governments of Great Britain, France, and the United States. These nations were extraordinarily worried about the threat that a Communist Russia might pose to their democracies and their imperial interests.

By 1920, the Bolsheviks, now officially renamed the Russian Communist Party, had

> ## "No more government," one soldier cried with a grin. "Slava Bogu! Glory to God!"

were coming was the palace switchboard operator, who called the ministers huddled in their chambers and reported that "a delegation of three to four hundred is approaching." The Bolsheviks broke into the palace and, without bloodshed, arrested the weary cadets and ministers.

END GAME

The revolution was never so genteel again. Lenin, now in power, named as ministers the likes of Leon Trotsky and Joseph Stalin, a Georgian clerk who had worked for the Bolshevik newspaper *Pravda* and risen through the Communist ranks with Lenin's support. Lenin had the czar and his family

triumphed. Kerensky fled to Paris and made his way to the United States, where he died in 1970. After Lenin's death from a stroke in 1924, there was a bitter power struggle. His obvious successor, Trotsky, was ousted and forced to flee by Joseph Stalin, who later had Trotsky assassinated in Mexico.

Stalin became the premier of the Soviet state for the next twenty years, and was responsible for the deaths of millions of the very people the revolution was supposed to free from oppression. The idea of liberating Russia from the cruel and inept rule of the czars had been a natural one. But the unfortunate result was the replacement of the czars with an equally cruel and ineffecent state.

The Wall Street Crash

The Stockmarket Sell-off That Sparked a Worldwide Depression

ONE MAN POISONED HIMSELF, his wife, and his two young children. Another dropped dead in his stockbroker's office. Still another, who lived in a small town in North Carolina, went into his garage and shot himself, the echo careening around his quiet neighborhood.

Rich and poor alike were affected. Winston Churchill, staying at a fancy New York hotel, awoke to a commotion. "Under my very window," he later wrote, "a gentleman cast himself fifteen stories and was dashed to pieces." The songwriter Irving Berlin remembered it this way: "I had all the money I wanted for the rest of my life. Then all of a sudden I didn't."

It was "Black Tuesday," October 29, 1929. Earlier that morning, in the first thirty minutes of trading on the New York Stock Exchange, over three million shares of stock had changed hands, something that normally took five hours. All of the major companies — General Electric, Chrysler, Standard Oil — were plummeting. Gradually, a crowd, later estimated at about ten thousand, filled the tiny winding streets around the exchange. Though the New York police commissioner placed extra security on the streets of the financial district, the people weren't violent. Instead, they seemed to be in shock. A reporter for *The New York Times* described the scene as "a sort of paralyzed hypnosis." Inside the exchange, a broker, looking out a window, had the horrible feeling that he was surrounded by "haunted things."

And this was only the start. American companies, their stock prices collapsing, either went bankrupt or laid off employees, instituting sharp drops in the production of goods. As people lost their jobs, they went through their savings and often lost their homes, as well. Their purchases — of new cars, furniture, clothing — dropped, and more companies began to close. Without money from industries and personal savings (and without federal banking insurance,

An anxious crowd gathers on Wall Street on "Black Thursday," October 24, 1929. The final crash came on October 29, "Black Tuesday."

something that is mandatory in the United States today), banks began to fail.

The crash also had an international impact, too. With American businesses failing, the U.S. government instituted high tariffs on imported goods, hoping to stimulate the economy. The effect on foreign trade was disastrous. European countries, already experiencing their own financial difficulties due to overspeculation in their markets, found that the tariffs made it impossible for them to compete in the U.S. marketplace. In response, they instituted their own tariffs, and international trade nearly ground to a standstill.

Driving these fads was the greatest fad of all: playing the stock market. Prior to this era, the buying and selling of stock had been a rich man's game. But by the twenties, one million Americans (out of a population of about 120 million) owned three hundred million shares of stocks in U.S. companies. This was in large part due to the advent of radio, telephone, and, especially, the ticker-tape machine — a small electronic machine from which a paper tape issued showing stock price quotations, allowing one to check each "tick" (upward or downward movement) of a stock, and communicate buy and sell orders almost instantly.

If you just stuck your money in a bank, you were, in the parlance of the day, a sucker.

ROARING TOWARD DISASTER

Along with the 1960s, the so-called Roaring Twenties is the twentieth-century decade most likely to be stereotyped. The name conjures up Prohibition, gangsters, flappers, and bizarre fads. In fact, much of the stereotyping has a basis in fact. People were fad crazy. They held competitions to see how long they could sit atop flagpoles. They took part in dance marathons. They loved the new talking movies, the Marx Brothers, grand musical extravaganzas on Broadway, and sneaking down to the corner "speakeasy" for a little snort of bonded Canadian whiskey — or so the proprietor claimed — on the sly.

The practice of buying stock "on the margin" — paying only a portion of the stock's price and borrowing the rest from a stockbroker — became so widespread that it seemed that you would have to be crazy *not* to play the market. As in the dot-com boom of the 1990s, stories abounded of ordinary people — the minister of the local church, a great-aunt, that quiet girl working behind the perfume counter at Sears — amassing fortunes. If you just stuck your money in a bank, you were, in the parlance of the day, a sucker.

THE BUSINESS OF AMERICA

In the mid-1920s, most Americans were quite happy with this situation — and with their government. Following the trauma of the Great War and what had been shown to be a corrupt administration under President Warren G. Harding, Calvin Coolidge became U.S. president in 1923. "Silent Cal" came across as a country bumpkin – a man of few but trenchant words who did not suffer city slickers gladly. Generally, voters approved of his "common man" approach, feeling that it mirrored their own feelings about themselves and their country. However, Coolidge was not quite what he appeared to be. In fact, he liked nothing better than to hobnob with the heads of major corporations in America at the time – John D. Rockefeller, Henry Ford, Andrew Mellon. "The business of America is business," Coolidge proclaimed. And: "The man who builds a factory builds a temple." Despite his working-man persona, Coolidge made basic changes that favored the wealthy over the working class – for instance, he made Mellon his Secretary of the Treasury and then allowed him to reduce income tax rates for big businesses and the rich.

Under Coolidge's presidency, business boomed. New technologies and procedures, which included Henry Ford's assembly line and improved techniques for refining oil, allowed companies to produce more iron, steel, gas, and chemicals. But, unfortunately, this was a business and production boom, not an employment boom, since many of the new industrial methods had as their goal the elimination of manual labor. In a familiar story, the rich got richer as the poor got poorer – in the 1920s, according

to historians, ninety percent of the nation's wealth was concentrated in the hands of thirteen percent of the population (today, roughly seventy percent of wealth is held by ten percent of the population).

Indeed, this so-called "New Era" of prosperity was to a large extent a chimera – as Mellon's tax cuts took effect, corporations that were making little in the way of profits had more money to spend, and they spent it on the stock market. And anyone in America who could afford to follow suit did so.

There were four million unemployed people in the United States by the end of 1928, yet the Twenties roared on unabated. When Coolidge refused to run for president again in 1928, his wife told a friend, "Papa says there's going to be a depression," but those who heard this just laughed, elected another pro-business leader, Herbert Hoover, and kept on speculating.

RIDING THE ROLLER COASTER

During the summer of 1929, the stock market reached an all-time high, with record numbers of shares being purchased. But the situation was beginning to give pause to more sober observers. For not only were more and more shares being bought on the margin, but also, as of early fall 1929, only a third of stocks – about four hundred of twelve hundred listed on the New York Stock Exchange – had grown in value since the previous January. It was also noted that the huge "stock trusts" – groups of wealthy investors who pooled their money to purchase stocks –

could drive up almost any stock they wanted, simply by investing heavily in it.

In September, an influential economist named Roger Babson made a speech in which he said that a crash was coming, and that there would likely be "a stampede for selling which will exceed anything that the Stock Exchange has ever seen.". Babson had been saying this for a year or so, but few had paid any attention to him previously. Now, however, his words echoed secret fears harbored by many, and a sell-off began. The market righted itself a few days later, but throughout September and into October it plunged up and down like a roller coaster.

A FEEDING FRENZY

When the stock market finally crashed on Tuesday October 29, it was one of the bleakest days in U.S. financial history, becoming forever known as Black Tuesday. But five days prior to this, on October 24, a near-crash had already occurred. It became known as Black Thursday. Through early October, stocks had rebounded slightly as

prominent bankers made calming statements to the effect that the market was simply adjusting itself. But late on the afternoon of Wednesday October 23 there was a sharp and terrifying plunge in the Dow Jones average (an index of select industrial stocks whose status is seen as an indicator of the health of the market in general) as brokers were flooded with sell orders by those who, like Babson, had finally decided the market was going to crash. In those days, unless they were wealthy enough to afford their own ticker-tape machine, people congregated in brokers' offices all over the country to watch the progress of their stocks. Stock panics, even in today's era of personal computers, are highly contagious. Think how much more virulent they would have been when your fellow investors were sitting right next to you, sweating and yelling sell orders.

By the end of trading on Wednesday, six million shares had changed hands, with losses of four billion dollars. That evening, stockbrokers began to make margin calls to those customers who had borrowed money

A Favorite Way Out

Did as many people commit suicide after the 1929 crash as is often rumored? Almost certainly not. John Kenneth Galbraith, in his book *The Great Crash*, studied U.S. death statistics and found that the number of suicides actually went down during the period from 1929 to 1932. And although some people did

kill themselves, jumping out of windows was by no means the favorite way to go, dramatic as that was. According to William Klingaman, in his book *1929: The Year of the Great Crash*, gas was the preferred means of shuffling off this mortal coil, followed by a gunshot wound straight to the heart.

to buy their stocks. In other words, the stockbrokers forced their clients to instantly repay the money they had borrowed to purchase the stock — the equivalent of a bank with whom you have a home mortgage suddenly contacting you to say that you need to pay off your entire mortgage at once or the bank will sell your house.

Shortly after the market opened on Thursday, it sped downward like a space rocket plummeting back to earth. Panicked crowds in Wall Street and around the country pushed their brokers to sell and speculators dumped stock quickly. When those who had been called for cash to meet their margins were unable to come up with it, the brokers sold the stocks at once, to recover whatever part of their losses they could. It was a horrible feeding frenzy, made worse by the fact that the overwhelmed ticker-tape system broke down and most stock quotations were forty-five minutes late. Since stocks were dropping twenty points in that interval, speculators and brokers were left in the dark about real values and began to sell blindly.

By mid-afternoon, stocks had crashed to the tune of $11.25 billion. The only thing that saved the market for another "black" day was the fact that a consortium of bankers quickly pooled together about $250 million and sent one of their members to walk the floor of the New York Stock Exchange making loud buy orders, often at *above* the asking price. By the end of the day, the market had stabilized, but was still down to the tune of three billion dollars.

THE BLACKEST DAY

Between this penultimate day of tragedy for Wall Street and Black Tuesday, the Federal Reserve Board, prominent bankers and President Herbert Hoover worked feverishly to restore public confidence. "The fundamental business of this country … is on a sound and prosperous basis," Hoover said. (It was the kind of irrationally optimistic comment the nation would come to expect from this president. Later, when bankrupted doctors and businessmen were forced to sell apples on the street to make ends meet, he told a reporter: "Many people have left their jobs for the more profitable one of selling apples.") But many people had been wiped out on Black Thursday, and those who hadn't began to wonder if they hadn't better sell in order to hang on to whatever savings they had left. Consequently, on Monday October 28, despite the reassurances, there was another plunge and near-crash.

And on Tuesday, October 29, the devastation really began. The day started with thousands of people congregating in Wall Street, as if they needed to be present at what they sensed was going to be a historic moment. All of the major stocks — those linchpins upon which the market depended — began to crash before the horrified eyes of those on the floor of the stock exchange. AT&T lost 105 points in a few hours that morning. RCA plummeted from 110 to 26. Brokers received sell orders from their clients, and went into a frenzy trying to place them. In two hours, eight million shares of stock were sold. One broker, apparently driven to a nervous breakdown by the pace of the activity, began screaming and rushed from the exchange, knocking over anyone who got in his way.

In the meantime, further margin calls ruined almost everyone who had borrowed to buy stocks. As the day wore on, people began to fall into shock. A reporter for *The New York Times* perceptively wrote that "to most of those who have been in the market it is all the more awe-inspiring because their financial history is limited to bull markets." In other words, these ordinary investors had never faced the full, clawing fury of a Wall Street bear market.

At three o'clock, after five hours of trading, the market closed. Sixteen million shares had been traded. The nation had suffered an estimated fifteen billion dollars in losses. The Dow Jones had tumbled from 290 to 260 points, furthering its slide of 120 points since September.

The stories of suicides began – as the humorist Will Rogers was to write sardonically, "you had to stand in line to get a window to jump out of." While these tales are as exaggerated as some of the earlier boom tales of clerks gaining instant riches from stocks, there *were* some who took their own lives as a result of their financial ruin. Businesses began to die as well. The first to go were the investment firms, followed by companies that had overspeculated in stocks, and banks. Like a house of cards, the Roaring Twenties tumbled to an end.

RISKS REMAIN

Herbert Hoover had entered office in the greatest bull market of all time. By the time he left it, overwhelmingly beaten by Franklin Delano Roosevelt in 1932, he was surrounded by mobs chanting "We want bread!" These days, historians do not place the blame for the Great Depression only on the 1929 Crash, but also on the Hoover Administration. Its economic policies, including high tariffs that stifled international trade and not issuing enough money, created a shortage of cash and did little to help stimulate the economy.

There would be other stock market crashes, one in October 1987, another at the end of the dot-com boom after 2000, but these did not have nearly so catastrophic an effect on the world. Among the lessons learned after the 1929 Crash was that margin lending had to be controlled, that the government needed to provide insurance to banks – the glorious "free market" needed in some sense to be regulated. Today, stocks, although they provide the highest return on the investment dollar, are still risky; and most ordinary investors cast concerned eyes upon their investment funds and pensions on a regular basis. The stories from 1929 of bodies thudding to the sidewalk – even if not all are true – remain a salutary warning.

In 1930, a year after the Crash, an unemployed man makes a heartrending appeal for a job, on a street corner in Detroit.

The Battle of Britain

How the Heroic Airmen of the RAF Halted
Hitler's Cross-Channel Invasion

I N JUNE OF 1940, GREAT BRITAIN was in mortal danger. Germany, under Adolf Hitler, had conquered all of Western Europe and was even now beginning preparations for an invasion of Britain. It was the most serious threat to its security that Great Britain had faced since the Spanish Armada in 1588. If Hitler's panzer divisions were able to cross the Channel and land on British territory, they would almost certainly overwhelm the exhausted British army.

Winston Churchill, the new Prime Minister of Great Britain, knew that his country faced a daunting challenge. On June 18, he stood before the House of Commons and said, "The Battle for France is over … the Battle for Britain is about to begin. Upon it depends our own British life, and the long continuity of our institutions and our Empire. The whole fury and might of the enemy must very soon be turned on us. Hitler knows that he will have to break us in this Island or lose the war … Let us therefore brace ourselves to our duties, and so bear ourselves that, if the British Empire and its Commonwealth last for a thousand years, men will still say, 'This was their finest hour.'"

These were ringing and inspiring words — but the reality, for many in Great Britain, was that this was also their country's darkest hour.

OPERATION SEA LION

Operation *Seelowe*, or "Sea Lion," was the Nazi plan to invade Great Britain. As Churchill knew only too well, if the Nazis conquered Britain (and, therefore, its many colonial possessions), the war was over. The United States, which had not yet entered the war, would almost certainly be forced to accept Hitler's control over Europe as a fait accompli; the führer's "thousand-year Reich" might then become a reality.

German war planners fixed an invasion date for mid-September; the idea was to strike the south coast of England with a huge amphibious force while at the same time parachuting troops deep into the English countryside. German strategists knew that Britain had one major strength: a powerful navy consisting of fifty destroyers and numerous battleships and cruisers, a navy that outnumbered the German navy, the Kriegsmarine, and could blow any invasion fleet out of the water. Therefore, the German air force, the Luftwaffe, was charged with clearing the skies above the English Channel of British Royal Air Force (RAF) planes, so that it could then destroy the Royal Navy at will. Then the invasion could begin.

Reich Marshal Hermann Göring considered victory in the air to be a foregone conclusion. The Luftwaffe was stationed in three "air fleets" in bases in Norway, Belgium, and France, and had about 2,670 planes, including bombers and fighters — compared to a British fighter force of just 640, led by Air Chief Marshal Sir Hugh Dowding.

The battle of Britain — the first large-scale battle to be fought exclusively in the air — was about to begin.

SHIFTING STRATEGIES

The epic air battle, which for all intents and purposes lasted from July to September 1940, was fought in three successive phases, as Germany adjusted its tactics to try to beat the RAF into submission. In the first phase, the Luftwaffe launched heavy air attacks against Britain beginning on July 10, when bombers and fighters struck shipping, coastal convoys, and ports in the south of England. In addition, they went after Britain's new defensive weapon, RDF, "radio direction finding," now known as radar, which was able to give advance warning of German planes coming across the British coast.

These first attacks were intended to destroy the British capacity to resist

The RAF's most effective weapon was the speedy and reliable Spitfire fighter, introduced in 1938 and steadily enhanced over the course of the war.

an invasion, but they also had a further purpose: to draw the RAF into the air and destroy it. By all rights, the Germans should have achieved this. Not only was the Luftwaffe superior in numbers, but in pilot training as well. German pilots – many of whose combat experience had been honed in the Spanish Civil War, where Germany supported the Nationalists – had an average of at least six months' training, and usually a good deal more, and recent victories had instilled in them a strong sense of confidence.

Most of the British pilots, on the other hand, were inexperienced. Though the stereotype of the British pilot is of a dashing

attack plan wasn't working. Despite the inexperience of the British pilots and the much larger Luftwaffe force, the RAF was more than holding its own. A great part of this was due to the superiority of the British fighter planes. The Germans depended on their Messerschmitt 109 single-engine and 110 double-engine fighters to protect their bombers and engage the RAF in dogfights. But the 110 in particular was relatively slow and had limited endurance compared to the British Hawker Hurricane, and, especially, the subsequently iconic Supermarine Spitfire, which gradually proved its superiority over the Messerschmitt 109, too.

> The Luftwaffe was superior to the RAF in numbers and training – most British pilots were inexperienced.

young man who had attended a top public school, only 200 or so of the 3,500 British pilots who took part in the battle of Britain had received a public school education. Instead, these men who formed the front line of defense came from all walks of life: they included bankers, teachers, clerks, factory workers, shop assistants. What they shared, as one of them said, was a sense that, "You wanted action because you were twenty or so … you knew how to fly and you had to fly because there was a war on."

EAGLE DAY
It soon became apparent to the German high command that the first phase of their

On August 13 – a day they codenamed *Aldertag*, or "Eagle Day" – the Germans shifted into the second phase of their offensive: targeting the RAF airfields with heavy bombing as well as dive-bombing attacks. This partially reflected Göring's mistaken impression that the Germans had knocked out the British radar system and had thus blinded its air defenses.

The goal of the second phase was to force the RAF to abandon its air bases in southern England within four days, and to completely destroy the RAF within four weeks. But on Eagle Day the Germans lost forty-five planes, while the RAF had only thirteen downed. More importantly, half the downed

RAF crews lived to fight again, since they had bailed out over friendly territory, whereas surviving German airmen were usually captured and thus lost to the Reich.

AERIAL COMBAT

This stage of the battle of Britain is the one most often portrayed in movies, with brave fighters putting down their cups of tea to race for their planes or dashing to their bases from a night of partying in London. In fact, this has some basis in fact. All across Britain, at dozens of air bases (but particularly at Fighter Command Group 11, stationed in southeast England), pilots waited to "scramble" after enemy aircraft. One of them described having pajamas on under his flight uniform, so that he could quickly take a nap on a bed if needed. Then the call would come – "Dover, 26,000 [feet], 50 bandits [German aircraft] coming from the southeast" – and he would race to his plane.

Each side had varying tactics. The Germans flew in "fingers" of four fighters in line, or in widely spaced groups of four (to make them harder to spot at a distance). At first, the British fought in stiff, closely packed group but these were vulnerable to the more mobile Luftwaffe formations. So they altered their tactics to allow a few planes to function as "weavers," outlying aircraft that moved at will, searching for "bandits."

Adventurous Americans

Beginning on July 15, 1940, a small advertisement appeared in some U.S. newspapers. It read: "The Royal Air Force is in the market for American flyers as well as American airplanes. Experienced airmen, preferably those with at least 250 flying hours, would be welcomed by the RAF."

Most people ignored it, but it did catch the eye of a certain type of American, as it was intended to do. These were adventurous-minded flyers, who chafed at having to sit on the sidelines while the epic air battle of all time was being fought in the skies over Britain. Despite the fact that at this time the United States's Neutrality Act made it a crime punishable by loss of citizenship to join the armed forces of a "belligerent nation," some young Americans – possibly as many as several hundred – joined the British fight against the Nazis. Normally, they crossed into Canada and either joined the Canadian armed forces or simply booked passage from there to Britain. Once in the RAF, they served as fighter pilots, navigators, gunners, and bombers. One such individual, Flight Lieutenant James Davies of New Jersey, shot down six enemy planes and was deemed worthy of the Distinguished Flying Cross. Tragically, he was killed on the day the king was to present it to him, and the medal was awarded posthumously.

The experience of aerial combat was both beautiful and extraordinarily cruel. One pilot, Richard Townshend Bickers, wrote: "We struggled to gain every inch of height in the shortest possible time and we gradually emerged out of the filthy black haze which perpetually hung like a blanket over London. Suddenly at about twelve thousand feet we broke through the smog and a different world emerged, startling in its sun-drenched clarity."

This crystal world was a murderous one, with no quarter given. One pilot described a head-on encounter between himself and an ME-109 pilot: "We appeared to open fire together and immediately a hail of lead thudded into my Spitfire." Then the German, though crippled, rammed directly into the British pilot's plane, sending him spiraling down to earth. He only just survived.

TARGETING CIVILIANS

Despite the initial British victories in this wave of the German attacks, the RAF was being slowly eroded by losses of both men and planes. By the end of August, Dowding and his staff were making contingency plans to move the most important airfields north, there to await the inevitable invasion. Fortunately for the British, however, the Germans did not realize that the RAF was in such dire straits. And then something happened that changed the course of the campaign again.

In mid-August, German bombers, which had not heretofore been bombing British

civilians, accidentally dropped a load of bombs over South London. The enraged British government retaliated on August 25 by bombing Berlin. The shocked German government, which had promised its civilian population that it was safe from the war, then decided to retaliate against British civilians, reasoning, too, that the direct attack on the RAF was not working.

What followed was the last phase of the battle of Britain. Beginning on September 7, two hundred German bombers a night assaulted London, using incendiary devices to create fires and high-explosive bombs to destroy structures. On September 15, two massive waves of German bombers attacked England – the largest air fleet ever to attack the country – but were repulsed by furious RAF counterattacks. German losses were sixty aircraft shot down, as compared to twenty-six RAF fighters. Another bomber force was repulsed two days later. As a direct result of this, Hitler postponed his invasion of Britain, and would finally abandon the idea altogether in December.

From June to September, the British had lost 915 fighters, with 481 men killed and missing (and another 422 wounded). But the much-vaunted Luftwaffe had suffered 1,733 planes lost (although the British claimed this number was closer to 2,600).

The threat of invasion had been lifted, though the British were unaware of it at the time and the bombings continued. On the terrible evening of October 15, nearly five hundred German planes dropped 386 tons

British pilots race to their fighters after receiving a warning of approaching German planes from coastal observation stations.

of high explosives and an astonishing seventeen thousand incendiary devices on London. During this period, raids killed forty-three thousand British civilians and wounded perhaps five times that number. The "Blitz" of the winter of 1940–41 was particularly terrifying, and German planes continued to haunt the skies well into the following spring. One incendiary attack against London, on May 10, 1941, killed or wounded three thousand people. But it was the last major attack. Five weeks later, as Hitler invaded Russia, most Luftwaffe squadrons along the Atlantic Coast were redeployed for duty in the East.

The British people had not broken, and the battle of Britain had, indeed, been the country's "finest hour." Many things contributed to the eventual Allied triumph in World War II, including the entry of the United States into the conflict in December 1941. But without the RAF's desperate victory, the war would almost certainly have been lost in 1940.

Next page: St. Paul's Cathedral seen through the flames and smoke of blazing buildings after a German air raid on London.

The Attack on Pearl Harbor

The Surprise Raid That Brought the United States into World War II

ON NOVEMBER 26, 1941, THE main Japanese aircraft carrier battle group, the *Kido Butai*, steamed out of the Kuril Islands (then part of Japan), in the gale-blown waters of the northern Pacific. The *Kido Butai* was made up of six aircraft carriers and numerous support vessels, and constituted the largest fleet seen to date in the Pacific, as well as the greatest number of carriers that had ever banded together. It was of the utmost importance that the fleet not be discovered, so much so that a force of submarines and escort aircraft spread out before the armada to destroy any ship that might stumble upon it.

The fleet was commanded by Vice Admiral Chuichi Nagumo, who had been tasked with the most momentous naval mission in Japanese history: to destroy the U.S. fleet at anchor in Pearl Harbor, on the Hawaiian island of Oahu, two thousand miles to the southeast of the Kurils. Eager to resume its empire-building in the East and stymied by the United States in its attempts to obtain badly needed resources, Japan had decided that war on the Western power was its only option. It expected that its attack would cripple America's naval capacity, allowing it to move in on other Asian nations. But although the raid would inflict a devastating military and psychological blow on the United States, it would – disastrously for the Japanese – fail to completely destroy the U.S. Navy, which would rapidly re-establish itself and help push Japan's armed forces back across the Pacific.

CHOKING JAPAN

Japan's entrance as a major player upon the twentieth century stage had begun in 1905, when it had comprehensively defeated Russia in the Russo-Japanese War. Building up its navy, army, and air force along Western lines, Japan soon had the finest military force in the Pacific Rim, and this buildup was accompanied by a parallel economic expansion. But to sustain this expansion Japan required additional natural resources, and it had long had designs on the bountiful neighboring

Japanese Zero fighters being prepared for takeoff by crewmen on the aircraft carrier *Hiryu* before their raid on Pearl Harbor.

lands of China and Southeast Asia. In 1931, Japan invaded Manchuria, populated the region with Japanese, and began to use it as a base for incursions into other parts of China. Then, in 1937, it launched a full-scale invasion of China, beginning a prolonged war. Three years later, Japan signed the Tripartite Pact, effectively becoming an ally of the fascist states of Germany and Italy, which were already at war with Great Britain and France, and in 1941 Japan invaded Indochina.

In response to these actions, the United States and Great Britain placed embargoes on shipments of oil and scrap metal to Japan. Enraged that the Western powers were objecting to the very type of expansion that they themselves had indulged in, and with supplies of oil dwindling, Japan felt it had no recourse but to take military action. But in order to buy time while its strategists formulated their plans, it began to discuss a possible truce with the United States.

The plan to attack Pearl Harbor was finalized by September 1941, but the Japanese continued extensive negotiations through their ambassador in Washington D.C. with President Franklin Roosevelt's Secretary of State, Cordell Hull. The two sides were far apart, however, with Japan wanting the United States to lift all trade embargoes and abandon the defenses it was preparing in the Philippines, and the United States demanding that Japan respect the boundaries of all Pacific Rim nations and pull back from expansion into Asia.

TOWARD "CERTAIN VICTORY"

Late on December 6 (by Tokyo time; across the International Dateline in Hawaii it was December 5) the *Kido Butai* steamed along in the dark at 14 knots, bucking gale-force winds. The fog was so dense and the winds so high that five or six lookouts were washed overboard, never to be seen again. The ships had already undergone a successful but risky refueling at sea – such maneuvers are dangerous in rough weather as they can result in collisions. Yet the atmosphere aboard the Japanese ships was one of quietly intense excitement.

That same night, five Japanese midget submarines were launched from larger submarines. Just eighty feet long and carrying a two-man crew, they were to advance ahead of the fleet toward Pearl Harbor and rendezvous there with the air attack.

Before dawn on the morning of December 7, the main fleet reached its air-force launching point, 275 miles north of Oahu. The Japanese pilots and their crews were awoken and ate a special ceremonial meal of *sekihan*, rice boiled with tiny beans. They put on their flight suits, and headbands bearing the legend *Hissho*, or "Certain Victory," took emergency rations, and went topside.

The big carriers had turned eastward into the heavy wind for the launch of the planes, and they pitched heavily – dangerous conditions for taking off. Waving green lanterns as a signal, the ground crews on each carrier sent the planes aloft, timing the pilots' runs so that the carriers' bows were pointed up when the planes roared off the carrier decks. Within fifteen minutes, the first wave of 182 fighters and bombers – there would be two waves of 350 planes in all – had departed.

The sky in the east was turning pale. Under the command of Commander Mitsuo Fuchida, the Japanese planes turned south, toward Pearl Harbor. In Honolulu, the time was 6:15 a.m.

"TORA! TORA! TORA!"

It was a quiet, partly cloudy Sunday morning on Oahu, with very little movement on the massive naval and air base of Pearl Harbor. Skeleton crews manned many of the proud battleships along "Battleship Row" in the harbor, all, as tradition insisted, named after states: *Arizona, Oklahoma, California, Nevada, West Virginia, Tennessee, Maryland, Pennsylvania.*

Some sailors were sleeping off a late night on leave; others were rising to prepare for church services.

Outside the entrance to Pearl Harbor, waiting for the massive anti-submarine net to swing open, was a navy minesweeper. Its captain saw a dark shape in the water and realized that it was a submarine. It appeared to be rolling slightly and was closer to the surface than a sub would normally be. He soon understood that this was not a friendly underwater apparition, however, but a Japanese midget submarine.

The minesweeper captain trained his guns on the sub and blew it out of the

this was a prearranged code to signal to the Japanese commanders that the Americans had been caught completely by surprise.

"I WISH IT HAD KILLED ME"

Admiral Husband Kimmel, naval commander of the Pearl Harbor base, watched from the window of a headquarters building as an armor-piercing Japanese bomb tore into the ammunition magazine of the *Arizona*, which blew up with a violent explosion, killing over one thousand U.S. servicemen. A spent .50-caliber machine-gun bullet came through the open window and struck his left chest, but was deflected

Hopping over Oahu's peaks, the Japanese planes swooped, and for two hours tore Pearl Harbor apart.

water before it could enter the harbor (two Japanese midget subs eventually did get inside the submarine net, and one may have torpedoed an American destroyer). The Americans had drawn first blood in the engagement. But the submarine probe was not seen as part of a larger assault, so no alarm was raised.

At 7:53 a.m., the first wave of Japanese planes flew in from the north, banked to circle around the west coast of the island and then, hopping over the volcanic peaks above Pearl Harbor, came roaring straight in from the south. Commander Fuchida radioed back to his carriers: "Tora! Tora! Tora!" *Tora* means "tiger" in Japanese and

by his thick glasses case. Kimmel leaned over and picked it up: "I wish it had killed me," he said. Both Kimmel and his army–air force counterpart (at the time, those two parts of the U.S. forces were combined), General Walter Short, knew at once that their careers were over for having allowed Pearl Harbor to be caught so unawares by the Japanese attack. And, indeed, both were forced to resign in quick order.

For two hours, Japanese planes tore Pearl Harbor apart. Soon after the attack began,

Next page: Smoke pours from wrecked U.S. warships, including, left to right, the USS *West Virginia* and the USS *Tennessee*.

an American radioman sent out a message that was later to become famous: "AIR RAID PEARL HARBOR. THIS IS NO DRILL." The message was picked up by U.S. military installations from the Philippines to San Francisco.

On Battleship Row, a seaman on the *Oklahoma* heard an explosion and looked up to see his friend dead: "The boy just slumped over. Blood was all over everything. I still didn't know what [had] happened." Two bombs struck the *West Virginia*, greatly

Continuing Controversy

Pearl Harbor remains as controversial as the assassination of John F. Kennedy and the terrorist attacks of September 11, 2001, and for the same reason: many Americans believe the government was complicit in the events, or, at least, ignored clear warnings.

Prior to Pearl Harbor, U.S. intelligence had been intercepting suspicious Japanese messages for some time. One, intercepted on the morning of December 6, was a message to Japanese pilots to watch for beacon lights in the windows of sympathizers on the ground at Oahu. An earlier message had asked for the exact location of Admiral Kimmel's headquarters. Intelligence also knew that the Japanese fleet was moving east across the Pacific. Yet at no time were Kimmel or General Short given any information that might have placed them on alert.

Even more controversial are accusations that President Roosevelt deliberately allowed the attack to occur because he wanted to join the war on the British side and thought a Japanese strike would persuade the American people to back him. As evidence for this, conspiracy theorists point to the fact that on the evening of December 6, at

a White House dinner party, Roosevelt was passed an intercepted message from the Japanese to their U.S. ambassador, which the ambassador was ordered to transmit to U.S. authorities — but not until 1 p.m. the next day. The message rejected the latest American negotiation offer. Roosevelt is said to have turned to his chief of staff, Harry Hopkins and said, "This means war." He did not alert his defense forces, however.

But although recent evidence from files released under the Freedom of Information Acts indicates that Roosevelt and his advisers knew of the Japanese fleet and Japan's hostile intentions, there is no proof that they allowed the attack to occur. The conspiracy theorists' presuppose perfect knowledge on the part of the government, but the intercepted messages were among thousands collected, many of them innocuous or contradictory.

In 2000, President Bill Clinton did, however, reverse the findings of previous investigations and found that Admiral Kimmel and General Short had been denied crucial information about Japanese intentions. Nearly fifty years later, with both dead, their names were cleared.

pleasing the Japanese pilot Matsumura Midorai, who had launched one of the torpedoes that hit the ship and who later recalled: "A huge waterspout splashed over the stack of the ship and then tumbled down like an exhausted geyser. What a magnificent sight." On board the *Utah*, seaman John Vaessen prayed as the ship capsized after being torpedoed: "I was hanging on to everything," he remembered, "the door and anything I could grab, and the deck plates came flying at me, fire extinguishers and anything loose … I was just lucky that God was with me, that's for sure."

Guns pumping, fighters, bombers, and torpedo bombers continued to pound the U.S. base. On Hickham Field, the planes had been placed close together on the runway, to protect against saboteurs, which, however, made them an easy target. Only a few U.S. fighters were able to take off, and all were shot down. In total, the army–air force lost 250 planes during the battle.

Along Battleship Row, great clouds of black smoke rose in the air. The *Arizona* had disintegrated, the *Oklahoma* had capsized, the *California* and *West Virginia* were sunk at their moorings. Eleven other vessels were sunk or damaged. The Japanese were uncanny in their aim, in part because they had developed a new type of dive-bomber-launched torpedo that skipped along the shallow waters of Pearl Harbor, and in part because a Japanese navy ensign, serving as a spy with the consulate in Hawaii, had carefully photographed the positions of the U.S. vessels.

American soldiers and sailors fought back bravely, managing to shoot down twenty-eight Japanese planes. But by the time the last Japanese planes had departed, the Americans had lost 2,330 killed and 1,145 wounded. Their grand Pacific Fleet was in tatters.

However, one vital component of the fleet had escaped the destruction. At the time of the attack, America's three aircraft carriers just happened to be out at sea, operating on maneuvers to the west. Around this solid core, the fleet would quickly be rebuilt and play a leading role in the subsequent victory over Japan.

"A DATE WHICH WILL LIVE IN INFAMY"

At about 1:30 in the afternoon, Eastern Standard Time, Americans clustered around their radios to receive the news that the Japanese had launched a surprise attack against their territory. At the same time, the Japanese had bombed the Philippines and Hong Kong, and landed troops in Malaya. On December 8, addressing a special joint session of the U.S. Congress, President Roosevelt called December 7 "a date which will live in infamy," and asked for a resolution of war against Japan, which was swiftly voted in. A few days later, the United States declared war against Germany as well. An enraged U.S. public was now completely behind Roosevelt, and the American nation quickly mobilized its massive industrial might and manpower for the conflict.

D-Day

The Daring Invasion That Was the Beginning of the End for Hitler

A T ABOUT 2:30 ON THE GRAY, cloudy morning of June 6, 1944, three divisions of Allied paratroopers — about twenty thousand men of the U.S. Eighty-second and One Hundred and First, and the British Sixth Airborne — took off from airfields in southern England, and flew east. Through breaks in the cloud cover, the pilots of the planes could look out to see the English Channel roiling darkly beneath them. The planes kept formation until they hit the French coast, when heavy antiaircraft fire and machine guns reached up for them. Bullets passed through the thin skins of the lumbering C-47 transport aircraft, sounding, one man remembered, like "corn popping." The arcing tracers were brilliant — red, yellow, blue, orange — and mesmerizing in their beauty, until the soldiers remembered that for every colored bullet, six more followed, invisible.

Some planes were hit and exploded in mid-air. Others crashed into the ground below, burning. Still others took evasive action, scattering across the night skies. Leveling off where they could, the pilots gave the signal and the jumpmasters ordered the paratroopers out the door. The U.S.

paratroopers' goal was to block approaches to the Normandy beaches to keep the Germans from reinforcing their defenses there. The British were to seize bridges over the Orne River. In the confusion, however, few men found their assigned drop zones — it has been estimated that only one in twenty-five landed where he was supposed to. Despite this, bands of men of different companies hooked up and began fighting the Germans wherever they found them.

One group of American paratroopers was captured just behind what would become known as Utah Beach, and placed as prisoners in a pillbox overlooking the waters. The Germans couldn't understand why the Americans kept begging to be taken farther to the rear. But as dawn approached and the mist began to lift slowly from the water, the German pillbox gunners finally understood. Blinking in disbelief, they looked out at the greatest amphibious landing force in the history of the world — 6,500 ships spread out in the English Channel along a fifty-mile stretch of Normandy's coast, from Caen in the east to the base of the Cotentin Peninsula in the west. In those ships, and others still in port in England, a total of

150,000 soldiers waited to land. Overhead, just beginning a fierce bombardment, were B-17s, each carrying sixteen five-hundred-pound bombs with which to pulverize the German coastal defenses — part of the force of 11,500 aircraft that would attack that day.

OPERATION OVERLORD

The Germans were witnessing the beginning of Operation Overlord, the long-awaited Allied invasion of France. Both sides had known for some time that the only way the Allies could destroy the German defenses in Europe any time soon would be with a major land offensive. British and U.S. forces were then moving north through Italy, but that was proving to be a hard, slogging conflict. On the eastern front, Soviet forces were pushing the Germans west, but making slow progress. American and British bombers were nightly pounding targets in Germany, but that alone wasn't going to crack the Germans either. Only a major ground offensive from the west was going to break the stalemate. And using Britain as a staging area for the hundreds of thousands of troops needed was the only possible approach.

The question for the Germans was: where along the Channel coast would the Allies attack? The Germans' Atlantic defenses extended all the way from Scandinavia to Spain, but they could not possibly station enough troops to repel an invasion at every point along this line, so they kept a mobile reserve force back from the coast, ready to commit when the invasion began. Most of

this reserve — the Fifteenth Army, consisting of about one hundred thousand men — was stationed near Pas de Calais, the region around the port of Calais. The Germans had placed their bets that this was where the attack would come, as it was the area of France closest to England and could provide deep-water harbors for Allied ships, as well as a direct route to Paris.

Allied war planners, working since the summer of 1943, had decided to take advantage of these German preconceptions. They launched a massive disinformation campaign, code-named Operation Fortitude, involving fake radio traffic, dummy troop emplacements, and German "spies" in England who were really Allied agents, to make the Germans believe that an attack on the Pas de Calais was imminent. This highly successful subterfuge also convinced the Germans that any attack on any other part of the coast would be simply a diversion.

Meanwhile, the Allies developed a plan for a massive offensive on the Normandy coast, Operation Overlord. The commander of the operation was U.S. General Dwight D. Eisenhower, who was in charge of SHAEF (Supreme Headquarters, Allied Expeditionary Force). General Bernard Montgomery of the British army led the Allied ground forces. Preparations at SHAEF were meticulous. Over a period of two years, men and materiel were built up all over Britain, so that the total number of combat-ready troops at the time of the invasion was eight hundred thousand, some forty-seven divisions.

Five beaches would be assaulted by Allied divisions: moving from east to west, they were code-named Sword (to be targeted by the British Third), Juno (Canadian Third), Gold (British Fiftieth), Omaha (U.S. First and Twenty-ninth), and Utah (U.S. Fourth).

"THE MOMENT OF OUR LIFE"

After the Allied bombers had pounded the German shore defenses, the navy began a massive bombardment in an attempt to destroy the gun emplacements along the shores, as well as mines and other obstacles at the water's edge. The troops who were waiting offshore from the beaches in their landing craft watched in awe as the shock waves from the battleships' blasts pushed the huge vessels sideways, in turn creating waves that rocked the landing craft up and down. One newspaper correspondent described the bombardment as "the loudest thing I have ever heard in my life." Listening to it, "most of us felt that this was the moment of our life, the crux of it."

At 6:20 in the morning, the bombardment let up and U.S. landing craft approached Omaha Beach, which was now shrouded in smoke. Shortly after, the invasions began at Juno, Sword, Gold, and Utah. Unfortunately, the bombardment had done little to destroy the German defenses. This was a testament to the work of Field Marshal Erwin Rommel, commander of the German Seventh and Fifteenth Armies, who had insisted that the German pillboxes be made of thick concrete reinforced with steel rods. Thus the defenders, while shocked and deafened, were able to rise as the bombardment lifted, and meet the Alies with stiff resistance all along the coast.

On Juno Beach, Canadian casualties in the first wave were fifty percent overall, but whether men lived or died depended to a great extent on which sector of Juno they landed on. The Regina Rifles, arriving on

Allied commanders General Dwight D. Eisenhower (foreground) and General Bernard Montgomery (background) reviewing troops.

"Mike" sector, made it ashore backed up by the dependable amphibious tanks of the First Hussar Division, which were able to help neutralize the pillboxes that naval gunfire had been unable to destroy. By afternoon, they were off the beach and fighting house-to-house in the village of Courseulles-sur-Mer.

But less than half a mile away, the Winnipeg Company on the western edge of the beach was severely battered by machine-gun fire from the pillboxes. There, the artillery bombardment had completely missed the mark and the tanks meant to support the men had landed elsewhere by mistake. The subsequent slaughter was terrifying. The Winnipegs finally made it past the beach defenses, but lost three-quarters of their company. By the end of the day, however, the Canadian Third Infantry had pushed farther into France than any other unit.

HELP FROM HOBART'S FUNNIES

On Sword Beach, the British Third were confronted with minefields and beach obstacles, but fortunately they came equipped with one of the oddest-looking weapons of the war: tanks known as Hobart's Funnies, after their inventor, Percy Hobart. Some of these vehicles had been modified to carry long arms like giant rolling pins, which whipped heavy chains into the sand, exploding mines harmlessly and allowing the infantry to follow in their wake. Others carried long extending platforms, rather like the extension ladders on fire trucks, with

which to span ditches and walls. The British eventually managed to land twenty-eight thousand troops (suffering only six hundred casualties) and push to within four miles of their target, the key town of Caen, before German counterattacks stalled them.

On Gold, the British Fiftieth suffered heavy casualties initially, in part because their tanks went astray. But by the end of the day, they, too, were advancing off the beach.

At Utah Beach, however, there was mass confusion. Stiffer currents than expected had carried the landing boats of the U.S. Fourth Division about a mile south of where they were supposed to be, so that the troops, trained via aerial photographs, had no idea where they were.

Landing in the wrong place turned out to be a stroke of luck, however, as the Fourth's original target was much more heavily defended than the sector where they now found themselves. The German defenses were quickly silenced, the seawall breached, and men and materiel began to pour ashore. At eleven o'clock, forward elements of the Fourth linked up with paratroopers from the 101st, who had been dropped the night before. It was the Allies' first such linkup.

OMAHA'S DAUNTING DEFENSES

Historians have commented that if there was one place where the Germans might have stopped the Allied onslaught anywhere in Normandy, it was at Omaha Beach. Because it was the only stretch of open beach for some way, it was considered to be an obvious

target for landing, and thus was heavily defended. Yet the Allies had no choice but to attack at Omaha – if they picked a beach farther west, there would be too great a gap between them and the British sectors.

Omaha Beach is about six miles long and perhaps 400 yards across at low tide, which is when the invasion was occurring. Much of the ground was shingle, or small, round stones, which would not support the weight of tanks. There were high bluffs facing the beach and on either side of it, making it into a kind of amphitheater. The Americans could not therefore outflank the German defenses; they had to go right at them.

And what defenses they were. Interlocking firing trenches made sure that every inch of ground along the beach was presighted by machine guns, mortars, and artillery. A trench system on the tops of the bluffs gave soldiers cover as they moved between pillboxes. Underground ammunition chambers protected the supply of shells.

Previous page: The view from inside one of the landing craft after the first wave of U.S. troops hit the water off Omaha Beach.

Five "draws," or small ravines, led up the cliffs; overlooking each was a strongpoint containing the dreaded German 88, the ubiquitous light artillery gun.

When the German defenders saw the Americans swarming ashore that morning, they almost felt sorry for them. "They must be crazy," one of them said. "Are they going to swim ashore? Right under our muzzles?"

WITHERING FIRE

But right under their muzzles the Americans came – forty thousand of them over the course of the day. Once again, few units landed where they were supposed to, due to the heavier than expected tidal currents caused by the strong winds. By the time that A Company (First Division) landed, the soldiers had been in their boats for

A Moving Target

One of the most daring assaults in a day filled with them was the attack by the U.S. Second Rangers on Pointe du Hoc, a one-hundred-foot-high promontory that juts up between Omaha and Utah beaches. Here, the Germans had emplaced six six-inch artillery guns that could wreak havoc on troops on both Utah and Omaha. The Rangers had trained intensively to capture these guns by scaling the cliffs by means

of ropes and metal extension ladders provided by a London fire company. Under heavy fire, they got to the top of the cliffs – only to discover that the guns had been moved about a mile inland to protect them from bombardment, and had been replaced with dummy wooden guns under camouflage netting. Undeterred, the Rangers found the guns and destroyed them, and then held off repeated German counterattacks.

four hours and were wet, seasick, and exhausted. When the first landing craft hit the beach, it was pulverized, either by a mine or German artillery fire, killing all on board. Other GIs hit the beach at the same time, but withered under the volume of fire (one German machine-gunner alone fired twelve thousand rounds that day). As the navy coxswains brought the landing craft in, many were stopped by the barrage and let their ramps down too early, causing the heavily loaded troops to disembark into deep water. A good many soldiers drowned.

Men ran onto the beach and then froze in fear. Long snaking lines of soldiers

There were more than three thousand casualties on Omaha Beach that day, and most occurred in the first few hours. By nightfall, however, the Americans had a precarious toehold.

A FATAL DELAY

Allied forces suffered eleven thousand casualties on D-Day, but managed the most important thing in any amphibious assault: not to be driven back into the sea. Over the next week or so, the troops cleared German opposition between the beachheads and linked their forces, forming a secure area eighty miles long and ten miles deep. The

One survivor remembered: "The beach was covered with bodies, men with no legs, arms ... it was awful."

formed behind the X-shaped beach obstacles. One survivor remembered: "The beach was covered with bodies, men with no legs, arms ... it was awful."

Bad as the fire was, if the attackers simply stayed where they were, they would die. They had to move, and, one by one, groups of men (often without officers to lead them) raced for the seawall near the base of the cliff, where the machine-gun fire from above could not reach them, although they were still subject to murderous mortar fire. As subsequent waves of men came in, the GIs were able to force their way up the draws and, once on top of the cliffs, attack the German fortifications from the rear.

German commanders, many of whom thought the real invasion was still to come at Pas de Calais, were slow to react, and by the time it finally dawned on them that Normandy was the Big One, the Allies were too securely ensconced to drive out.

In late July, the British and Canadians finally secured the city of Caen and then mounted major offensives. These drew more and more German reserves, allowing the Americans, farther to the west, to break out from the coast. Allied forces then pushed through France en masse and by August had captured Paris. The success of the D-Day landing meant that Hitler's Third Reich was all but doomed.

The Battle of the Bulge

The Titanic World War II Struggle That Cleared the Way
for the Allies' Final Conquest of Germany

A MOMENTOUS MILITARY engagement that took place on the European western front between December 16, 1944, and January 17, 1945, the battle of the Bulge was one of the biggest and bloodiest battles of World War II. It involved over one million soldiers — half a million Germans, six hundred thousand Americans, and fifty-five thousand British — and cost the combatants almost two hundred thousand killed and wounded. The American casualties of eighty-one thousand, which included nineteen thousand killed and almost twenty-four thousand captured, made the Bulge the most costly U.S. engagement of the entire war. Yet ultimately the battle was a triumph for the Allies, for it broke the back of the German defense of western Europe, paving the way for an attack on Germany itself, and for ultimate victory.

The battle's curious name is another reason why people remember it. The "bulge" was the dent, or, in military terms, salient, punched into the thin Allied line by the surprise German counteroffensive that began the battle — a bulge that protruded as much as fifty miles in some areas. Not that this was, technically speaking, a single battle at all, but rather a series of small and large encounters that took place over the following five weeks between a determined German Army making a last-ditch attempt to win the war and an equally determined Allied force trying to stop it. Most historians call it the Ardennes Offensive, after the rugged, wooded Ardennes area of southeastern Belgium where the dramatic events unfolded.

THE SUMMER OF '44

Beginning in early June with the Allied invasion of Normandy, the summer of 1944 had been a long, hot and weary one for the German army. At the end of July, the Allies broke out of Normandy, where they had been contained by ferocious German fighting. With the Americans, British, and Canadians proceeding on three separate fronts, two German Armies were sent

reeling back toward their homeland, suffering ten thousand dead and leaving behind fifty thousand prisoners. On the eastern front, an entire German Army group in Poland had been shattered by a massive Soviet offensive, while two more German Armies were retreating back up the Italian boot and more American forces were landing in the south of France.

But in early September, the Allied offensive in the west came grinding, almost literally, to a halt. The reason? Supplies.

American soldiers running down a village street during the German counteroffensive that began the battle of the Bulge.

The Allied army, moving at a faster rate than anticipated, could not be provided with as much fuel, ammunition, and spare parts as it needed. This was in part because of the extensive damage done by the Germans to France's infrastructure of railways and bridges, but also because the only deep-water port the Allies held was Cherbourg, at the tip of the Cotentin Peninsula in Normandy. They had also captured the port city of Antwerp, but it could not be used until the Germans were pushed away from the surrounding area, which would not happen until late November.

With the Allies having paused, the Germans stopped their flight. The two Armies then faced each other across the Ardennes, and the ever-resourceful Germans sought for a way to take advantage of the situation.

SENT REELING

About 5:30 on the morning of December 16, sleepy American troops on the seventy-five-mile-long Ardennes front, extending from Monschau in the north to Echternach in the south, were awakened by a massive artillery bombardment that shattered trees in the rugged terrain, blew soldiers out of their foxholes, and scrambled communications systems. Much to the Americans' surprise, the Germans — whom many in the U.S. ranks considered to be licking their wounds after being pushed back through France — were attacking, and attacking in force. Even the scattered and confused reports reaching the headquarters of Supreme Allied Commander Dwight Eisenhower indicated multiple German divisions (there were in fact twenty — hundreds of thousands of men) attacking along the entire front. Soon reports came through of whole American regiments surrendering and others reeling back.

Not Playing by the Rules

One of the most controversial tactics of the entire war was implemented by the Germans during their Ardennes Offensive. Dubbed Operation *Greif* ("Condor"), it was led by the daring commando Colonel Otto Skorzeny, who, at Hitler's personal command, had earlier rescued Benito Mussolini from a mountaintop prison in Italy. In preparation for Operation Greif, Skorzeny trained a team of commandos to speak U.S. English. Then he put them in captured jeeps and U.S. uniforms, and sent them behind American lines on December 16. There they were not only to create suspicion, but also to seize bridgeheads and hold them for the panzer divisions coming after them.

While Greif did cause confusion — all along the front GIs famously queried unfamiliar soldiers to see if they knew who had won the World Series that year — most of Skorzeny's troops were captured. Ultimately they were executed as spies, which was permissible since they were wearing U.S. uniforms, contrary to international law, as set out in the Hague and Geneva conventions. After the war, Skorzeny himself was tried as a war criminal for letting his men fight in enemy uniforms. But he was acquitted when Allied officers testified that U.S. and British commandos had done exactly the same thing.

The bombardment haunted many a survivor's dreams thereafter, for it involved over 600 light, medium, and heavy guns, as well as 347 *Nebelwefer* (multiple rocket launchers), whose screaming missiles were terrifying to hear. The German Sixth Panzer Army, commanded by General Sepp Dietrich, attacked in the northernmost part of the sector, supported to the south by the Fifth and Seventh Panzer Divisions. At the same time, two special units were brought into play. Colonel Friedrich von der Heydte led a thousand paratroopers in a drop behind Allied lines, planning to fight off any reinforcements coming from the

the American lines, but many of the GIs were green replacement troops and gave up without firing a shot.

HITLER'S DARING GAMBLE

The massive German counteroffensive against the U.S. Army in the Ardennes was the brainchild of one man: Adolf Hitler. During a September briefing at his headquarters at Wolf's Lair, in East Prussia, Hitler was told that, following the halt of the Allied advance due to dwindling supplies, German forces had made a few small and successful counterattacks. A briefing officer pointed

All at once, the quiet hills and forests of the Ardennes became a terrifying killing ground.

north. Colonel Otto Skorzeny disguised a small group of Germans in U.S. uniforms and led them through to the American rear, where they disrupted communications and sowed confusion.

The quiet hills and forests, covered with snow, became a terrifying killing ground. One American noncommissioned officer, raising his head after the bombardment, realized the telephone lines had been cut at the same time as he saw, coming through the early morning snow and darkness, "opaque figures," who turned out to be German soldiers in snowsuits. (The Americans had no such camouflage gear.) Ferocious running battles began all along

to a map of the Ardennes and the Netherlands as he described these small successes – some of the few the German army had experienced lately. Suddenly, Hitler stood up. "I have come to a momentous decision,", he said. "I shall go over to the counterattack!"

Striding to the front of the room before his surprised officers, he took the pointer and tapped the map. The counteroffensive would originate "out of the Ardennes," just where the successful German thrust into Belgium had begun in 1940, and its goal would be Antwerp. If German troops could break through to Antwerp, they would starve the Allied army of supplies while

splitting it in two, with the Americans to the south and the British and Canadians to the north. Such a bold stroke might make the western Allies sue for peace and allow the Germans the chance to turn all their attention to fighting Russia in the east.

The plan was on paper not strategically unsound, but in practice extremely perilous. It depended on total secrecy, on bad weather to halt the Allied bombers and spotter planes, and on one assumption that Hitler took as gospel: that the Americans were inferior fighting troops and would be easily overwhelmed.

An American Sherman M4 tank creeps through the Ardennes Forest. Conditions were hazardous for armored vehicles.

SKYLINE DRIVE

In fact, while many Americans did surrender, many more carried on the fight of their lives. During the early days of the attack, the veteran Twenty-eighth Infantry Division held half of the ground attacked by the Germans, from St.-Vith in the north to Medernach in the south. Part of their line was the so-called "Skyline Drive," a road running along a ridge for about ten miles. When the Germans attacked in force, the Twenty-eighth held their ground. Some American soldiers, manning machine guns, noted that the German infantry attacked in columns rather than in line abreast, making it easy to mow them down. This was a sign of a major German weakness: although the Germans held the numerical advantage, many of their troops were green conscripts, either very young or very old, and often poorly led and trained.

The Germans' immediate goal was to reach the Meuse River and protect the river crossings in order to allow the panzers to break through and drive toward Antwerp, which was held by British forces. To protect the Meuse crossings, the British assembled a makeshift group of air-force personnel, rear-echelon clerks, and cooks. Meanwhile, members of the British Twenty-ninth Division, which had been refueling in the rear, fought their way back to the front. Units of the British Corps also fought bitter actions at the Meuse crossings of Dinant, Givet, and Namur, sustaining heavy casualties but holding off the Germans.

The Americans, in the meantime, fought desperately at the village of St.Vith, on the north side of the "bulge." There, the Seventh Armored Division put up a roadblock that held the German panzers in place from December 17–23, inflicting enormous casualties and destroying their timetable. With precious time running out, Field Marshal Walter Model, the German commander in chief who had been instructed by Hitler to oversee the offensive, decided to redouble his efforts to push through the Allied lines farther south.

THE ELEMENT OF SURPRISE

How had the Americans not noticed that twenty divisions of the German army with 2,600 artillery pieces, 1,400 tanks, and self-propelled guns had gathered only a short distance across the front from them? There were several reasons for this. One was that the Americans had long come to depend on their top-secret code-breaking program, known as Ultra. Ultra only read radio traffic. With the Germans back in their native land, they could and did impose radio silence while at the same time using their excellent and extensive telephone and telegraph systems to communicate.

The Germans were also extremely clever at disguising their troop movements, making them appear to be defensive preparations (the code name for the entire attack *Wacht am Rhein*, meaning "the Watch on the Rhine," was deliberately devised by Hitler himself to connote homeland security rather than aggressive action). In addition, the Allies had also become a little complacent. The prevailing point of view of many high-ranking officers was that the Germans were too beaten to attack. A few days before the German offensive, an American staff officer told top brass, "The enemy divisions ... have been cut by at least fifty percent ... the [German] breaking point may develop suddenly and without warning."

Finally, there was the weather. Here, the Germans got a lucky a break. Although the skies in that part of Europe are usually cloudy in December and January, in 1944–45 they were unusually so, and parts of the front were covered in dense fog and snow – it was one of the worst winters in decades. Allied planes were grounded, and therefore unable to follow German movements.

A DEFIANT RESPONSE

With the German attack slowed in the north around St.Vith, Model directed the Fifth Panzer Division to attack and seize a vital road junction at a village called Bastogne. But the U.S. 101st Division, along with elements of other divisions, dug in around the village and fought back valiantly against German attacks that began on December 20.

The defenders of Bastogne were under the command of a tough, no-nonsense officer named General Anthony McAuliffe. Some of his troops wore only summer uniforms (resupply of winter ones had been slow) and had little ammunition – McAuliffe had had to order his artillery to fire only ten rounds per day. A few did not even have guns. Nevertheless, under heavy snow and leaden grey skies, they repulsed attack after attack. Gradually, however, German armored troops advanced around the village and soon it was surrounded.

On December 22, a four-man German delegation, carrying a white flag, came into the town and demanded to see McAuliffe. They carried a note, in German and English,

asking for his "honorable surrender," since "the fortunes of war" had changed. If this surrender were not forthcoming, the Germans would destroy Bastogne.

When McAuliffe was informed of this, he wrote down the following reply:

To the German Commander:
Nuts!
The American Commander

Word of McAuliffe's response spread around the troops at Bastogne, stiffening their morale, even though they expected a heavy attack at any moment. Fortunately for the Americans, on December 23 the skies finally cleared. Tons of ammo and supplies were airlifted into the town, while U.S. fighter planes provided close support. When the Germans finally did attack, they were repulsed.

THE TIDE TURNS

With the skies clearing and American reinforcements pouring in, the tide began to turn against the Germans. On Christmas Day, the U.S. Second Armored Division struck the Germans at the center of the bulge and after a two-day battle began pushing them back where they had come from. In the meantime, U.S. General George Patton's tanks forged a narrow corridor to Bastogne, through which relief was able to flow. In early January, Model began to pull back his troops on every front, breaking contact with the Allied lines so skillfully that the Allies didn't know the Germans had

gone from some areas. By January 17, the Allies had eliminated the salient in their lines and reformed an unbroken front.

The lengthy campaign had delayed the Allies from moving forward for six weeks, but had cost the Germans casualties and materiel that they could not replace. As a result, Hitler was left with almost no

German troops, some in winter camouflage, surrendering to members of the U.S. First Army during the fighting in the Ardennes.

reserves at all, and, with the Russians pressing in from the east, it was only a matter of time before the Allies would secure the total defeat of Germany.

The Bombing of Hiroshima

*How the Most Powerful Weapon Yet Created
Ended World War II, Began the Cold War,
and Raised the Specter of Nuclear Catastrophe*

THE ATOMIC BOMB THAT THE United States dropped on the Japanese city of Hiroshima on August 6, 1945 – as well as the one unleashed three days later on Nagasaki – changed the world utterly. In the short run, these massive weapons of destruction ended World War II almost immediately, a not inconsiderable consequence for a single weapon. In the long run, the unleashing of atomic weapons shaped global history, giving rise to the Cold War, during which the great superpowers of the United States and the Soviet Union engaged in a nuclear arms race. In turn, and even after the end of the Cold War, it affected the consciousness of almost everyone on Earth.

RELATIVELY UNSCATHED

It wasn't as if, in the summer of 1945, Hiroshima was untouched by the war. At least fifty thousand people, many of them children, had been evacuated from this, Japan's seventh largest city. Military fire marshals had demolished hundreds of houses to create firebreaks, hoping to protect Hiroshima from the fate suffered by other places during the ongoing and intense U.S. bombing campaign that had already targeted sixty Japanese cities – Tokyo had been devastated in March by a firestorm. Yet, except for an incident when an American bomber had accidentally jettisoned its bombs on the city, Hiroshima had fared far better than many comparable urban centers.

Despite having a population of some 250,000 people, Hiroshima still had the feel of a small, peaceful town. Located in the western part of Japan's main island of Honshu, it was a pleasant place, noted for its many fruit trees. Mountains flanked the city on three sides and seven rivers flowed through it (Hiroshima means "wide island"). More than forty bridges crossed these rivers, the largest and most famous one being the Aioi Bridge.

The mushroom cloud from "Little Boy," the first atomic bomb, dropped on Hiroshima on August 6, 1945, rises above the city.

Why hadn't the Americans bombed them, the people of Hiroshima often asked themselves? There were certainly military-supply industries in the city, although not necessarily the most crucial ones. A rumor sprang up that President Truman had an aunt who lived in Hiroshima and thus wanted to spare the city. It is a measure of how much people wanted to grasp at straws in the summer of 1945 that many of Hiroshima's residents believed this.

As July turned into early August, Hiroshima's luck continued, so much so that the town's children, when they saw the silver shapes of the U.S. B-29 bombers high in the sky, winging their way elsewhere in the country, would laugh and cry out, "B-san!" Which means, "Mr B."

A RUTHLESS CAMPAIGN

After initial successes in China and Southeast Asia, the Japanese had been slowly pushed back toward their homeland as American forces retook island after island in the Pacific in vicious, no-holds-barred combat. With the capture of the Mariana Islands in June of 1944, the Americans arrived within striking distance of Japan and were able to unleash the might of their air force. The mainstay of that force was the four-engine B-29 Superfortress, which featured cutting-edge innovations — a pressurized cabin, a fire-control system, and remote-control machine-gun turrets. It could fly as high as forty thousand feet, higher than most fighters and antiaircraft guns could reach.

At first, however, the bombing results that came from Japan were disappointing to the U.S. high command. Far above Japan, strong prevailing tailwinds made the planes hard to stabilize and the B-29's chief weakness — an engine that could overheat under stress — proved to be a significant problem. But then General Curtis E. LeMay was appointed to take over the bombing campaign.

Later to become infamous to another generation of Americans for threatening to "bomb Vietnam into the Stone Age" during the 1960s, LeMay was an inspirational figure in the U.S. military during World War II. He conceived the tactic of low-level, nighttime bombing raids using incendiaries. Since Japan's air defenses were mainly visual ones, operational only in daytime, nighttime bombing helped neutralize whatever Japanese antiaircraft resistance was left.

LeMay's perfect storm of tactics came together on the night of March 9–10, 1945, during the bombing of Tokyo, when 335 B-29s, stripped of most of their defensive armaments to allow them to carry extra bombs, went in low and slow, dropping incendiaries or napalm every fifty feet. Within two hours, Tokyo was engulfed in a firestorm. Estimates of the dead civilians that night range from seventy thousand to a hundred thousand. One million Japanese were left homeless.

During the raid, American pilots were forced to wear oxygen masks to filter out the stench of burning flesh. Even the American planners were aghast at the devastating results of the campaign. (LeMay acknowledged later: "I suppose that if I had lost the war, I would have been tried as a war criminal.")

The purpose of this bombing campaign aimed directly at Japan's civilian population was to force the country to surrender. However, the ferocious fighting on the Japanese islands of Iwo Jima and Okinawa that spring had made the U.S. high command realize that Japan would not capitulate easily. Even more extraordinary force was needed.

who hurried across the Aioi Bridge to work. To them the bridge was a familiar object of pride, the longest of Hiroshima's spans, joining the east and west sections of the city.

At the same moment, high above Hiroshima, a twenty-six-year-old American bombardier named Major Thomas Ferebee, aboard the second B-29 (the first had been a weather-monitoring plane), squinted through his bombsight, searching for that very same bridge. Ferebee had personally selected the Aioi Bridge from reconnaissance photographs as his Aiming Point, or AP. His commander, Colonel Paul Tibbets, the pilot of the B-29, had agreed with his

The American B-29 seemed to circle overhead, but the children in the playground below paid little heed.

A PERFECT TARGET

The morning of August 6 dawned partly cloudy and warm in Hiroshima. Nurses in Shima Hospital, a small, private medical institution next to the Aioi Bridge, gently awakened their patients for breakfast. Children and their teachers gathered at the adjacent Honkawa Elementary School. Around 7:30, an American B-29 flew overhead and seemed to circle, but the children playing in the Honkawa school playground paid "Mr B" little heed.

Just after eight o'clock, another U.S. bomber appeared. This one, too, was ignored by the nurses, teachers, and children, and by the citizens of Hiroshima

choice, saying, "It's the most perfect AP I've seen in the whole damned war."

It was just after 8:15 a.m. The "perfect AP" filled Ferebee's precision bombsight and he said: "I've got it."

A DEADLY DILEMMA

The ten-thousand-pound bomb Ferebee was about to release was called, with typically sardonic American humor, "Little Boy," and it was the first of only two atomic bombs in history to be used in conflict. Little Boy was the end result of the most extraordinary secret program of the war.

After nuclear fission had shown a select group of scientists around the world that enormous energy could be released by splitting an atom, Germany had begun developing an atomic bomb. In response, the Americans, Canadians, and British had initiated the Manhattan Project in 1942 to develop one, too. The Nazis, as it turned out, never got very far with their bomb, but the Americans, driven by the specter of atomic weaponry in Hitler's hands, proceeded at a furious pace, spending over two billion dollars and eventually producing a nuclear weapon. The "gadget," as the scientists called it, was successfully detonated in New Mexico on July 16, 1945.

The new weapon gave U.S. President Harry S. Truman a chance to end the war quickly. But was dropping such a bomb on Japanese civilians ethically permissible, even in wartime? This was an immensely problematic issue, the morality of which is debated to this day. Truman was aware of the power of the bomb and its potentially devastating effect. But he was also under intense pressure to limit further loss of life as a result of a prolonged conflict. Though the war in Europe had been over since April of 1945, the human toll in the continuing war against Japan was still soaring. On top of the almost 300,000 Americans already killed in both theaters of war, recent fighting against the Japanese on Okinawa had cost 72,000 American casualties, as well as 125,000 Japanese deaths, of which over 40,000 were civilians. If the Americans went ahead with Operation Olympic, their planned invasion of the Japanese mainland, projected for the fall of 1945, they expected casualties in the hundreds of thousands, as well as millions of Japanese deaths.

On July 26, America joined with its allies in issuing the Potsdam Declaration, demanding Japan's unconditional surrender.

Show of Strength?

Some historians, particularly in the 1960s, believed that the Truman Administration was mainly motivated by fear of the Russians, and that the atomic bomb was primarily a way of displaying U.S. power to the Communist government of Joseph Stalin. At the time, Russia was considering entering the war against Japan, something the Truman administration saw as a bald power grab and wanted to forestall. Dropping the bomb, some say, was a way to cause the Russian bear to back off – and to keep it from sharing in the spoils of a defeated Japan, particularly territory in Manchuria. In fact, the U.S. Secretary of State, James Byrnes, did tell Truman that the bomb should be dropped so that "Moscow would not [get in] on the kill." And whether or not this became Truman's main motivation, the dropping of the bomb may well have kept the Soviets from demanding a joint occupation of Japan, which Stalin had been hinting at only a week prior to the attack on Hiroshima.

Japan refused and seemed to dismiss the Allied demands out of hand. (In fact, Japan was in turmoil and its leaders were terrified that the Soviet Union might enter the war against it – which it did, on August 8.)

Even at this point, Truman still had alternatives to dropping the atomic bomb immediately, including demonstrating its power on a non-civilian target. But, tiring of the Japanese delays, he decided to proceed with the most forceful demonstration possible.

After some discussion, the peaceful city of Hiroshima was picked as the target. It had not yet been bombed, so the destruction caused by Little Boy could be well studied, and it was thought that the mountains on three sides of the city would have a "focus effect" on the blast, causing more casualties.

SHOCKING DESTRUCTION

As soon as Little Boy fell out of its bomb bay doors, the B-29 – the *Enola Gay*, it was called, after Paul Tibbets's mother – dived sharply and to the right before gaining altitude and heading back west, toward the sea. Ferebee watched the bomb as it fell, at first sideways, then turning nose down. It

was set to detonate in forty-three seconds and the crew waited breathlessly. They were wearing dark goggles to protect their eyes from the glare of the explosion, which they had been told could scorch their retinas. Since this first dropping of the bomb was a historic occasion, the intercom exchanges between the crew members were being recorded (and Tibbets had warned them to watch their language).

Nothing happened after the forty-three-second count, and many of the crew thought the bomb was a dud. But then there came an extraordinary flash of light and a shock wave so fierce that Tibbets thought the plane had been hit by antiaircraft fire. A huge column of smoke began to rise from a fiery red core, forming a mushroom-shaped cloud. Tibbets told the whirring recording device that he was "shocked" by "a destruction bigger than I imagined." But perhaps a more honest response came from the copilot, Captain Robert Lewis, who wrote

The *Enola Gay* crew, left to right: Major Thomas Ferebee, Colonel Paul Tibbets, Captain Theodore Van Kirk, Captain Robert Lewis.

in his notes as the plane sped from the target: "My God, what have we done?"

GROUND ZERO

Ferebee missed the Aioi Bridge by roughly 800 feet, and Little Boy exploded at about 1,850 feet above Shima Hospital. The hospital courtyard was directly under the explosion and was thus the Ground Zero, or "hypocenter," of the blast. All hospital staff and patients were instantly vaporized. Eighty-eight percent of people within five hundred yards died instantly. Heat waves at temperatures of 5,400 degrees Fahrenheit caused first-degree burns within about two miles of Shima Hospital.

A man stands by a gutted tram amid the desolation of Hiroshima, a few months after the dropping of the atomic bomb.

The Aioi Bridge buckled but was not destroyed. At the Honkawa Elementary School about one hundred yards away, teacher Katsuko Horibe was tossed through the air but survived, as did the only other survivors near the blast, because the school had concrete walls. The children in the playground were burned beyond recognition.

Everyone close to Katsuko Horibe suffered horrible burns. As she wandered with her surviving children onto the streets, she noticed that the burned men and women were holding their arms straight up in the air, a natural response to prevent the raw skin rubbing on the body, but one that made it look as if the whole city were a hell full of supplicating people.

The Ota River, spanned by the Aioi Bridge, was the first place these people raced to, to dive into the water, but the river itself seemed like it was on fire, being filled with burning debris and burning bodies. Scenes of horror abounded. One survivor, sixteen years old at the time, remembered that "what impressed me very strongly was a five- or six-year-old boy with his right leg cut at the thigh. He was hopping on his left foot to cross over the bridge." Another noted that a black rain began to fall an hour after the attack, yet it did not put out any of the fires.

Hiroshima was so short of workers that thousands of high school students had been mobilized to operate telephones and trams. Seven thousand of them were to die that day. One who survived, a fifteen-year-old girl who was disfigured by the blast, remembered: "I saw something shining in the clear blue sky. I wondered what it was, so I stared at it. As the light grew bigger, the shining thing got bigger as well. And at the moment when I spoke to my friend, there was a flash, far brighter than one used for a camera. It exploded right in front of my eyes … I thought the bomb had been dropped on the central telephone office. The dust was rising and something sandy and slimy entered my mouth." It was her blood, mixed with the dust.

Looking down from his weather station on a hill above the city, Isao Kita, a meteorologist, wrote: "I could see that the city was completely lost. The city turned into a yellow sand. It turned yellow, the color of the yellow desert."

"THE GREATEST DAY IN HISTORY"

Estimates of the death toll vary, but perhaps one hundred thousand people died in Hiroshima almost immediately, and another thirty thousand, due to burns and radiation poisoning, by the end of the year. This was a far greater toll than the Manhattan Project planners had expected. Nevertheless, Truman immediately declared August 6 "the greatest day in history," and again called on Japan to surrender, promising "a rain of ruin from the air" if it again refused. But the shocked Japanese government did not respond at once and on August 9 another atomic bomb was dropped, this time on Nagasaki, where the death toll reached sixty to seventy thousand. After this, on August 15, Japan surrendered.

The war was over. But the use of the nuclear bomb echoed through subsequent generations. After August 6, 1945, human beings would always be possessed of the knowledge that there exists a weapon that can do awful damage, and can be carried in a missile-tip or even a suitcase. Not only that, but the use of one of these weapons might cause yet more of them to be unleashed, so that the world might ultimately be destroyed. This consciousness – nuclear anxiety – is a fixture of our modern age, and is here to stay.

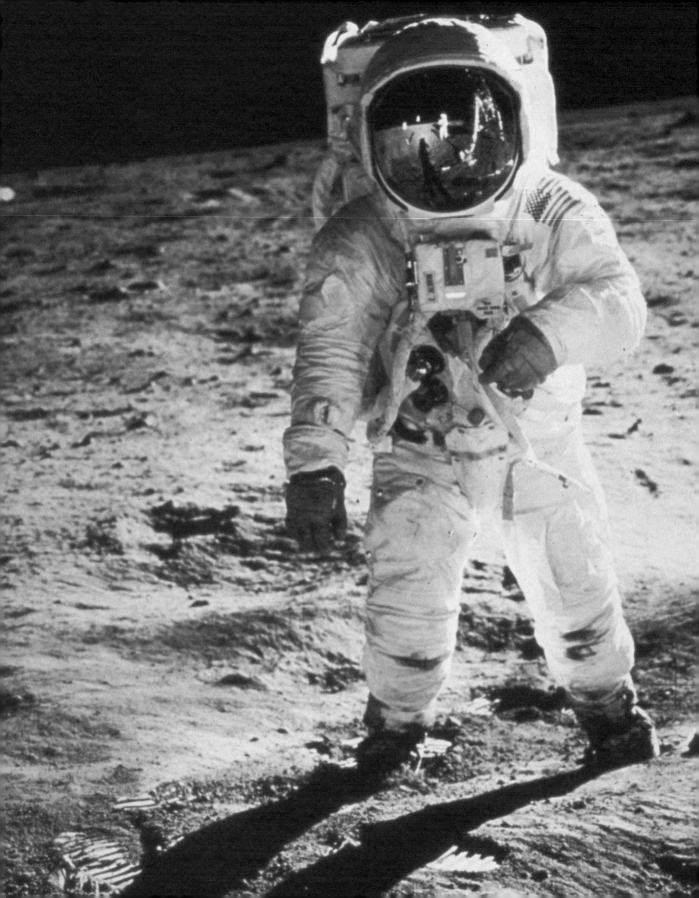

The Cold War
and Beyond

1950–2001

The Cuban Missile Crisis

How a Standoff Between the Superpowers
Brought the World to the Brink of Nuclear War

VERY EARLY IN THE MORNING of October 15, 1962, a U-2 spy plane took off from McCoy Air Force Base in Florida, in the United States. The U-2 was the best aerial reconnaissance plane in the world — sleek and lightweight, supersonic and capable of snapping clear pictures from heights of seventy thousand feet. Yet it was not without flaws, one of them being its vulnerability to well-aimed surface-to-air missiles, or SAMs. In one incident in May of 1960, a U-2 had been shot down over Russia, becoming a major public embarrassment for the Eisenhower Administration in its waning days. And on September 9, 1962, another had been shot down over western China, tarnishing the image of the new administration of President John F. Kennedy. U-2 flights were therefore considered risky from a public relations point of view, but the one taking place over Cuba on October 15 was deemed too important to forgo.

The U-2 crossed Cuba at almost exactly 7 a.m., just the right time for spy photos as the sun is high enough to create shadows which give dimension to objects on the ground. The camera in the plane's belly clicked and hummed. In fifteen minutes, the U-2 had finished its job and turned back toward its base. By the middle of the day, the pictures were in the hands of analysts at the CIA headquarters in Langley, Virginia.

At 7:30 on the following morning, McGeorge Bundy, President Kennedy's National Security Adviser, met with the CIA analysts in his office in the White House basement to review the images. They directed Bundy's attention to a rectangular-shaped clearing in the Cuban jungle. Military trucks could be seen, as well as some long sheds. Based on their knowledge of similar sites in the Soviet Union, the analysts were sure that some of the shapes were missile ramps. Indeed, it was the CIA's conclusion, they told Bundy, that the Soviet Union was installing medium-range nuclear missiles in Cuba.

The briefing chilled Bundy to the bone. For this meant that Russia had, or would

MISSILE TRANSPORTERS

12 PROB GUIDELINE MISSILES

HEAVY EQUIPMENT

5 MISSILE DOLLIES

20' LONG CYLINDRICAL TANKS

MISSILE TRANSPORTERS

OPEN STORAGE

soon have, nuclear weapons in place about one hundred miles from America's shores. Bundy immediately called the president.

This reconnaissance photograph, taken over Cuba on October 15, 1962, highlights the features of a Russian missile base.

TO THE BRINK

For fourteen days in the middle of October 1962, the world came the closest it has ever come to nuclear war. During those fourteen days, a nuclear holocaust was a very, very real possibility, so much so that one Russian participant in these events said that at one point he was "counting the minutes" — not days or hours — until missiles were fired. People in America bought food supplies with which to stock "bomb shelters" (usually cellar rooms) in their homes, while schoolchildren practised taking cover under their desks. Around the world, people nervously read newspapers and watched the crisis on television. Demonstrations demanding a peaceful resolution to the standoff took place in Paris and London.

When the crisis eventually subsided, John F. Kennedy, the charismatic and youthful President of the United States, would be hailed in America as a hero for having faced down the Russians. Yet what many people do not know to this day is that Kennedy made a secret deal with Premier Nikita Khrushchev, the leader of the Soviet Union, to get the Russians to dismantle their missile

woke up on the morning of October 16 to be told for the very first time that Khrushchev had installed nuclear missiles in Cuba. In fact, the warnings had been arriving for some time. In early August, CIA director John McCone had received a highly reliable report that at least one such missile had been installed in a cave with a hole drilled through its ceiling near the little Cuban harbor town of Mariel; McCone personally told the president this on August 20. U-2 reconnaissance flights in early September had also revealed the presence of SAM missile sites, submarine pens, and Soviet MiG fighters in Cuba. Further reports

One Russian official said he was "counting the minutes" – not days or hours – till missiles were fired.

sites – a deal even some intimates in his administration were not aware of.

What became known as the Cuban Missile Crisis was caused by a number of factors. They included Russia's unsettling knowledge that the United States had it completely outgunned when it came to nuclear missiles, and the Kennedy Administration's near-clinical paranoia about having a socialist state in Cuba. But, as with many dramas, both on the world stage and in our own backyards, the chief cause was hubris.

"THERE IS NO EVIDENCE"
It is part of the many myths surrounding the Cuban missile crisis that President Kennedy

indicated that five thousand to ten thousand Soviet troops were also present.

Despite this, Kennedy had said at a press conference in early September: "There is no evidence of any organized combat force in Cuba from any Soviet bloc country." The main reason for his secrecy was that the Americans were then planning an attack on Cuba to rid themselves of this taunting presence. An earlier attempt to do this, the so-called Bay of Pigs invasion, in 1961, carried out by Cuban exiles and funded by the CIA, had been a poorly planned disaster. The new invasion, however, was to be an all-American one, with the full power of U.S. military might behind it.

But the Kennedy Administration could not simply invade Cuba; it needed to provoke President Fidel Castro into some belligerent act that justified such a response. Since late 1961, the CIA had been running Operation Mongoose, in which operatives made small hit-and-run raids on Cuba, hoping that Castro would lash back.

TIT FOR TAT

Khrushchev's decision to place nuclear warheads in Cuba had been prompted by numerous considerations. One was the United States' far greater nuclear firepower – at the time, America had 27,297 nuclear warheads to Russia's 3,332. Another was

Castro's request, made in January of 1962, that Russia station men and weapons in Cuba in case of another American attack. The Russians believed the Americans would attack again, as well – one Russian diplomat later told a historian that "in the spring of 1962, we in Moscow were absolutely convinced … that a new military invasion of Cuba was at hand – but this time with all the American military might, not only with proxy troops."

But what had finally convinced Khrushchev to position his missiles close to America's shores was the decision by the Kennedy Administration to place fifteen intermediate-range ballistic missiles in

The Bay of Pigs

On April 15, 1961, a CIA-backed invasion force of Cuban exiles hit the beaches of the Bay of Pigs (Bahía de Cochinos) in southwestern Cuba in an attempt to overthrow the new government of Fidel Castro. After initial successes, the invasion force, lacking promised support from the U.S. Navy and Air Force, was soundly defeated and most of its members imprisoned. (The U.S. was later forced to ransom them for fifty-three million dollars.)

The Bay of Pigs was the worst disaster of the Kennedy Administration and haunted U.S.-Cuban relations for decades to come. The plan had originated and been approved during the Eisenhower Administration, prior to Kennedy's term in office. Even

then, U.S. government officials were seeking a way to overthrow the unfriendly socialist government that had come to power in a neighboring country that had previously been an ally – indeed, almost a colony.

On coming to office, Kennedy gave his approval for the invasion. But once he realized that the United States would have to take a public, rather than a covert role in the fighting, he baulked and withdrew military backing at a late stage. This was one of the main reasons why the invasion failed. Another, revealed in 2000, was that the Soviet Union and Cuba knew about the invasion, including its date, all along – thanks to a KGB mole in the CIA.

Khrushchev's decision to back down from confrontation brought praise in the West, but condemnation from hardline Communists.

Turkey in 1961. From then on, any Soviet official vacationing along the shores of the Black Sea could easily imagine an American nuclear warhead arcing across the shore and fifteen hundred miles into Russia. From the Russian point of view, these missiles were a direct challenge to Soviet security.

THREE OPTIONS

The president's reaction to the call from Bundy on October 16 was swift. He ordered an immediate top-secret meeting of a dozen leading foreign policy officials, including Bundy, Secretary of State Dean Rusk, Secretary of Defense Robert S. McNamara, and the president's brother, Attorney-General Robert Kennedy, whose influence on the president went beyond the domestic purview of normal attorneys-general. Also part of the group were Chairman of the Joint Chiefs of Staff General Maxwell Taylor, Vice President Lyndon Johnson, and the Ambassador to Russia, Chip Bohlen. Known as the Executive Committee, which would soon be shortened to "Excomm," this group would meet daily for the next two weeks. The meetings were taped – U.S. presidents had been taping important moments in office since World War II – and the tapes are now a matter of public record.

At the first meeting, President Kennedy was told the extent of the buildup in Cuba. The Russians were constructing nine missile sites, which could launch SS-4 and SS-5 missiles a distance of 2,400 miles into the United States. There were indications that up to forty launching sites were planned, which would mean nearly seventy percent of the Soviet nuclear capability was resting on America's doorstep. The scale of the buildup came as a surprise, even to Kennedy.

Three types of response were discussed. One, advanced by Maxwell Taylor, was an air strike: "We're impressed, Mr President, with the great importance of getting a … strike with all the benefits of surprise … Hit 'em without any warning whatsoever." Another option was a blockade, to keep any more Soviet men and materiel from entering Cuba. And then, as Robert Kennedy put it, "We have [a third choice] … which is the invasion." At the same time as he said this, Robert Kennedy passed a note to his brother, which read: "Now I know how Tojo felt when he was planning Pearl Harbor" (a reference to the popular, but inaccurate, perception that Japanese Prime Minister Hideki Tojo had personally planned the surprise attack on December 7, 1941).

THE BIGGER PICTURE

On October 18, out of a secret location deep in the Russian steppes, the Soviets launched *Cosmos X*, their very first spy satellite. Primitive by today's standards, and less advanced than U.S. satellites, *Cosmos X* rose to a height of about 122 miles and headed off on a course which put it directly above U.S. military bases, on land and at sea, in the southern and southwestern United States. As a result of this, the Soviet Union was able to see for the first time at close quarters the massive American military buildup that had been going on since October 16. A day later, the official Soviet newspaper, *Isvestia*, published a warning: if America attacked Cuba, the Soviets would go to war against the United States. This warning was without a doubt approved by Khrushchev.

On October 22, President Kennedy went "live" with the crisis. Addressing the American nation and an anxious worldwide audience on television, he announced the discovery of the missile installations and proclaimed that he was placing a naval blockade – or "quarantine," as he called it, since blockades were illegal under international law – around Cuba. Kennedy had fought off the military demands for a massive bombardment or invasion of Cuba, mainly because he felt Khrushchev would retaliate with military action in Berlin (then still divided into Eastern and Western sectors), which would call for a U.S. response, thus escalating the situation even further.

Khrushchev responded by declaring the quarantine illegal (which it was) and vowing that Russian ships would ignore the blockade. The Russians, through Soviet Ambassador Anatoly Dobrynin, also claimed that there were nothing but "defensive" weapons in Cuba, which the Americans knew to be a lie.

On October 24, the blockade went into effect. U.S. intelligence knew that nineteen Soviet ships were at that moment en route to Cuba. As the Western world held its collective breath, the Strategic Air Command (SAC) went to a DEFCON 3 alert. (In U.S. military lexicon, DEFCON alerts gauge the readiness of the country's defenses against attack. DEFCON stands for Defense Readiness

Condition, with DEFCON 5 meaning normal peacetime conditions and DEFCON 1, which has never been used, standing for imminent attack.) Sixteen of the ships turned away. Two moved toward the 180 U.S. ships strung out around Cuba, escorted by a Russian submarine. As a U.S. destroyer prepared depth charges to blow the Russian sub out of the sea, the two surface vessels stopped dead in the water and waited.

EYEBALL TO EYEBALL

At this point, famously, Dean Rusk is said to have turned to McGeorge Bundy and said: "We're eyeball to eyeball, and I think the other fellow just blinked." But this wasn't quite the case. On the evening of October 24, Khrushchev sent a private message to Kennedy, continuing to claim that the quarantine was "an act of aggression." This caused Kennedy to order the Strategic Air Command to DEFCON 2, for the first (and only) time in its history. By the morning of October 26, Kennedy was convinced that he needed to invade Cuba and increased the frequency of reconnaissance flights over the island to one every two hours. But then Kennedy received a letter from Khrushchev – one that Bobby Kennedy described as "very long and emotional" – which stated that Soviet missiles and personnel would be removed if Kennedy announced that he would not invade Cuba.

As Kennedy considered this, a U-2 was shot down over Cuba on October 27, killing its American pilot, and other reconnaissance planes were fired on. These attacks were nevertheless against Khrushchev's orders, but tensions rose extraordinarily, leading the U.S. military to once again push for war. On the evening of October 27, Khrushchev sent yet another missive, this time demanding that Kennedy remove the U.S. nuclear warheads from Turkey.

The official version at the time had it that Kennedy simply chose not to respond to the second letter, only replying to the first and agreeing not to attack Cuba. But, in fact, through a secret avenue of communications Kennedy also agreed to remove the missiles from Turkey. This agreement was known only to a few intimates, because Excomm at large was against the deal, which was felt to undermine NATO and Turkey.

WINNERS AND LOSERS

However the agreement had been achieved, people around the world breathed a huge sigh of relief. The crisis had shown how close the planet could come, at any time, to nuclear war, and it caused many people around the world to join peace movements, particularly those that sought the banning of nuclear arms.

While Kennedy – who would be president for only little more than a year, before being shot down in Dallas – was not the all-out victor he was initially credited with being, he can be applauded for resisting military urgings to go to war, urgings that could very well have led to a nuclear holocaust. But it was American hubris, in thinking it could

Anxious Americans listen to President Kennedy's analysis of the tense stand-off. Scenes like this took place the world over.

invade Russia's ally Cuba with impunity while positioning missiles in Turkey, so near Russia, that had initiated the crisis.

Khrushchev had also made mistakes, however, in thinking he could get away with placing missiles in Cuba and in under-

estimating American resolve. Afterward, he lost face around the world and in October 1964 was forced to resign, at least in part because the Soviet Union had been cast as the loser in this ultimate global confrontation.

All in all, for the statesmen the result could be seen as a draw. The true winners, however, were the citizens of the world, who had only narrowly escaped being vaporized by atomic weaponry.

The Assassination of President Kennedy

The Slaying of a Much-loved Leader Leaves a Nation in Shock and Gives Birth to Countless Conspiracy Theories

ALMOST EVERYONE IN THE Western world who was an adult on November 22, 1963, can remember where they were and what they were doing when they heard the news that President John Fitzgerald Kennedy had been assassinated in Dallas, Texas. The young American president had won international renown as the gracious, charming symbol of the Second World War generation's coming of age; of a hoped-for end to the Cold War; and of the beginning of what Kennedy himself called a "New Frontier" that would include the eradication of poverty and the spread of democracy worldwide. The shock of his death reverberated far and wide.

Without doubt, the assassination is the single most controversial event in U.S. history. Well over two thousand books have been written on the subject. Two government commissions have studied it in depth. Numerous movies and documentaries have been devoted to dissecting that day, those scant six seconds, those three (or four, or five) shots.

It all boils down to this. If we have to believe that a lonely, maladjusted, arrogant sociopath like Lee Harvey Oswald was alone responsible for killing the charismatic, altogether extraordinary JFK – just Oswald himself, without the aid of some massive and covert machinery of conspiracy – then we have to believe that we live in a world where random luck can fall on the side of creeps as well as handsome heroes.

If, on the other hand, we believe, as some conspiracy theories suggest, that the Mafia, Fidel Castro, the Soviet Union, or the CIA – or Kennedy's own vice president, Lyndon Johnson, for that matter – used Oswald as a pawn (a "patsy" is what Oswald said he was) to get to the president, then we can believe that JFK was killed for a purpose, that he died because his perceived goodness threatened the wrong people or global interests. And that is truly a hero's death.

GOING ON A CHARM OFFENSIVE

The day of the assassination began for the glamorous presidential couple in Forth Worth,

Texts, about thirty miles from Dallas. It was cool and overcast, raining slightly. A crowd of twelve thousand people gathered in front of the Hotel Texas, where the Kennedys were staying. Coming out without Jackie – a fact that he knew disappointed the crowd – Kennedy made a few short remarks before

Lee Harvey Oswald after his arrest. In the two days he had left to live, he continued to proclaim that he was a mere "patsy."

commenting wryly that his wife's tardiness was due to the fact that "she always looks so much better than the rest of us."

This was not the first time that Kennedy had used his cultivated young wife – she was thirty-three to his forty-six – to charm slightly hostile crowds. And this trip to Texas was in fact one huge charm offensive. The following year, 1964, would be a reelection year for Kennedy, and Texas was one of the states in the country not swayed by his aura, since along with it came many stances – including civil rights and his reluctance to re-invade Castro's Cuba – that did not endear him to the heart of conservative Texans. This was not merely a matter of polite political disagreement. Numerous violent fringe groups were known to exist in Dallas, and security along the president's motorcade route would be stringent.

A VIOLENT LONER

As Kennedy was preparing to leave Fort Worth, a twenty-four-year-old man named Lee Harvey Oswald – who sometimes used the pseudonym Lee Hidell – was preparing to leave for his job at the Texas School Book Depository, a textbook distribution center located in Dealey Plaza, a small park on the outskirts of Dallas's downtown. Oswald had a bland, almost meek appearance that disguised numerous secrets. Born into a poor New Orleans family, he had never known his father, who had died two months before his birth. He grew up to be a lonely child – "lone" or "loner" were words that would follow him all his short life – who was fascinated with guns. As a teenager, he developed leftist

views. He could also be violent, striking his mother, Marguerite, on several occasions; once he pulled a knife on her.

Despite his early socialist leanings, Oswald joined the U.S. Marines when he was seventeen, in 1956. By the end of 1956, after only a few weeks of training, he had attained a "sharpshooter" qualification on the firing range. That meant he could hit a ten-inch bull's-eye from two hundred yards away, eight times out of ten, without the aid of a telescopic sight.

THE FATEFUL JOURNEY

President Kennedy and his entourage – which included Vice President Lyndon Johnson, a native Texan, and his wife, Lady Bird, as well as Texas Governor John Connally and his wife, Nellie – flew into Dallas's Love Field to be greeted by cheering crowds. Special plaudits were reserved for a smiling Jackie Kennedy, lovely in a pink suit and pillbox hat. The Kennedys and Connallys then entered their limousine (the Johnsons would follow two cars behind) for the motorcade to the Dallas Trade Mart, where Kennedy would make a speech. The Kennedy car was an open-topped Lincoln Continental.

The skies had cleared, the weather was warming, and crowds had already begun to gather along the motorcade's route, which had been published in the local newspapers. The penultimate leg of the trip took it through Dealey Plaza, in front of the Texas School Book Depository building. Some of the depository workers gathered at the windows for a bird's-eye view of the proceedings. Lee Harvey Oswald was alone on the sixth floor, in the southeast corner of the building. None of his fellow workers saw him, because he was hidden behind cartons of books he had placed there.

In his hands was an Italian-made Mannlicher-Carcano rifle, complete with telescopic scope, which he had purchased for $24.45 from a Chicago mail-order rifle and ammunition company. Conspiracy theorists would later disparage the Mannlicher-Carcano as a poor rifle, impossible to use to hit a moving target, but FBI tests found it to

unsuccessfully to renounce his citizenship, and moved to the Soviet Union, where he worked in a factory in Minsk and met and eventually married Marina Nikolayevna Prusakova. But after an attempt to obtain Soviet citizenship failed, he tried to kill himself and was placed in a mental asylum.

Upon his release, upset over his rejection by the Russians, Oswald returned to America and settled in the Dallas–Fort Worth area with Marina and their new daughter, June. When he wasn't working in a series of menial jobs, Oswald made fitful attempts to live out his socialist beliefs. He volunteered briefly for an organization

Oswald was trained to hit a ten-inch bull's-eye from 200 yards away, eight times out of ten.

be extremely accurate. It fired a 6.5-millimeter bullet at about two thousand feet a second. The Mannlicher-Carcano could also be broken down and reassembled quickly; Oswald had walked into work that day with a long brown package that contained, he said, "curtain rods."

By 12 noon, Oswald was ready.

THE MAN BEHIND THE BOXES

A study of Lee Harvey Oswald reveals a personality typical of lone assassins. After a short, unhappy time in the Marine Corps, where he was bullied for his socialist sympathies, his Marxist leanings became more pronounced. He attempted

called Fair Play for Cuba, and went to Mexico, where he visited both the Cuban and Soviet embassies, trying to get visas to live in their countries.

All of this later provided fodder for conspiracy theorists, who believed that Oswald was working for the Russians or the Cubans, or even the CIA. A problem with all these theories, however, is Oswald's extraordinary instability, which impressed almost everyone with whom he came into contact. He was just too weird for professional intelligence operatives to use as a spy, let alone as an assassin.

In any case, Oswald had already carried out a similar act, alone. In April of 1963, he

The President and Jackie Kennedy at the start of the motorcade. In front of them are Governor Connally and his wife, Nellie.

had sneaked into the backyard of a former U.S. Army general and arch conservative segregationist named Edwin Walker, who had recently made an "anti-Communist" speaking tour – and shot at him. The shot hit a wooden windowsill and was deflected, although bullet fragments grazed Walker. Oswald's involvement was not suspected until after the Kennedy assassination, when police found surveillance photos Oswald had taken of Walker's house.

Having missed Walker, Oswald's restless anger – at the world, at authority figures to both the right and the left of the political spectrum – had gone unassuaged.

THE ZAPRUDER TAPE

Even today, explanations of the assassination that posit Oswald as the "lone" shooter can prompt a vitriolic response from passionate conspiracy theorists. "Ridiculous!" they say, or "What about Umbrella Man?" Umbrella Man is a figure who appears in a famous film of the assassination and who, for no apparent reason, on a sunny day opens and closes his umbrella just as JFK's motorcade passes and shots ring out. Many conspiracy theorists suggest that this man must have been signaling to someone.

The film in question was made by Abraham Zapruder, a fifty-eight-year-old clothing manufacturer, who had offices in the Dal-Tex building in Dealey Plaza. He was an avid Democrat and supporter of President Kennedy, and he went home in the middle of the day to get his eight-millimeter film camera to record the president's visit.

He then went with his secretary to Dealey Plaza, walked down Elm Street past the book depository, and climbed up on a concrete pergola near the grassy knoll and the triple underpass through which Kennedy's motorcade would drive. The innocent and enthusiastic film Zapruder subsequently made has become essential evidence in all investigations of the assassination.

KENNEDY'S LAST MOMENTS

At just before 12:30 p.m., Kennedy's motorcade entered Dealey Plaza on Main Street, turned right on Houston Street, traveled one block and turned left onto Elm Street beneath the book depository. This was a 120-degree turn, which slowed the motorcade down to a speed of just about ten miles per hour.

First came two motorcycles, then Kennedy's limousine, with the President and First Lady in the back seat and John and Nellie Connally in the front seat. The crowds along Elm Street began to scream and wave. "Mr President," Nellie Connally said at that moment, "you can't say that Dallas doesn't love you." "No, you certainly can't," the president said.

At this point, as Kennedy and his wife smiled and waved, Oswald fired his first shot. It missed. While no remnants of the bullet have been found, it appears that it nicked the branch of an oak tree and ricocheted against a kerb – a chip of concrete flew off and grazed the cheek of a bystander.

Within three seconds, Oswald had fired again. This second shot entered Kennedy's upper back. Although it didn't touch his spine it created a shock wave that damaged his sixth cervical vertebra, which in turn caused a neurological reflex sometimes called Thorburn's Position. This can be seen quite clearly in Zapruder's film: Kennedy's arms go up almost parallel to his chin, elbows jutting out and fists clenched, and remain locked there. The same bullet then struck John Connally, seriously injuring him.

Watching the Zapruder film at this point, one sees the situation in the lead limousine quickly unravel into chaos. The driver, disastrously, slows the vehicle to a near crawl. Governor Connally has collapsed with his head on his wife's lap. Kennedy is leaning toward Jackie, his arms locked.

She reaches to him, trying to pull down his left elbow from this strange position.

Then, suddenly, a large portion of the right side of Kennedy's skull flies off. In the film, it looks like the bullet has hit him on that side, but what can be seen is really an exit wound. The bullet had entered the back of Kennedy's head and exploded outward. Nellie Connally remembers Jackie Kennedy saying, "His brains are in my hand."

The film captures Jackie, her pink suit blood-spattered, trying to climb over the back of the car, where a Secret Service man was reaching to her. Some speculated that she was trying to escape the carnage, but she later provided a simple explanation: a piece of her husband's skull had blown back over the car. She wanted to get it, in case it was needed.

"JUST A PATSY"

Oswald hid the rifle behind some boxes and sprinted down a rear stairwell of the book depository. A police officer who had already entered the building, gun drawn, stopped him, but Oswald's supervisor identified Oswald as an employee, and he was allowed to leave. He returned to a rooming house where he had been staying, picked up a pistol, and headed out once more. He was seen acting suspiciously enough – ducking into storefronts as police cars went by – that an officer named J. D. Tippet stopped him for questioning. Oswald shot him four times, killing him.

By this time, the rifle had been found in the book depository and an all-points bulletin had been issued for Oswald's arrest. Soon, he was caught in a movie theater where he was hiding and booked on suspicion of murdering both President Kennedy and Officer Tippet. Reporters saw him briefly; he claimed he was innocent, "just a patsy," he said, arrested because he had lived in the Soviet Union.

Meanwhile, the enormity of the assassination was sinking in. Film taken of the crowd in Dealey Plaza after the motorcade rushed the mortally wounded president to the hospital shows men and women standing around in stunned silence, hands over their mouths, or with tears unashamedly running down their cheeks. The same reaction of shock, disbelief, and grief quickly spread worldwide.

OSWALD IS SILENCED

In his short time in custody, Oswald continuously wore a smug grin or sneer. Although he continued to deny killing the president, he seemed to be enjoying himself immensely – right up to the moment when, while being transferred to another jail, he was shot and killed by a strip-club owner named Jack Ruby.

Ruby's motive appeared to be simple revenge: he had idealized JFK. His friendship with members of the Dallas police force had allowed him to be on hand as Oswald was being moved. This was more fodder for conspiracy theorists, who postulated that the supposedly Mob-connected Ruby had been hired to shut

Oswald up. But Ruby's Mafia connections were never proven, and most of those close to him scoffed at the notion that he was part of a conspiracy. They considered him unstable – after he shot Oswald, Ruby cried, "This should show the world that Jews have guts!" – and to be acting out of violent emotion.

Ruby was convicted of murdering Oswald in 1964, then granted a new trial on appeal (over a technicality). But he died in jail of lung cancer in 1966, before the new trial, insisting on his deathbed that "there was no one else" involved in Oswald's murder.

Despite this, and the findings of the 1966 Warren Commission, which stated that Oswald had been the lone gunman, theorists continued to pore over pictures of Dealey Plaza on that day, looking for accomplices. They found smoke coming from the grassy knoll, which turned out to be leaf shadows. They found CIA men disguised as tramps, who turned out to be tramps. Shots that seemed to have come from all over the plaza turned out to be acoustical echoes.

Oh, and Umbrella Man? The simple truth about Umbrella Man is that he was a guy named Louie Witt, who came forward in 1978 when he heard of his notoriety among conspiracy theorists. Witt was an eccentric who waved his umbrella to heckle Kennedy; he still had the umbrella.

And the simple truth about the assassination appears to be that Lee Harvey Oswald, acting on a deranged impulse, was the sole killer of John F. Kennedy. Not a terribly satisfying answer – as mundane, in fact, as an old umbrella – but, nonetheless, unless new evidence is found, almost certainly the correct one.

Congressional Findings Discredited

In 1976, the U.S. House of Representatives convened a congressional committee to hear new evidence on both the Kennedy assassination and the later assassination of Martin Luther King. Their 1979 conclusion regarding Kennedy was that, while Oswald had fired three shots and killed the president, acoustical evidence presented a "high probability" that two more shots were fired at JFK from somewhere on Dealey Plaza, indicating the presence of a conspiracy.

The committee was relying on evidence that has now been discredited, however, particularly a Dictabelt recording from the motorcycle of a Dallas police officer, which supposedly picked up the sound of other shots. The police officer insisted that he was not in Dealey Plaza at the time the "shots" were recorded, but racing with the Kennedy limousine to the hospital. In 1982, a team of scientists backed him up, concluding that the sound of "shots" on the tape is probably static.

The Six-day War

*The Astonishing Military Triumph That Ensured the
Survival of Israel — and Lasting Insecurity in the Middle East*

IT WAS MOSHE DAYAN, THE charismatic Israeli Defence Minister, who first began referring to Israel's "War of Independence" against its Arab neighbors in June 1967 as "the Six-day War." The name quickly stuck, and it was a brilliant stroke, bringing with it echoes of the Book of Genesis: God had made the Earth in six days, and Israel had asserted itself as a nation in the same amount of time in a lightning war that saw it defeat Egypt, Syria, and Jordan. The difference was that in the biblical story God rested on the seventh day, whereas Israel's epic triumph brought it no rest at all. Today, Israel remains the occupier of the land it won in the Six-day War, but, as a result, it is faced with repeated terrorist attacks, and its borders seem no more secure than they were prior to that conflict. Some might wonder, has Israel's victory turned to ashes?

A JEWISH STATE IS BORN

Beginning in roughly the mid-nineteenth century, the Zionist movement called for Jews in Europe, Russia, America, and the Middle East to return to their ancestral homeland of Palestine — especially to their sacred city of Jerusalem — and settle there.

At the time mainly populated by Arab peoples, the region had been under Ottoman rule since the early sixteenth century. When Great Britain took control of Palestine after World War I, it promised through the Balfour Declaration, a formal statement of policy intentions in the post-war Middle East issued by its Foreign Secretary Arthur James Balfour, to create a Jewish state. However, each successive wave of Jewish immigration was met with violent resistance from Palestinian Arabs, some of whom were then seeking independence for Palestine, and Britain soon reneged on its promise.

After World War II, when the Holocaust created sympathy worldwide for the Zionist cause, the British handed over the Palestine problem to the United Nations. It sought to resolve the situation in November of 1947 with General Assembly Resolution 181, which partitioned Palestine into two states, one Arab, one Jewish. Zionists welcomed this proposal, but Arabs rejected it because large numbers of Palestinian Arabs would be left living in the Jewish state. The day after the resolution was passed, Palestinian fighters attacked Israel, and what Israel called its War of Independence began.

Fighting through 1948 against Palestinian nationalists and their Arab supporters from Iraq, Syria, Egypt, and Transjordan – all of its neighbors – Israel eventually conquered thirty percent more territory than the partition had given it. Although the Old City of Jerusalem ended up in Jordanian hands – a blow to the Jews, who had been expelled from this ancient city by the Romans in the first century AD – and the Israelis suffered heavy losses, by the end of 1948 the Israeli state had been born.

COUNTDOWN TO WAR

It would take almost another decade of war – through to the Israeli victory in the second Arab-Israeli war of 1956 – for the Israelis to solidify their position. After 1956, Palestine settled into an uneasy calm. However, in a manner typical of the Middle East, the two successive and overwhelming Israeli victories simply sowed the seeds of another war. Pan-Arabism – the philosophy that the Arabs, no matter what their country, were all one people – took hold in the region at this time and found its chief proponent in Gamal Abdel Nasser, President of Egypt, who had driven the British out of the all-important Suez Canal and nationalized it for his people.

For the next ten years, Nasser made preparations for a new and final war against Israel. He joined forces with Syria, to Israel's east, and spoke of liberating the Palestinians living in land held by the Israelis. The radical Baathist Party controlling Syria was even blunter: it wanted, a spokesperson said, "to push Israel into the sea."

Meanwhile, the Israeli Defense Force (IDF) continued to build up its army and air force with munitions and planes from the United States and France. Egypt and Syria did the same, with weaponry supplied by the Soviet Union.

"A CHILD'S GAME"

By 1967, Israel was ringed by thousands of miles of hostile borders and more than thirty Arab divisions. With a few simple strokes, Egypt could close off Israel's vital shipping links through the Strait of Tiran to the Red Sea. Jordan talked openly of diverting the Jordan River, Israel's main water supply. One Egyptian government official said that his peers in the military considered "the destruction of Israel a child's game." A Syrian general thought that the Arab allies could conquer Israel in four days.

In May of 1967, Egyptian forces began to concentrate in the Sinai Peninsula to the southwest of Israel. Under intense pressure from Nasser, the United Nations agreed to remove its Emergency Force, which had acted as a buffer in the area since 1957. On the night of May 22–23, the Egyptian navy blockaded the Strait of Tiran, something Israel had always said would be tantamount to a declaration of war. Israeli Prime Minister Levi Eshkol pleaded unsuccessfully to Britain, America, and the United Nations for help. At the end of May, Nasser signed a defense pact with King Hussein of Jordan,

The Public Face of the IDF

At the time of the Six-day War, Defense Minister Moshe Dayan was the most glamorous soldier the Israelis had, instantly recognizable in his signature eyepatch (he had lost his left eye to a sniper's bullet while fighting with the British against the Vichy French in the Second World War). Born on a kibbutz in Palestine in 1915, he had distinguished himself in the 1948 battle against the Arabs and became known in the next twenty years as Israel's top warrior. He was a man who did not shun the spotlight, and this was especially evident during the Six-day War. Although he had only recently been appointed Defense Minister and had not taken part in the planning of the war, Dayan kept a high profile, repeatedly meeting with reporters and even ending up on the cover of *Time* magazine. Generally cynical and irreverent, he made excellent copy. His political fortunes sank when he, like the rest of the Israeli government and military, was caught off guard by the sudden Arab attack that launched the Yom Kippur War of 1973. He died of a heart attack in 1981.

and Jordanian troops began massing along the border with Israel, while Syrian forces massed on the Golan Heights. "Our basic objective will be the destruction of Israel," Nasser said on May 27.

Conferring with Yitzhak Rabin, commander of the IDF, Eshkol finally realized that Israel had no choice: it had to go to war to survive. And it was quickly established that the best way to do this was to take preemptive action against the Arab states that threatened it.

The decision was so nerve-wracking that Rabin suffered a nervous breakdown and was treated for acute anxiety and depression.

maintaining strict radio silence, the planes flashed into Egyptian air space and launched devastating attacks against Nasser's airfields. The raid was perfectly disciplined and methodical: the first planes dropped huge concrete-busting bombs to destroy the runways, then other fighters roared in to bomb and strafe.

The attack caught the Egyptians completely off guard. Within two hours, after twenty-five Israeli sorties against eleven airfields, the Egyptians had lost more than half of their air force — approximately three hundred fighters, bombers, and helicopters.

On May 27, Egyptian President Nasser said, "Our basic objective will be the destruction of Israel."

But with chief of staff Ezer Weizman running operations — and the aggressive Moshe Dayan pushing for a massive surprise attack — the Israelis made their move.

OPERATION FOCUS

At about 7:30 on the morning of June 5, 250 Israeli French-made fighter-bombers rose from their airfields, flew out over the Mediterranean, and then banked and headed straight for Egypt. This was the start of Operation Focus, one of the most carefully planned and complete surprise attacks of this or any other war.

Flying low across the desert — sometimes just thirty feet above the ground — and

Operation Focus was a brilliant move. Striking first against their most powerful enemy brought the Israelis time to turn and face Jordan and Syria. And Israel's resulting domination of the skies allowed its forces to advance against the dug-in Egyptian troops in the Sinai. There, the Egyptian army was quickly pushed back all along the line.

In the east, despite Israeli diplomatic efforts to keep their eastern neighbors from attacking, the Jordanian's launched an offensive against IDF forces, shelling and bombing targets within Israel, which included Tel Aviv and the Jewish portion of Jerusalem. But another quick Israeli air strike destroyed much of the Jordanian air power.

By nightfall, Israeli forces held strong positions along all their borders. Ironically, citizens in Cairo were told that the Egyptians were destroying the Israelis and celebrations there went on into the night.

EGYPTIAN ERRORS

Despite these Israeli victories on the first day, the Egyptians were far from defeated. Nasser sent out a desperate plea to other Arab countries for more planes and soon fifty Soviet-built MiGs were on their way from Algeria. Since most Egyptian planes had been destroyed pilotless and on the ground, scores of pilots stood ready to fly the replacement fighters.

But Egyptian generals now made several tactical mistakes. Instead of digging in to repel the advancing IDF (which was tired and suffering from ammunition shortages), they decided to retreat through the Sinai toward defensive positions along the Suez Canal, thus ceding great amounts of territory as they went. On June 6, however, Nasser began a propaganda war that was more effective than his war on the ground, claiming that the attacks were being made by waves of American bombers, piloted by Americans. Protests sprang up against the United States all over the Arab world.

In the meantime, fighting was occurring between the IDF and Jordanian forces in Old Jerusalem. The Israeli attack had begun early in the morning of June 6, as huge searchlights behind Israeli lines illuminated the dug-in Jordanian forces and blinded them. The fighting was vicious, bunker to bunker, machine-gun nest after machine-gun nest, hand-to-hand.

By the end of the day, the Israelis had taken all of Jerusalem except the Old City, where the Jordanians were still entrenched. Early the following morning, Israeli artillery bombarded these positions, driving the Jordanians back across the West Bank, and then IDF paratroopers entered the Old City en masse. It was a time of extraordinary emotion for the Israelis. The assault commander, Colonel Motta Gur, sent a message to his officers: "The ancient city of Jerusalem, which for generations we have dreamed of and striven for — we will be the first to enter it."

The Israelis took the Old City with little resistance, moving to the site of the First and Second Temples, a place of pilgrimage for both Muslims and Jews. Despite sniper fire, they made their way to the Western Wall, one of the most sacred places in the Jewish religion, the only portion of the Second Temple still standing, the rest having been destroyed by the Romans in AD 70. There, General Shlomo Goren, chief rabbi of the IDF, blew his *shofar*, a traditional Hebrew trumpet used in religious ceremonies, and proclaimed: "I have come to this place never to leave it again."

On the evening of June 7, the United Nations was successful in arranging a ceasefire between Israel and Jordan. King Hussein of Jordan, who had lost half of his kingdom in a few days — the half

that brought him a good deal of tourist revenue – retired to lick his wounds.

From the opposite side of the Suez Canal, an Israeli soldier studies an oil refinery at Port Suez set alight by Israeli shelling.

SLAUGHTER IN THE SINAI

In the Sinai, the Israelis raced after the retreating Egyptians. They stopped taking prisoners, advising any Egyptians they encountered to run in the direction of the Suez Canal and attempt to cross back into Egypt. But when they caught and trapped Egyptian troops in the mountain passes leading back toward the canal, they indulged in great slaughter. Israeli artillery poured fire down on traffic jams of Egyptian trucks and tanks; soon, wrecked machinery and dead bodies littered the narrow passes – in Mitla Pass, on June 8, thousands of Egyptians lost their lives.

On that same day, the IDF in the Sinai, having heard of the recapture of Jerusalem, sought some glory for itself. Despite having standing orders to stay twelve miles away from the Suez Canal, and despite the fact that the retreating Egyptians had blown the bridges over the waterway, some Israeli soldiers jumped into the canal and bathed gleefully in its all-important waters.

Egypt now accepted a ceasefire, too, leaving Syria as Israel's only undefeated enemy. Syria remained in control of the strategically important Golan Heights, east of the Jordan River, from whose summits it could pour down artillery fire on Jerusalem. On June 9, the IDF attacked the Syrian positions. The fighting was as vicious as that for Jerusalem, but on June 10, driven by their grand successes and racing now for as much territory as they could gain before the expected ceasefire, the Israelis drove the Syrians out and captured the Golan Heights.

PEACE REMAINS ELUSIVE

It had been an incredible war, an astonishing six days unlike any other six days in history. Eleven thousand Egyptian troops had been lost, as well as six thousand Jordanians and one thousand Syrians, while the IDF had suffered only seven hundred dead. The territory Israel had gained was beyond its wildest expectations a week before — twenty-six thousand square miles, which included the Sinai and the Gaza Strip from Egypt, East Jerusalem (including the Old City) and the West Bank from Jordan, and the Golan Heights from Syria. The Arab nations and President Nasser (who was to die in 1970) had been totally humiliated.

In November of the same year, the United Nations passed an American-backed resolution that called for Israel to withdraw from the occupied lands; in return, the Arab combatants would recognize Israel's statehood. But the Arabs would not agree to this "land for peace" deal, so Israel not only remained in the so-called Occupied Territories, but also began to fortify them and populate them with Jewish settlers.

Such settlement, some of it illegal, has ever since fueled the rise of Palestinian nationalism and sparked terrorist attacks on Israel, which has responded on many occasions with military strikes on the homes of Palestinians and their supporters. "Land for peace" continues to be the operative philosophy when other countries try to broker peace in the Middle East, but it has not worked terribly well. After forty years, Israel remains an occupying power. And no matter how just its cause may have been in 1967, as such it has caused a good deal of harm to Palestinians living within and close to its borders.

War goes on now, as it did in 1967, but it is a far different war, and one whose eventual victor — if there can be one — is anybody's guess.

Israeli paratroopers stand reverently beside the Western Wall of the Old City of Jerusalem, after its capture on June 7, 1967.

The Tet Offensive

*The U.S. Victory That Brought Down a President
and Turned Public Opinion Against the Vietnam War*

EARLY IN THE MORNING OF January 31, 1968, Michael Herr, an American war correspondent, was visiting Special Forces troops at their base camp near Can Tho in South Vietnam. As he sat smoking marijuana with the Green Berets, he heard the sound of fireworks coming from the nearby town. It was Tet, the annual Vietnamese celebration heralding the beginning of the lunar New Year. That year, 1968, would be the Year of the Monkey. All over Vietnam, similar celebrations were going on.

But as Herr and the Green Berets sat there, the fireworks got closer and closer and louder and louder, until the men realized that these were not fireworks at all, but grenade explosions and automatic weapons fire. The Americans were under attack.

That night, as he describes it in his classic work of war reportage, *Dispatches*, Herr changed from observer of war to participant, fighting alongside the Special Forces troops, who were surrounded on all sides and under heavy fire: "I slid over to the wrong end of the story, propped up behind some sandbags at an airstrip in Can Tho with a .30 caliber automatic in my hands."

A PYRRHIC VICTORY

The attackers were the Viet Cong and North Vietnamese Army (NVA), the Communist forces fighting for control of Vietnam against the South Vietnamese Army of the Republic of Vietnam (ARVN) and their U.S. allies. As their massive and historic Tet Offensive began, numerous noncombatants like Herr, from journalists to staffers at the U.S. Embassy to civilians in the ancient and elegant city of Hue, found themselves on the front lines of the war. The journalists quickly relayed their experiences home. Vivid reports made front pages around the world; scenes of carnage were shown nightly on television.

The impact of the offensive and the effect of these images would ultimately force the U.S. president, Lyndon Johnson, not to seek reelection — a shocking result for the leader and his advisers, given that the offensive would end with an American victory, the devastation of the Viet Cong as a fighting force, and the severe mauling of the NVA. But this would be the public's way of making the president and the military pay for their propaganda — for lying about the war. They had told the public that the battle was almost won.

U.S. troops wounded during the Tet Offensive. Images like this one shocked the American public and heightened opposition to the war.

Tet, with its attacks right at the heart of U.S. interests in Vietnam, showed graphically that it wasn't.

THE IDEOLOGICAL BATTLEGROUND

The war in Vietnam that became such a flashpoint of the 1960s was a continuation of a war that had been going on since World War II had ended. After the Japanese surrender, the French attempted to take back their former colony, but the Viet Minh, Vietnamese nationalists led by the Communist Ho Chi Minh, defeated the French at the battle of Dien Bien Phu in 1954 — a battle that signaled the end of Western colonialism in Asia. In the peace settlement that followed, Vietnam was divided into two separate states at the seventeenth parallel, in recognition of gains made by the Viet Minh. In the North, Ho Chi Minh, with aid from the Chinese, set up a Communist state. In the South, a democratic Western-backed state was born. A demilitarized zone (DMZ) was created in order to keep the two sides apart, but from the start the Viet Minh infiltrated the South and launched hit-and-run guerilla raids meant to undermine the South Vietnamese government. The United States, fearful that a North Vietnamese annexation of South Vietnam would lead to Communist takeovers of other nations in Southeast Asia — the so-called "domino theory" — ramped up the supply of military aid, advisers, and support troops.

The first American ground combat troops, 3,500 in all, landed in Vietnam in 1965. By December, faced by a wily and determined guerrilla foe, the United States had increased its presence to two hundred thousand troops. By November 1967, despite protests in the United States against the war, there were nearly half a million Americans fighting the Viet Cong and the NVA.

To counter the protests at home, a carefully orchestrated "success offensive" was set in motion. General William C. Westmoreland, commander of the U.S. Military Assistance Command, Vietnam (MACV), claimed to anyone who would listen that America was winning the war. President Lyndon Johnson appeared on the deck of the aircraft carrier USS *Enterprise* in late 1967 and declared that the war would not last "many more nights."

Within weeks, the Tet Offensive would highlight the absurdly misplaced optimism of these words.

THE EMBASSY ATTACK

At about 2:45 a.m. on the night of January 31, at the same time as Herr and his Green Berets were roused from their stoned state, a group of nineteen highly trained Viet Cong guerillas struck at the prime symbol of the American presence in Vietnam: the U.S. Embassy in Saigon. Blowing a hole in

the outside wall of the embassy compound, they stormed the buildings and killed five U.S. Marine guards and numerous military police (MPs).

Many of the attackers had worked by day as gardeners and drivers at the embassy and thus knew the layout intimately. While the highest-ranking American diplomat present — the Deputy Chief of Station — was pinned down in his house, the attackers fought a six-hour gun battle with reinforcing marines. By the end of it, the attack had been halted and the attackers wiped out. But television footage of the battle and pictures of the Viet Cong dead littering the embassy grounds were flashed around the world. Many Americans were left wondering how such a thing could have happened in a war they were supposed to be winning.

PLANNING TET

The operating genius behind the Tet surprise attack was North Vietnamese General Vo Nguyen Giap. It was his belief that the previous two years of guerrilla warfare against the Americans had done nothing to appreciably change the fortunes of North Vietnam and had in fact left the country, through attrition, in a steadily weakening position. Despite the fact that the conventional wisdom behind guerrilla warfare is not to engage the enemy in set-piece battles (and, in fact, at places like the Ia Drang Valley in Vietnam's Central Highlands in 1965, the NVA had done just this and been battered by U.S. firepower),

Giap wanted to shake up the enemy with a dramatic attack. Giap also believed that the population of South Vietnam was sick of the Americans and the corrupt South Vietnamese puppet government, and that the planned Tet Offensive could be the spark that would fan the flames of a broad popular uprising. In this last calculation, however, the normally pragmatic Giap was well wide of the mark.

Under Giap's plan, preparations for the Tet Offensive had already begun in the autumn of 1967, when North Vietnam struck at U.S. bases such as Khe Sanh and Con Thien along the DMZ, attempting to

battalions hitting over one hundred targets in South Vietnam – could not be kept secret for long. In fact, a Viet Cong soldier's notebook, containing a fairly precise description of the attack, was even captured on January 5.

However, in what one U.S. Army general later called "an allied intelligence failure ranking with Pearl Harbor," the MACV failed to put two and two together. And although a heightened state of alert was called for, it was in the main ignored by American commanders. After all, it was estimated that they were on high alert nearly fifty percent of the time, anyway.

U.S. television presenter Walter Cronkite said, "What the hell is going on? I thought we were winning the war."

draw U.S. reinforcements away from South Vietnam's cities. But the main offensive was to be launched at the time of the Tet celebration. While secretly planning this attack, North Vietnam announced that it would participate in a truce for the duration of the festival. In response, the South Vietnamese Army gave half of its troops permission to go on leave.

AN INTELLIGENCE FAILURE

There has long been a myth that the United States was completely surprised by Tet, but in fact this was not the case. Such a huge buildup – for an attack that would involve almost two hundred Viet Cong and NVA

On the night the Viet Cong guerillas blasted their way into the U.S. Embassy, two hundred U.S. colonels went to a raucous party at a fellow officer's quarters in Saigon. Only one extra guard had been assigned to the embassy.

RUNNING BATTLES LIVE ON SCREEN

In the days before the attack, thousands of NVA and Viet Cong stripped off their uniforms and infiltrated Saigon. Thousands more did the same in other cities. Still more waited in the countryside, ready to attack military bases. Overall, about seventy thousand North Vietnamese and Viet Cong were involved. These fighters hit hard, and with a vengeance, attacking thirty-six of forty-four provincial capitals, five large cities, and about one hundred other towns. Twenty-five military bases were assaulted. In and around Saigon, the enemy blew up a good portion of the massive Long Binh ammunition dump, briefly took over the national radio station, and attacked the Presidential Palace. General Westmoreland found himself under siege at the MACV headquarters and ordered his personal staff to find weapons to aid in the defense of the perimeter. The Saigon suburb of Cholon — inhabited mainly by Chinese — was turned by the NVA into a virtual staging ground for their attacks. In one running gun battle, U.S. military police — whose role normally was restricted to rousting drunken marines out of bars — fought better-armed, better-trained guerrillas in a side alley near the U.S. embassy. Sixteen MPs were killed and twenty-one wounded.

Thousands of people on both sides were to die in the ensuing days. The United States was faced with an enemy that had dug in, literally in its midst, and would fight to the death.

In the meantime, the world saw a constant barrage of television images of battles going all over the southern half of the country — battles in which the U.S. forces appeared to be being overwhelmed. The war had been beamed to American television and around the world since the first U.S. troops had arrived in 1965, but most of the early reports contained very

little combat footage, since obtaining it involved extreme risks for reporters. Now, however, all reporters had to do was point their cameras through their hotel windows in Saigon and viewers would see street battles in progress and hear the sound of gunfire.

This was where Lyndon Johnson's "success offensive" worked against him; expectations had been set so high that the American people simply could not comprehend how the North Vietnamese could pull off such a coup. After the few first days, the U.S. television presenter Walter Cronkite said, "What the hell is going on? I thought we were winning the war." It mattered little that within weeks the North Vietnamese were being pushed back, with heavy losses. The dramatic images stuck in people's minds.

THE BATTLE FOR HUE
After the embassy raid, the battle that became most emblematic of the Tet Offensive was the pitched combat that took place for a month, beginning in early February, as American and South Vietnamese forces attempted to recapture Hue City, in central Vietnam. Situated on the banks of the Perfume River, Hue is the ancient "Imperial City" of the Nguyen dynasty and is filled with historic artifacts and the tombs of the ancient Vietnamese dynastic rulers. In 1968, it had a population of about 140,000 people, and was also noted for its graceful parks and a French-designed university campus, whose student body included a large number of Catholics.

The Photograph that Turned the Tide of Opinion

On the morning of January 31, 1968, an Associated Press photographer named Eddie Adams wandered the streets of Saigon with a Vietnamese NBC television cameraman, looking for a story. They came upon a group of South Vietnamese soldiers holding a man dressed in shorts and a checked shirt, who had his hands tied behind his back and appeared to have been beaten. As they approached, Nguyen Ngoc, the chief of South Vietnam's National Police, walked up to the man with a pistol in his hand.

It was common practice for the South Vietnamese to interrogate VC suspects by pointing a gun at their head; Adams raised his camera and snapped a picture – just as Ngoc fired a bullet into the man's head. The subsequent photo, catching the VC suspect grimacing as the bullet hit him, became an iconic image of the Tet Offensive, won Adams the Pulitzer Prize, and brought opprobrium down upon the head of Ngoc. This was something Adams always regretted: the VC suspect was a Viet Cong officer who had been identified as the assassin of a South Vietnam official's entire family, and Ngoc therefore had reason for doing what he did. But Adams' photograph became, in the words of *Harper's* magazine, "the moment when the American public turned against the war."

Bewildered residents returning to the city of Hue soon after North Vietnamese forces were forced out by U.S. bombing.

When the Tet Offensive began, a division of NVA and Viet Cong attacked and seized much of the city. The North Vietnamese hoisted their flag over the Citadel, the fortified inner city of the ancient kings, and quickly reinforced it with ten thousand troops. Then they commenced another mission: to cleanse the city of those who had spoken out against the Communists in the north. NVA commanders carried lists of these people, who included government officials, teachers, priests, and others, many of them foreign-born. Many were rounded up and executed, some by shooting, others by being buried alive. Thousands of graves were dug.

In early February, however, three under-strength battalions of U.S. Marines, aided by the South Vietnamese, counterattacked. The weather was cold and rainy. The Americans engaged in running battles with their NVA counterparts, fighting for the city block by block – the only house-to-house fighting seen in Vietnam.

At first, out of respect for the historic value of the ancient city, the Americans did not bomb Hue, but the NVA was so well dug in that they finally decided they had no choice. Plane after plane then hit enemy positions with napalm and high explosives, turning seventy percent of the city to rubble and making 116,000 civilians homeless. For many watching at home, it was another example of an ill-advised and counter-productive U.S. policy of using massive amounts of firepower to achieve a pyrrhic victory. This strategy was famously summed up in a television interview by a U.S. major involved in heavy fighting for another town, Ben Tre on the Mekong Delta. "It became necessary to destroy the town to save it," he said.

VICTORY FROM DEFEAT

The popular uprising that Giap expected did not eventuate. By the beginning of March, the NVA and Viet Cong forces had been pushed back from every position they had seized on January 31, and suffered a staggering forty-five thousand men killed. The offensive became a calamitous defeat for Giap and for North Vietnam. After Tet, the Viet Cong ceased to function as a fighting force and the NVA struggled to rebuild itself.

But although they had lost on the ground, the North Vietnamese had won where it counted: in the hearts and minds of the public in the West. Americans in particular now saw that their government's strategy was resulting in massive casualties, both American and Vietnamese, and that the war seemed to have no clearly defined goal and no end in sight.

Shortly after the offensive, the news was leaked that General Westmoreland wanted an additional 206,000 troops in Vietnam. Westmoreland saw the situation from a military point of view – after defeating the enemy he wanted to press home the attack. But Americans saw it as sacrificing more precious lives for a lost cause.

In the presidential election year of 1968, Lyndon Johnson became so unpopular that after narrowly winning the important Democratic primary contest in New Hampshire – normally a shoe-in for a sitting president – he announced in March that he would not run for another term of office. He also declared a halt to U.S. air strikes above the twentieth parallel in an attempt to bring the North Vietnamese to the negotiating table.

After tumultuous months that saw yet more angry antiwar protests in the United States and elsewhere, formal peace negotiations began in Paris, in November of 1968. It was the first step in the de-escalation of the war, which would eventually lead to a full U.S. withdrawal in 1973.

From the point of view of Giap and his commanders, the forty-five thousand men lost in the Tet Offensive had not died in vain.

The First Moon Landing

*America's Rapid Triumph in the Space Race
Brings Lunar Exploration to a Halt*

IT'S ALWAYS BEEN UP THERE, nice and yellow and juicy, an allure to lovers, waxing and waning, in charge of tidal pulls, rhyming with "June" and "spoon." Human beings have worshiped it, steered by it, and been driven mad by it. There are rock drawings five thousand years old that depict it. In the second century AD, the Roman writer Lucian wrote a romance in which travelers went to the Moon – the first of many efforts in the genre that would eventually be known as science fiction. People right into the twentieth century imagined there might be extraterrestrial life of some kind there, teeming away beneath the surface or on the so-called "dark side." Yet, for all of human history, no one had ever landed on it. Two hundred and thirty-eight thousand miles away, it sat there, tantalizing us.

It took two things to make a lunar expedition possible in the late 1960s. First, technology had to advance to a point where rocketry could hurl capsules out of the Earth's gravitational field and into the much weaker gravitational pull of the Moon.

Secondly, the Russians had to act like they were going to get there first. For, first and foremost, landing a man on the Moon was, in those days at the height of the Cold War, a political act. With the United States and Russia competing in every aspect of life, from education and technology to the arms race, such an achievement would demonstrate the superiority of one system, democracy or Communism, over the other. And not only to the citizens of the USA and the USSR, but also to other nations, most notably developing nations taking their first steps toward political independence.

In this contest of one-upmanship, science, ironically, was sidelined. And in this lay the seeds of the demise of lunar exploration.

BEATING THE SOVIETS

On July 16, 1969, three astronauts lay strapped on their backs in their space module atop a massive *Saturn V* rocket.

Apollo 11 takes off from Cape Canaveral, Florida. The tip of the rocket carried the command module, *Columbia*, and the lunar module, *Eagle*.

Neil A. Armstrong, Edwin "Buzz" Aldrin Jr., and Michael Collins were the finest products of the National Aeronautics and Space Administration (NASA), and they – like the pioneers of the Age of Exploration, to whom admiring editorial writers often compared them – were going on a journey into the unknown. In a few moments, they would lift off into the bright Florida sky and head for a landing on the Moon.

The mighty U.S. Apollo space program had begun just eight years before, in April of 1961. On the twelfth day of that month, the Russian cosmonaut Yuri Gagarin had become the first person to travel into space and orbit Earth. This had stirred U.S. President John Fitzgerald Kennedy's strong competitive streak. Shortly after Gagarin's single, ninety-minute orbit, Kennedy wrote to Vice President Johnson, then chairman of the National Space Council, asking: "Do we have a chance of beating the Soviets by putting a laboratory in space, or a trip around the Moon ... or by a rocket to go to the Moon and back with a man?"

At the time, the American space program was not far behind the Russians in its ability to launch a man into space – on May 5, 1961, Alan Shepard became the first American to orbit the Earth – but lagged in developing the technology to reach the Moon. The Russians had succeeded in launching at least three so-called hard-landing rockets – unmanned spacecraft that had been shot up with the goal of simply hitting the Moon – and

America was at least two years away from achieving this. But buoyed by Shepard's triumph, Kennedy issued a famous challenge when addressing a Joint Session of Congress that summer: "I believe this nation should commit itself to achieving the goal, before this decade is out, of landing a man on the Moon and returning him safely to Earth."

HEADING INTO ORBIT

With a mighty roar which thrilled the million people who had gathered on the beaches around Kennedy Space Center near Cape Canaveral, Florida, and the millions more watching on television, *Apollo 11* lifted off into space. Only eleven minutes after blast-off, it was in orbit with the three astronauts aboard beginning to feel the sensations of weightlessness.

They were used to it. Neil Armstrong, the commander of the mission, was thirty-eight years old, a veteran of seventy-eight combat missions during the Korean War, a test pilot of some of America's most advanced rocket airplanes, and a veteran of an earlier Gemini space flight. Armstrong had been selected to become the first man to walk on the Moon.

Thirty-nine-year-old Buzz Aldrin would be Armstrong's partner on the Moon landing. He, too, had been a Korean War fighter pilot and was a Gemini veteran. Aldrin would pilot the lunar module, *Eagle*, which would separate from the command module, *Columbia*, once in the

Moon's orbit and bring the two astronauts down to the surface of the Moon.

The third man was Michael Collins, thirty-eight, pilot of *Apollo 11* and the *Columbia* command module. Another Gemini veteran, Collins would not get a chance to touch the Moon's surface but had the essential job of making sure the *Eagle* was launched correctly and ensuring that it redocked safely for its journey back to Earth.

A TURBULENT DECADE

While only eight years had passed since Kennedy's challenge, they had been tumultuous ones. Kennedy was dead of an

United States abroad at the expense of the ten million people who lived below the poverty line at home.

But nothing deterred NASA from attempting to reach its goal. With Project Apollo, named after the Greek and Roman god of the Sun (among other things), it devoted all its energies to finding a way to land a man on the Moon and began a series of unmanned and manned missions. Efforts intensified in 1966, when the Russians managed to reach the Moon with a so-called soft landing module – a rocket-launched landing vehicle that did not crash on impact and was able to send back lunar pictures.

While millions watched with admiring eyes, others felt space travel was a hugely expensive vanity project.

assassin's bullet, as was his brother, Robert, and another iconic figure of the sixties, Martin Luther King, Jr. The war in Vietnam had torn the United States apart, pitting patriotic conservatives against those who thought the conflict misguided or immoral. The counterculture of drugs, sex, and rock 'n' roll was in full swing. And America was riven by racial divisions and, in some places, crushed by poverty.

Therefore, while there were millions who watched the journey of *Apollo 11* with admiring eyes, there were others who felt that space exploration, at the cost of billions of dollars, was a kind of vanity project meant to enhance the image of the

In 1967, tragedy struck the U.S. program when three astronauts on *Apollo 1* – the first manned launch, which was intended merely to test systems by sending the men into Earth orbit – died in a fire on the launching pad. By July 1969, however, Apollo had made four successful manned flights, which had put spacecraft in orbit around the Moon and tested the lunar module.

Unfortunately for the Russians, at this crucial stage one of their chief scientists died and their N1 rocket exploded at least four times during top-secret launch attempts. The Soviet program quickly unraveled, and even Soviet politicians privately ceded the race to the Americans.

Now, on July 16, 1969, with Armstrong, Aldrin, and Collins speeding to the Moon, and with the eyes of the world upon them, the United States was about to publicly claim its prize.

"YOU CATS TAKE IT EASY"

It took the astronauts three days to reach the Moon. On July 19, in the command module *Columbia,* they passed behind the Moon and while on its "dark" side initiated rocket burns that slowed the spacecraft down and corrected its course so that it could enter lunar orbit, about sixty miles above the surface of the Moon. Armstrong and Aldrin then entered the *Eagle,* and, on July 20, separated from *Columbia.* "You cats take it easy on the lunar surface," Collins told them, his jocularity masking a real concern, for his fellow astronauts were literally going where no human being had gone before.

After it coasted down to an altitude of twenty-one thousand feet, the *Eagle* began a powered descent at the rate of twelve hundred feet per second. The surface of the Moon began to appear around the astronauts, pocked with deep craters and with boulder fields scattered on all sides. Suddenly, a computer overload alarm went off, meaning that one of the navigational computers was in danger of malfunctioning.

This famous image of Buzz Aldrin walking on the Moon was taken by Neil Armstrong, who is visible in the reflection on Aldrin's visor.

Mission Control in Houston, confident it was a false alarm, never even thought of stopping, however. "Roger, we're GO on that alarm" was their response, meaning that the mission would continue.

The computer was bringing the *Eagle* down into a deep, wide crater, about two hundred yards in diameter, called West Crater. The area around the crater was covered with boulders as much as ten feet high. Noting this, the astronauts decided to override the computer. "We elected to overfly this area in preference for smoother spots a few hundred yards farther west," Armstrong said after the mission. Their final approach took them between two boulder fields, where they touched down.

Since lunar gravity is only about one-sixth that of Earth, and since the *Eagle*'s rockets had blown dust everywhere, Aldrin and Armstrong were not entirely sure that they had landed until a contact light lit up on one of the *Eagle*'s landing pads. "Houston, Tranquility Base here," Armstrong reported. "The *Eagle* has landed." There was pandemonium in Mission Control in Houston — joyous celebrations, hugging and kissing, the lighting up of cigars. It was 4:18 p.m., U.S. Eastern Daylight Time, on June 20, 1969.

"ONE SMALL STEP"

While the world waited in awed wonder, the two astronauts rested and checked their gear. The *Eagle*'s cameras sent back ghostly, almost surreal images of a moonscape that was stark and lifeless. At 10:40 p.m., after resting, Armstrong put on his backpack with its portable oxygen system and began climbing down a nine-rung ladder to the surface. Before stepping down, he prudently looked at the ground below him. "The surface appears to be very, very fine-grained," he said. Then his left foot touched the ground. "That's one small step for man, one giant leap for mankind."

This utterance, heard through hissing static, immediately became famous around the world. But Armstrong always insisted, with irritation, that he had said "one small step for *a* man," and so his words were officially changed to this, although the recording does not reflect it. Whatever he said, Armstrong — a man of few words, not comfortable with rhetoric — had made history.

Around the world people watched in astonishment. Some held "moon parties" and toasted the yellow orb with champagne, or stood on rooftops, staring up at the Moon, trying to imagine that human beings were, right at that moment, walking on its surface. It was hard not to feel that something had changed irrevocably in the universe.

MEN FROM PLANET EARTH

Soon after, it was Aldrin's turn to climb down to the Moon's surface. The two men then began their scientific tasks, which consisted of taking soil and rock samples and setting up a sort of aluminum-foil windsock, designed to capture solar wind particles (charged particles ejected from the upper atmosphere of the Sun).

The two men also set up seismic equipment, to measure moonquakes, and a laser mirror. The latter would reflect back a laser beam sent by an observatory telescope in California, allowing scientists to determine the precise distance between the Earth and the Moon; even more importantly, scientists could use the laser mirror to monitor movements of the Earth's crust.

The astronauts also planted a U.S. flag and placed a stainless-steel plaque that read: "Here men from Planet Earth first set foot on the Moon. July, 1969." It was inscribed with the names of the three astronauts and President Richard Nixon.

Finally, after more than two hours on the surface of the Moon, Aldrin, and Armstrong climbed back up the ladder and into the *Eagle*. It was just after 1 a.m. At 12:54 p.m. that day, after resting and preparing for another twelve hours, Aldrin fired the *Eagle*'s ascent engine and the craft climbed into the sky, where it rendezvoused with the *Columbia*, piloted by Michael Collins. Then all three astronauts flew home.

After splashing down in the Pacific Ocean on July 24, 1969, Collins, Aldrin, and Armstrong were placed in quarantine for three weeks, just in case they had brought unknown microorganisms back from the Moon with them. They reemerged to fame and adulation.

THE END OF APOLLO

Most people assumed the success of *Apollo 11* would pave the way for not only more trips to the Moon but also manned voyages to other planets. As it turned out, there were four more manned missions to the Moon, including one, in 1971, in which America's premier astronaut Alan Shephard famously stroked a few golf balls. But following the return to Earth of *Apollo 17*, on December 19, 1972, the program was scrapped.

A telling fact about that last mission was that it was the only one whose crew included a real scientist, geologist Harrison Schmitt. All other Apollo astronauts were military men, talented and savvy in many areas, but not scientists. The program had been driven by political ambition — the desire of an American president to beat a rival. It had never really become the scientific fact-gathering program it ought to have been.

The public's attention span, never long, soon shifted in another directions. Moon walks became old hat. Moreover, as the 1970s and recession set in, there was no longer the money to fund this incredibly expensive program. And with the Russians having fallen out of the race, there was a growing sense that the Americans had sealed their victory and had nothing more to prove.

Human beings have not been to the Moon since 1972, and the beautiful orb in the sky has returned to the world of our imaginings, only a little marred by a stainless-steel plaque and one or two golf balls. It seems only fitting.

All a Hoax?

Predictably, some people thought the Moon landing never happened, that the whole thing was staged to distract Americans from the war in Vietnam, or to gain Cold War prestige over the Russians. These conspiracy theorists, mainly fringe writers and commentators, pointed out several facets of the landings that they found suspicious. The images broadcast back from the Moon had a surreal quality. The men bouncing around the Moon's surface — unrecognizable in their heavy suits and tinted helmets — could have been almost anyone. And there were certain strange details. For example, how could Armstrong's first step be filmed when there was no one outside to film it? And how could the American flag flutter at the end of its pole when there was no air?

The answer to the first question was that when he was halfway down the ladder, Armstrong pulled open an outer compartment on the *Eagle* and activated a television camera that had been set up to film his first step onto the Moon.

And the fluttering flag didn't really flutter. It had been packed in a tight roll and, due to the lack of air and gravity, the wrinkles simply took a long time to smooth out.

The Fall of the Berlin Wall

The Symbol of a Divided Europe is Demolished, Bringing an End to the Cold War and Reuniting Germany

MOST FAMOUS WALLS IN history — the Great Wall of China, Hadrian's Wall, the walls of Troy, to name a few — were constructed to keep people out: Mongols, barbarians, Greeks, whoever. However, the purpose of the Berlin Wall, built in 1961, was the exact opposite: to keep people in. Specifically, it was designed to prevent the people living in the eastern half of the German city of Berlin, which, since the Second World War had been part of the Communist German Democratic Republic (GDR), from leaving for the western, democratic, "free" half of the city, then part of West Germany, or the Federal Republic of Germany.

Of course, the powers that be in the GDR at the time would not admit to this and told the world that their only goal had been to build a protective shield against Western espionage agents and other pernicious influences. But the people who lived in East Berlin knew differently — which is why thousands sought a way over or under the wall and why about two hundred died doing so.

In the end, the wall amounted to a propaganda victory for the West and a failure of imagination on the part of the Communist regime for, during the twenty-eight years that it stood, it became symbolic of the fact that a person living in the Eastern Bloc lacked the freedom to move about as he or she chose, a basic tenet of democracy. The wall also severely restricted the East Berlin economy by limiting the free flow of goods and currency, so that while West Berlin boomed, East Berlin stagnated.

The end of the nightmare of the Berlin Wall was a long time in coming, but when it came it was accompanied by one of the most joyous celebrations of freedom the world has ever witnessed.

LIVING IN A DIVIDED CITY

After the end of the Second World War, Berliners got used to living in a divided city. The victorious Allies divided Germany into four zones, one each for the Americans, British, French, and Soviets. Although Berlin lay inside the zone belonging to

An East German border guard patrols
a checkpoint in Berlin, soon after the
construction of the Berlin Wall in 1961.

the Soviets, it was also divided into four sectors, so that the victorious powers could govern the country jointly from the capital.

But the beginnings of the Cold War interfered with this setup. In 1948, responding to the reality that they were united against Joseph Stalin and Soviet Russia, the three Western powers merged their German zones into one, creating, in 1949, West Germany. In response, the Soviet zone became East Germany. West Berlin in turn became a part of West Germany, and consequently an island of Western control at the heart of a Communist state.

Berliners made the best of the situation, making shopping trips back and forth, visiting relatives and landmarks, going to theaters. Everyone needed to carry identity cards and the checkpoints were a nuisance, but those who had lived through the Second World War had lived through far, far worse.

THE TRAP IS SPRUNG

At about midnight on Saturday August 12, 1961, the S-Bahn trains traveling from East Berlin to West simply stopped running. West Berliners who happened to be spending the evening in East Berlin were forced, grumbling, to get out and walk.

Soviet tanks. Then trucks arrived, carrying pneumatic drills, barbed wire, and concrete posts. In an obviously carefully planned operation, GDR troops began tearing up the pavement just inside the East German border, sinking the posts, stabilizing them with poured concrete, and stringing barbed wire between them. The tanks fanned out to block any movement along East–West boulevards, and other streets were ripped up to hinder any possible attacks from the West.

When the people of East Berlin awoke on Sunday June 13, they quickly realized they were completely cut off from the West. No longer could they visit relatives or go

> East Berliners realized they were now cut off from the West. The "iron curtain" had become reality.

When they reached the checkpoints, they were stopped by East German border guards, and only allowed back into the Western part of the city after their papers had been checked and double-checked. Any East Berliners trying to get over to the West were firmly turned away. East Berliners who happened to be in the West at that point realized that they had to make a daunting decision: they could return – to family and friends – but never cross into the West again; or they could start a new life, alone, and never turn back.

Meanwhile, the generally quiet streets along the West Berlin–East Berlin border filled with troop carriers, armored cars, and

shopping in the Western part of the city. No longer could the sixty thousand East Berliners who worked in the West reach their jobs. The "iron curtain," a metaphor that Winston Churchill had famously used in a 1946 speech to describe the division between Communist nations and the West, had become reality.

HOW THE OTHER HALF LIVES

During the 1950s, the citizens of East Berlin, able to view the city's Western half at first hand, had gradually realized that it had a far better standard of living. In fact, in that decade, infused with American aid, West Germany experienced a phoenix-like rise from the ashes of the Second World War. By 1960, West Berlin had built (and publicly celebrated) its one hundred thousandth new apartment; raised luxury hotels; constructed museums, galleries, and concert halls; and seen numerous industrial plants – many destroyed during the war – resume production.

In East Berlin and the GDR, in contrast, the economy was stagnant. Basic human needs – food and clothing – were sometimes hard to come by, and the ruins of buildings bombed by the Allies during the war remained as a stark reminder of the city's failure to advance. Little wonder then that during the 1950s a total of two and a half million East Germans fled to the West, almost half of whom were under the age of twenty-five. One million of these refugees escaped through East Berlin, where there were no walls or barbed wire because the agreement between the four occupying powers specifically prohibited this.

It became clear that if this situation were allowed to continue, not only would East Berlin be almost entirely drained of workers, but also the claim that the GDR was a happy socialist state would be disproved. So Walter Ulbricht, Chairman of the Council of State of the GDR, and his boss in all but name, Soviet Premier Nikita Khrushchev, decided to build themselves a wall.

WORK IN PROGRESS

The Berlin Wall was a work in progress that the GDR sought constantly to perfect. At first, it was just barbed wire. Where houses or apartment buildings lined the boundary, GDR troops (no Russian troops were involved, lest it seem like a Soviet initiative) initially bricked up just the ground floor and windows. But East Berliners jumped across the barrier from upper windows or climbed from them along ropes to the windows of neighboring apartments, so the authorities responded by bricking up entire buildings.

Through the fall of 1961 and into the early winter, the barbed wire gave way to a concrete-slab wall thirteen feet high. Soon this barrier extended for a hundred miles, completely encircling West Berlin. (Twenty-eight miles of the wall were directly between East and West Berlin, the rest between West Berlin and East Germany.) Only eight crossing points were left – one specifically for the transfer of deceased persons to relatives in the other half of the city (which were allowed to pass in either direction every Wednesday, after their coffins had been carefully checked), one for the mail, and the rest for foreigners or East Berliners with special passes. One crossing – in the middle of the broad and busy Friederichstrasse – became famous as "Checkpoint Charlie," where spies were exchanged, where East met West with an air of steely tension.

RUSH FOR FREEDOM

At first, when the barrier was mere barbed wire and gaps still existed, frantic East Berliners escaped in droves – almost fifty thousand in that first month of August 1961 alone. They slipped through the wire at night, swam across canals, sneaked across the boundary clinging to the undercarriages of cars. But then the local East Berlin GDR guards, some of whom turned a blind eye to such escapes, were replaced by guards from Saxony and other parts of the country, who had no ties to the city. These men, the *Volkspolizei* or "Vopos," were ordered to shoot escapees on sight. Sixteen had died by the end of the year. Several deaths were witnessed by helpless Western authorities, even the media, and became notorious symbols of the suffering caused by the wall.

Despite the fact that the wall was a violation of the agreement between the Allies, the Western powers weren't willing to confront the Communists over it. There were simply larger issues at stake: the division of Berlin paled in comparison to the space race and the attempts by both sides to control the outcomes of civil wars in various emerging countries. However, the wall did give U.S. presidents, from John F. Kennedy to Ronald Reagan, a perfect symbol of a dictatorial Communist regime.

Over time, the two sides of the wall developed distinctive characters. The Western side was covered with bright graffiti and became a kind of tourist attraction. In contrast, the Eastern side became a desolate death zone, the wall separated from the adjoining streets by a one hundred-yard-wide no-man's-land, every inch of which was covered by Vopos guns. As a result, escape attempts dwindled dramatically.

The only citizens who traveled from East to West on a regular basis were East German pensioners, who were allowed to visit their families in the West and stay as long as they liked. While the GDR presented this as a humanitarian gesture, many people pointed out that every pensioner who stayed in West Berlin was one less the East German government had to pay for.

COMMUNISM RESTRUCTURED

In June of 1985, twenty-four years after the construction of the wall, facing the reality that the Soviet Union had fallen far behind the rest of the world in economic output, Premier Mikhail Gorbachev introduced reforms under the heading of *perestroika*, or "restructuring." The reforms included the introduction of private ownership of businesses, the expansion of foreign trade, and permitting foreigners to invest in Soviet business ventures.

In turn, the states that made up the Soviet Union loosened their own trade laws, while nationalists in Eastern Bloc nations began clamoring for more freedom and a say in their own government. In 1989, for instance, the first free labor union was founded in Poland. In August of that year, Hungary removed its border restrictions with Austria. Thereafter, for any East German to escape to the West, he or she needed simply to get to Hungary, which was fairly easy.

Yet, even as most observers began to think that a change was soon to come in the long-static situation in Berlin, Erich Honecker, who headed the East German Socialist Party, decried *perestroika* and promised that nothing of the sort would take place in East Germany. The wall, Honecker said, would last "a hundred years." But Honecker and his other ageing politicians were soon being left behind by a new reality. Gorbachev had heralded a new era of détente, where there would be no need for an armed line between the two Germanys. And no need for a wall.

THE WALL COMES DOWN

In the autumn of 1989, thousands of demonstrators marched the streets of East Berlin – an unheard of sign of independence among the citizenry – demanding "Wir wollen raus.", or "We want to leave." Finally, on October 18, Honecker, lacking support

both within and without East Germany, resigned, citing health reasons.

After Honecker's resignation, more and more East Germans streamed to recently liberalized countries such as Hungary and Czechoslovakia, so many that the governments of these countries pleaded with East Germany to do something about the flow of refugees. On November 8, the East German government decided to issue passports to any East German who wanted one; all the citizens had to do was ask.

This decision was announced the next day at a press conference given by the East Berlin Minister of Propaganda, Günter Schabowski. In an almost offhand way, he said that people would now be able to cross between the two Germanys whenever they wanted and not have to go through any other countries. When asked when this

. . . .

Symbols of Oppression

One of the wall's earliest victims was an eighteen-year-old construction worker named Peter Fechter. Attempting to climb the wall in 1962, he was shot by the Vopos and fell to the ground on the Eastern side; though within sight of passersby in the West. As locals and journalists looked on, unable to help, he slowly bled to death.

The last of the almost two hundred people killed by the Vopos while attempting to climb or otherwise subvert the wall was

twenty-year-old Chris Gueffroy. On February 5, 1989, just short months before the wall would come tumbling down, Gueffroy, along with a friend, Christian Gaudian, tried to climb the barrier and nearly got to the top before being shot through the heart. Gaudian was wounded and sentenced to prison for the attempt, although he was soon released and turned over to the West Berlin government.

There are now memorials to both men in Berlin.

would take place, Schabowski said: "As far as I know, effective immediately, right now."

Schabowski's announcement was carried live by radio and television at about 7 p.m. Within twenty minutes, thousands of East Berliners had flocked to checkpoints, carrying their identification papers and demanding to be let through to West Berlin. At first, the Vopos attempted to turn them back, then to sort through the papers, but finally, they gave up, opened the gates, and a mass of humanity swarmed through.

There followed one incredible party, carried live on television around the world, as mobs of people, waving bottles of wine and beer, cheering and hugging and kissing, thronged the wall. One of the most remarkable scenes was the moment when a young man wearing a backpack walked through the no-man's-land on the eastern side of the wall, near the Brandenburg Gate, climbed on top of it, and began walking back and forth in a nonchalant fashion. For the crowds on both sides, this was a moment of extraordinary tension: no citizen had got this close to the wall for years without being shot. But, aside from drenching the young man with a hose, the Vopos did nothing. Soon he was joined by hundreds of others, dancing atop the most hated symbol of oppression in postwar Berlin history.

Beneath the Brandenburg Gate, Berliners celebrate the fall of the wall. The Brandenburg Gate was reopened in December 1989.

The party lasted for weeks. On Christmas Day, the American composer and conductor Leonard Bernstein led a concert which included Beethoven's Ninth Symphony (*Ode to Joy*), performed by an orchestra of musicians drawn from East and West Germany, as well as from around the world. People chipped away at the wall with hammers and pickaxes, taking away chunks of it for souvenirs. In 1990, heavy equipment was brought in to tear down the rest. The only portions of the wall left today are parts of memorials and a section in a Cold War museum.

GERMANY REUNITED

German reunification was officially declared on October 3, 1990, but the citizens of Berlin knew that the real uniting had begun on November 9, 1989, when the hated wall was at last breached for good.

Since reunification, the road has been a rocky one for East Germany and for many former Eastern bloc countries. In part, this is because, economically, the Communist states had fallen a long way behind the West during the time the wall was in place. Some economists estimate that even with a five to six percent annual growth rate, they will need another twenty years to catch up. Though Germany is still one of Europe's leading powers, its recent economic growth has been greatly hindered by reunification, and unemployment remains at high levels in the former East Germany. For some, the shadow of the wall remains.

9/11

*The Attacks That Traumatized America,
Stunned the World, and Launched a Global War on Terror*

T HEY WERE FOUR ENERGETIC and intense young men, the oldest of them born in 1968, the youngest a decade later. Three of them had studied city planning and engineering. All were well traveled, not only in their native Middle East but also throughout Europe and the United States, where all four, on temporary work visas, took pilot-training lessons. During the last days of their lives, they acted like anyone else might do in America – drawing cash from ATMs, eating at fast-food outlets, even having a few drinks at a bar. They might easily have been taken for recent immigrants, young professionals enjoying a new lifestyle and looking forward to a bright future in their adopted country.

But they were anything but. For on September 11, 2001, Mohammed Atta, Marwan al-Shehhi, Ziad Jarrah, and Hani Hanjour would lead fifteen other men onto four passenger planes. Turning these jets into deadly weapons, they would inflict the most devastating terrorist attack in history on the United States, in the name of an Islamic *jihad*, or holy war.

In doing so, they would transform the world. The 9/11 attacks not only led to a war in Afghanistan and a contentious and divisive conflict in Iraq, but also changed the way many people viewed their lives. After 9/11, travel became fraught. Danger could lurk on airlines, in nightclubs, on railway trains and buses. A lost suitcase could be a bomb, an approaching guard might arrest you at any moment. Public anxiety was – and to some extent remains – at its highest since the worst days of the Cold War.

PRIME TARGET

By the end of the twentieth century, the United States had become a prime target for Islamic terrorists, due to its long-term support of Israel and of Saudi Arabia, which it had supplied with funds, military equipment, and training. Chief among these was Al-Qaeda, an Islamic militant group, led by Osama bin Laden, which seeks to install fundamentalist regimes in all Muslim countries and eradicate all foreign, non-Muslim influence from those nations. As noted by the 9/11 Commission, a bipartisan U.S. government group that looked into the

The south tower of the World Trade Center starts to collapse at 9:59 a.m. The north tower would crumble half an hour later.

September 11 attacks, "Islamist extremists had given plenty of warning that they meant to kill Americans indiscriminately and in large numbers." Indeed, 9/11 was not the first time American interests, and even the country itself, had been attacked by such extremists, including Al-Qaeda.

The first attack on U.S. soil was the 1993 bombing of the World Trade Center, which caused some damage but failed due to bungles by the terrorists, most of whom were caught and jailed. In 1994, a plot to blow up thirteen American passenger jets over a two-day period was foiled. The following year, terrorists attacked a U.S. military base in

preparations began as much as eighteen months before September 11 occurred, and the operational mastermind was bin Laden's right-hand man, Khalid Sheikh Mohammed. Khalid was captured in Pakistan in 2003, and remains in custody in the U.S. prison at Guantanamo Bay, Cuba.

TRIAL RUNS

The four pilots had been in America for some time, perhaps from as early as January 2000, funded by Al-Qaeda money laundered through numerous sources and deposited regularly in their bank accounts. In early 2001, Osama bin Laden met with

The targets chosen by the terrorists were America's headquarters of finance, defense, and government.

Riyadh, Saudi Arabia, killing nineteen American servicemen and wounding hundreds of others. The U.S. embassies in Kenya and Tanzania were bombed in 1998, with a total loss of 260 lives; and in October of 2000 seventeen American sailors were killed when a motorboat filled with explosives was ignited next to the U.S. destroyer Cole, in the port of Aden in Yemen.

Al-Qaeda learned from these successes and failures. Having in the late 1990s re-established its headquarters in Afghanistan – then ruled by the Islamic fundamentalist Taliban regime – the group began planning a grand attack on the United States. According to the 9/11 Commission,

subordinates in Afghanistan in order to pick what the 9/11 Commission later referred to as "the muscle": the hijackers who would subdue and threaten the passengers while the trained pilots flew the planes. Twelve of the fifteen men selected came from Saudi Arabia, where bin Laden originated. Most of them were unemployed, with at most a high school education, and single. For the most part, they had been recruited after attending mosques that practised a more austere and radical form of Islam.

After undergoing basic training in Afghanistan, these men were sent to the United States. They began arriving there in pairs, on tourist visas, in April of 2001, and met up with the pilots, who helped them find places to live, open bank accounts, and become accustomed to American life.

During the summer of 2001, the pilots took cross-country reconnaissance flights, carrying knives through airport security and, once on a plane, watching to see when the cockpit doors would be opened.

In June of 2001, the hijackers received final word from bin Laden regarding their targets. They were to be the World Trade Center in New York, the Pentagon in Virginia, and either the White House or the Capitol Building in Washington DC – the nation's headquarters of finance, defense, and government.

A BEAUTIFUL DAY FOR FLYING

Up and down the eastern seaboard of the United States on September 11, people awakening and getting ready to go to work remarked on what an extraordinarily beautiful day it was. The sky was clear, the air nearly translucent, and the temperature mild, almost balmy. It was a beautiful day for flying.

At around 7:30 a.m., Mohammed Atta and his four muscle men boarded American Airlines Flight 11, bound for Los Angeles, at Boston's Logan International Airport. The plane took off at 7:59. At another terminal at Logan Airport, Marwan al-Shehhi and his four companions checked in for United Airlines Flight 175, also heading for Los Angeles. This plane took off at 8:14. Meanwhile, at Dulles International

Airport in Washington D.C., Hani Hanjour and his four-man team boarded American Airlines Flight 77, bound for Los Angeles. This plane lifted off at 8:20. At that same moment in the same airport, Ziad Jarrah and three companions boarded United Airlines Flight 93 to San Francisco, which rose up into the air at 8:42.

The flights had been chosen with great care. Each was bound for the West Coast, which meant that the planes would have plenty of fuel. The airplanes were Boeing 757s or 767s, simulators of which the pilots had trained in.

The terrorists took their first-class seats, in most cases two at the back of the first-class section and two at the front. Then they waited.

FLIGHT 11

At 8:14 a.m., American Airlines Flight 11 out of Boston reached twenty-five thousand feet, at which point the pilots had a routine conversation with the Logan control tower. By 8:25, two attendants on the flight, Betty Ong and Amy Sweeney, were making cell phone calls to American Airlines offices. Ong reported: "The cockpit is not answering … somebody is stabbed in business class. I think there's mace … we're getting hijacked."

Most likely, the muscle men had risen up as soon as the cockpit door was opened and stabbed two of the unarmed flight attendants in order to create terror. Another man, who had formerly been an Israeli army soldier, was also killed, probably because he tried

to stop the terrorists. Then the pilots were killed or incapacitated and Atta took over the controls. The plane executed a sweeping turn over Massachusetts and New York State's capital city of Albany, and headed south, down the Hudson River. Betty Ong reported that the plane was flying "erratically."

At around this time, air traffic controllers began to hear voice transmissions from Flight 11. At one point, a voice said: "Don't try to make any stupid moves. Just stay quiet and you'll be okay." A terrorist –

The devastated remains of the World Trade Center in Manhattan, subsequently known as the "Ground Zero" of the terrorist attack.

possibly Atta – had tuned into the wrong transmission channel and instead of talking through the cabin intercom was broadcasting his message over the air traffic control channel.

At 8:29 a.m., air traffic control notified the FAA that a hijacking had occurred. But it was too late for military aircraft to intercept. Flight 11, swooping down to 900 feet, was speeding over Manhattan Island at 450 miles per hour. Flight attendant Sweeney, looking out the window, cried out on her cell phone: "We are flying low. We are flying very, very low. We are flying way too low ... Oh my God we are way too low."

Then the phone went dead as American Airlines Flight 11 crashed into the north tower of the World Trade Center, tipping its wings at the last second to create maximum damage to the structure. The exact time was 8:46:40.

FLIGHT 175

The flight crew on United Airlines Flight 175, which had also taken off from Boston's Logan airport, heard what they considered to be a "suspicious transmission" from another plane (which turned out to be Flight 11) and reported this to air traffic control. Then Flight 175 itself stopped responding to enquiries from air traffic. At 8:51 a.m., the flight left its normal altitude and also began flying erratically.

As with Flight 11, passengers made panicked calls on their mobile phones. One man, Peter Hanson, called his father to say, "I think they've taken over the cockpit ... the plane is making strange moves." A flight attendant reported that both pilots were dead. At nine o'clock, Peter Hanson called his father again. "It's getting very bad on the plane," he said. "Passengers are throwing up and getting sick. The plane is making jerky

movements ... I don't think the pilot is flying the plane ... I think we are going down ... Don't worry, Dad: if it happens, it'll be very fast – my God, my God."

Flight 175 crashed into the south tower of the World Trade Center at 9:03:11.

FLIGHT 77

Before boarding American Airlines Flight 77 for Los Angeles at Washington's Dulles International Airport, two of the hijackers had set off metal-detector alarms. But they had then passed through manual checks with a hand-held metal detector and were allowed to proceed, although their luggage was held as a precautionary matter until it was ascertained that they were indeed on board. Videotape of one of the hijackers viewed later appears to show a box-cutter buttoned into his back pocket.

The flight reached its cruising altitude of thirty-five thousand feet at 8:46. At 9:16, one of the passengers, Barbara Olson, wife of Theodore Olson, the U.S. Solicitor-General, called her husband to say that the plane had been hijacked by men with box-cutters. Ted Olson told his wife about the two earlier crashes into the World Trade Center, but then the call was cut off. At about 9:30, the autopilot of the plane was disengaged when it reached 7,000 feet and then Flight 77 made a sweeping turn, descending to 2,200 feet. Hani Hanjour, the hijacker pilot, pushed the throttles to full power as the plane dived down into Arlington, Virginia, across the Potomac from Washington D.C. When it hit the Pentagon, at 9:37:46, Flight 77 was going at 530 miles per hour.

FLIGHT 93

The last of the airlines hijacked that day, Flight 93, carrying thirty-seven passengers, was twenty-five minutes late in taking off, finally departing at 8:42. It became the only plane out of the four in which all the passengers had full knowledge of what had occurred previously and time in which to attempt to do something about it.

At 9:26, a warning was sent out to all planes in the sky to beware of any "cockpit intrusions," along with the news that two planes had hit the World Trade Center. The puzzled pilot of Flight 93 asked for a confirmation of this strange message, but before that could occur, the plane suddenly dropped altitude and began putting out a Mayday distress call. Air traffic control in Cleveland heard the pilot crying, "Hey, get out of here!" The plane then turned back east.

As they did on the other planes, the hijackers told the passengers that there was a bomb on board and that if they didn't cause trouble they would be all right. But from mobile phone conversations the passengers soon knew that it was only a matter of time before the plane would be crashed into a building.

One caller told his wife that they had voted to rush the hijackers. They were planning to use anything they could as weapons. At 9:57, the passengers began their assault, the sounds of which were recorded on the cockpit voice recorder, which was recovered after the crash. The terrorist pilot Ziad Jarrah yelled at another hijacker to block the door and then rolled the plane side to side and pitched it up and down.

On the cockpit voice recording, at exactly ten o'clock, Jarrah says in Arabic: "Is that it? Shall we finish it off?" Another terrorist tells him to wait. Then a passenger is heard to yell, "In the cockpit. If we don't, we die." There are further sounds of commotion and then Jarrah yells: "Allah is the greatest!"

At 10:03, the airliner rolled over on its back and crashed at a speed in excess of five hundred miles per hour into a wooded area outside Shanksville, Pennsylvania, about twenty minutes' flying time from Washington. Because of the efforts of the passengers, either the Capitol Building or the White House was saved.

THE WAR ON TERROR

The 9/11 attacks took the lives of 2,749 people in the World Trade Center, 125 at the Pentagon, and 256 on the four planes. It was the worst-ever attack on the United States in its history, with a death toll greater than that of Pearl Harbor, when 2,330 died. The 9/11 Commission called it "a day of unprecedented shock and suffering in the history of the United States."

The attacks were witnessed on television by millions around the world. The reaction of the United States was swift. Based on evidence that Al-Qaeda and Osama bin Laden were operating in Afghanistan, President George W. Bush ordered an attack on that country by the United States and a coalition of allied nations, which began on October 7, 2001. It was successful in displacing the Taliban, although not in discovering the whereabouts of Osama bin Laden. In 2003, the United States and Britain also launched an invasion of Iraq, claiming that Saddam Hussein had links to Al-Qaeda (a claim since hotly disputed), sparking a long, bloody, and divisive conflict in that country.

Around the world, nations tightened up security in airports, along borders, and on public transport. This in turn gave rise to a debate about how to balance security and civil liberties, a debate that still rages as new terrorist attacks take place and new plots are uncovered.

The shock waves from 9/11 are still reverberating around the world. They will do so for decades to come.

The Twentieth Hijacker?

The United States missed its greatest chance to stop the 9/11 attacks when it failed to make the most of the fortuitous arrest of Zacarias Moussaoui, a French citizen of Moroccan descent, who may have been the twentieth hijacker. Moussaoui showed up at the Pan-Am International Flight Academy in Eagan, Minnesota, on August 13, 2001, and paid nearly seven thousand dollars in cash for training on a Boeing 747 flight simulator. Instructors became suspicious when it became apparent that Moussaoui, whose English was poor, knew little or nothing about flying and was mainly interested in take-offs and landings. They alerted the FBI, who arrested Moussaoui on an immigration violation. The FBI then tried but failed several times to get a warrant to open Moussaoui's laptop – it was considered that they had insufficient evidence to ask for one. Had they been able to do so, they would have found evidence connecting Moussaoui to the 9/11 plotters.

We may never know exactly what Moussaoui's role in 9/11 was. In 2006, he was convicted of conspiring to hijack planes and crash them into the World Trade Center, and sentenced to life imprisonment. But during the trial he vacillated between admitting his role, claiming that he was part of another planned terrorist attack, and denying everything. Khalid Sheikh Mohammed, the attack's mastermind, denied Moussaoui's role in the plot as well, but U.S. government officials believe that Moussaoui may have been training as a last-minute replacement for Ziad Jarrah, who, in the summer of 2001, was having second thoughts about his involvement.

Bibliography

Ambrose, Stephen E. *D-Day: June 6, 1944: The Climactic Battle of World War II*. New York: Simon & Schuster, 1994.

Black, Jeremy. *The Seventy Great Battles in History*. London, Thames & Hudson, 2005.

Bobrick, Benson. *Angel in the Whirlwind: The Triumph of the American Revolution*. New York: Simon & Schuster, 1997.

Bradford, Ernle. *Julius Caesar: The Pursuit of Power*. New York: William Morrow & Co., 1984.

Brugioni, Dino A. *Eyeball to Eyeball: The Inside Story of the Cuban Missile Crisis*. New York: Random House, 1991.

Cantor, Norman F. *In the Wake of the Plague: The Black Death and the World It Made*. New York: The Free Press, 2001.

Chang, Jung and John Halliday. *The Unknown Chairman Mao*. New York: Knopf, 2005.

Collins, Michael. *Liftoff: The Story of America's Adventure in Space*. New York: Grove Press, 1988.

Crankshaw, Edward. *The Shadow of the Winter Palace: Russia's Drift to Revolution* 1825–1917. New York: Viking Press, 1976.

Danziger, Danny and John Gillingham. *1215: The Year of Magna Carta*. New York, London: Simon & Schuster, 2003.

Davis, Burke. *George Washington and the American Revolution*. New York: Random House, 1975.

Der Spiegel Magazine: Reporters, Writers, and Editors. *Inside 9-11: What Really Happened*. New York: St. Martin's Press, 2001.

Devries, Kelly. *The Battles of the Medieval World: From Hastings to Constantinople*. New York: Barnes & Noble, 2006.

Dwyer, Jim and Kevin Flynn. *102 Minutes: The Untold Story of the Fight to Survive inside the Twin Towers*. New York: Times Books, 2005.

Foster, R. F. *Modern Ireland: 1600–1972*. London: Penguin, 1988.

Gardner, Brian. *The Big Push: A Portrait of the Battle of the Somme*. New York: William Morrow, 1963.

Herlihy, David. *The Black Death and the Transformation of the West*. Cambridge, Massachusetts: Harvard University Press, 1997.

Herr, Michael. *Dispatches*. New York: Alfred A. Knopf, 1977.

Hibbert, Christopher. *The Days of the French Revolution*. New York: William Morrow & Co., 1980.

Hough, Richard. *The Battle of Britain: The Triumph of RAF Fighter Pilots*. New York: Macmillan, 1971.

Howarth, David. *Waterloo: Day of Battle*. New York: Atheneum, 1968.

Kelly, John. *The Great Mortality: An Intimate History of the Black Death, the Most Devastating Plague of All Time*. New York: HarperCollins, 2005.

Klingaman, William H. *1929: The Year of the Great Crash*. New York: Harper & Row, 1989.

Kohn, George Childs. *Dictionary of Wars*. New York: Checkmark Books, 2007.

Leasor, James. *The Plague and the Fire: London, 1665/1666*. New York: McGraw Hill Book Company, Inc., 1961.

Leckie, Robert. *George Washingon's War: The Sage of the American Revolution.* New York: HarperCollins, 1992.

Lewis, Richard S. *The Voyages of Apollo: The Exploration of the Moon.* New York: The New York Times Book Co., 1974.

Lloyd, Alan. *The Spanish Century: A Narrative History of Spain from Ferdinand and Isabella to Franco.* Garden City: Doubleday & Co., 1964.

Lucie-Smith, Edward A. *Joan of Arc.* New York: W. W. Norton & Co., 1976.

McCourt, Malachy. *History of Ireland.* Philadelphia: Running Press, 2004.

McPherson, James M. *Abraham Lincoln and the Second American Revolution.* New York, London: Oxford University Press, 1991.

Madden, Thomas F. *Crusades: The Illustrated History.* Ann Arbor: University of Michigan Press, 2004.

Martin, Colin and Geoffrey Parker. *The Spanish Armada.* New York: W. W. Norton & Co., 1988.

Mattingly, Garrett. *The Armada.* Boston: Houghton, Mifflin Company, 1959.

Moorehead, Alan. *Gallipoli.* New York: Harper & Brothers, 1956.

Oren, Michael B. *Six Days of War: June 1967 and the Making of the Modern Middle East.* New York: Oxford University Press, 2002.

Parenti, Michael. *The Assassination of Julius Caesar: A People's History of Ancient Rome.* New York, London: The New Press, 2003.

Perez, Joseph. *The Spanish Inquisition: A History.* New Haven: Yale University Press, 2005.

Pernoud, Régine. *The Retrial of Joan of Arc: The Evidence at the Trial for Her Rehabilitation, 1450–1456.* New York: Harcourt, Brace & Co., 1955.

Posner, Gerald. *Case Closed: Lee Harvey Oswald and the Assassination of JFK.* New York: Random House, 1993.

Read, Anthony and David Fisher. *Berlin Rising: Biography of a City.* New York: W. W. Norton & Co., 1994.

Reston, James Jr. *Dogs of God: Columbus, the Inquisition, and the Defeat of the Moors.* New York: Doubleday, 2005.

Salisbury, Harrison E. *Russia in Revolution: 1900–1930.* New York: Holt, Rinehart & Winston, 1978.

Schama, Simon. *Citizens: A Chronicle of the French Revolution.* New York: Alfred A. Knopf, 1989.

Thompson, Josiah. *Six Seconds in Dallas: A Micro-Study of the Kennedy Assassination.* New York: Random House, 1967.

Thompson, Robert Smith. *The Missiles of October; The Declassified Story of John F. Kennedy and the Cuban Missile Crisis.* New York: Simon & Schuster, 1992.

Toland, John. *Infamy: Pearl Harbor and Its Aftermath.* New York: Doubleday & Co., 1982.

Townsend, Peter. *Duel of Eagles.* New York: Simon & Schuster, 1970.

Turner, John Frayn. *Invasion, '44: The Story of D-Day in Normandy.* New York: G. P. Putnam's Sons, 1959.

Ward-Perkins, Bryan. *The Fall of Rome and the End of Civilization.* Oxford: Oxford University Press, 2005.

Weintraub, Stanley. *Long Day's Journey into War: December 7, 1941.* New York: Dutton, 1991.

Wilford, John Noble. *The Mysterious Story of Columbus: An Exploration of the Myth, the Man, the Legacy.* New York: Alfred A. Knopf, 1991.

Wills, Gary. *Lincoln at Gettysburg: The Words That Remade America.* New York: Simon & Schuster, 1992.

Wyden, Peter. *Day One: Before Hiroshima and After.* New York: Simon & Schuster, 1984.

Acknowledgments

I'd like, once again, to acknowledge my debt of gratitude to Will Kiester, in whose fertile and creative imagination this book originally took shape. Also thanks to Scott Forbes, who must be atoning for sins of a previous life, but who has been, as always, a wise and patient editor.

I'm also very grateful to Peter Long for his elegant design, Amanda McKittrick for finding the images, and Emma Hutchinson for coordinating the project at Murdoch Books.

Image Credits

Index

This edition published in 2008 by Pier 9, an imprint of Murdoch Books Pty Limited

Murdoch Books Australia
Pier 8/9
23 Hickson Road
Millers Point NSW 2000
Phone: +61 (0) 2 8220 2000
Fax: +61 (0) 2 8220 2558
www.murdochbooks.com.au

Murdoch Books UK Limited
Erico House, 6th Floor
93-99 Upper Richmond Road
Putney, London SW15 2TG
Phone: +44 (0) 20 8785 5995
Fax: +44 (0) 20 8785 5985
www.murdochbooks.co.uk

Chief Executive: Juliet Rogers
Publisher: Kay Scarlett
Commissioning Editor: William Kiester
Project Manager: Emma Hutchinson
Editor: Scott Forbes
Concept and design: Peter Long
Photo researcher: Amanda McKittrick
Production: Monique Layt

Text copyright © Murdoch Books Pty Limited 2008
The moral right of the author has been asserted.
Design copyright © Murdoch Books Pty Limited 2008

ISBN 978 1 74196 186 7

Printed by Midas Printing (Asia) Ltd in 2008. PRINTED IN CHINA.